To Lucy,
with all best
wishes,

Rachel
and David.

GATHERING GREATNESS

Edited by Rachel Macfarlane & David Woods

Gathering Greatness is published by London Leadership Strategy
Copyright. London Leadership Strategy 2014.
ISBN 978-0-9930720-0-0

ACKNOWLEDGEMENTS

We would like to thank everyone at The London Leadership Strategy who has supported the Going For Great (G4G) programme, and also colleagues at the G4G schools who provided the capacity for the school leaders involved to attend seminars, and focus on producing their case studies. We are grateful to Andy Buck, Chris Husbands, Sally Morgan and Kevan Collins for coming to Going For Great seminars to share their thoughts and research – all were inspiring in their presentations, generous with their time and hugely supportive of the programme.

ABOUT THE AUTHORS

Rachel Macfarlane is a National Leader of Education in her 12th year of Headship. In 2011, Rachel joined ARK Schools to set up a new all-through academy in Ilford, East London. Isaac Newton Academy opened in September 2012 and takes a new primary and secondary intake each year. Since 2009, Rachel has been Project Director of The London Leadership Strategy's Going For Great (G4G) programme. She also led the Good To Great (G2G) programme from 2010-2014.

David Woods was the Chief Education Adviser for London Schools and the London Challenge until April 2011, as well as holding the role of Principal National Challenge Adviser for England. He was previously Head of the DfES Advisory Service, and before that the Chief Education Adviser for Birmingham Schools. David worked on many School Improvement policies and programmes and has written and spoken extensively about these. He wrote The A to Z of School Improvement – Principles and Practice with Tim Brighouse, which was published in April 2013, and Transforming Education for All: The Tower Hamlets Story with Chris Husbands in the same year. He is currently the Chair of The London Leadership Strategy and several Local Authority Education Challenge Boards, as well as being a visiting Professor of Education at Warwick University, and a Professorial Fellow at the London Institute of Education.

CONTENTS

CHAPTER 1

INTRODUCTION

RACHEL MACFARLANE

In February 2008, The London Leadership Strategy set up a leadership development programme entitled Good To Great (G2G), aimed at supporting good schools in their endeavour to become great. The programme provides access to conferences, teacher improvement support, training and knowledge sharing. Over 100 schools have been involved.

In June 2009, a second and complementary strand of the G2G programme was conceived, entitled Going For Great (G4G). It was designed to focus on 'outstanding' rather than 'good' schools (in Ofsted terms) and to support them in both maintaining this designation and becoming even more effective.

The aims of the G4G programme are:

- To encapsulate key features and qualities of schools which are consistently outstanding, in order to better understand how outstanding schools become great schools.

- To share exceptional practice demonstrated in outstanding schools and by the leaders of outstanding schools to support all schools on the G2G programme in moving towards becoming great schools.

- To support schools rated outstanding by Ofsted in maintaining this designation in subsequent inspections.

- To support outstanding schools in maximising their impact on the local, national and/or international community, through effective systemic leadership.

- To ensure that outstanding schools are helping to make education in London world class, contributing to the vision of London as the leading urban education service in the world through having system-wide impact.

- To support succession planning, both in outstanding schools and those with which they are working.

The programme was deliberately very ambitious and intended to break new ground in the sense that it sought to define and exemplify world-class practice and capture at least something of the essence of a great school. The outcomes were intended to add significantly to our knowledge and understanding of how schools become great and sustain greatness.

In June 2009, Heads of all outstanding secondary schools in London were invited to apply for a place as one of five or six pilot schools in Year 1.

The criteria for selection were as follows:

- Currently an outstanding school as judged by Ofsted in their most recent Ofsted report (newly accredited outstanding schools were considered on an equal footing with those which had achieved this designation in several successive inspections).

- Making a contribution to system-wide school improvement (locally, nationally or internationally).

- Evidence of a culture of research-based enquiry.

- Commitment to engagement with the G4G model.

- Commitment to striving to become a great school.

- Ambition to become a Teaching School.

Six schools (representing a range in terms of size, type and location) were chosen in September 2009 as G4G pilot schools. The G4G programme involved the Headteacher and another colleague (Project Champion) from each of the six pilot schools meeting for a half-day seminar each half term with the Project Director (Rachel Macfarlane) and Project Consultant (David Woods).

These seminars provided a forum for:

- Exploring the nature of greatness in schools, sharing and discussing research and recommending reading.

- Networking to share good practice and set up visits to observe in and learn from each other's schools.

- Preparing and writing a publication, aimed at showcasing areas of outstanding practice in each of the pilot schools as well as tracking each school's journey in moving an identified area of good practice towards being great practice.

In between the half termly seminars, colleagues from the G4G schools carried out reading and research into great schools, shared their findings with their own leadership teams, wrote up their case study of outstanding practice and maintained a log of action taken in the area of practice that they had identified for improvement. This led to the production of a publication, Going For Great, in the summer of 2010.

It had always been envisaged that a significantly greater number of outstanding secondary schools would be invited to participate in Year 2 of the Going For Great (G4G) project. All six pilot schools were keen to continue into year two of the programme and a model was devised whereby each of the original schools would lead a hub of four schools, with a total of 24 schools in cohort 2. The Heads of all outstanding secondary schools in London were invited to apply for one of the 18 new places.

The schools were chosen to represent a variety of institutions: mixed and single sex, non-denomination and faith, large and small, local authority and academy, selective and comprehensive, high and low Free School Meals (FSM) entitlement, high and low English as an Additional Language (EAL) percentages.

The structure of the G4G project in Year 2 was very much as in Year 1: four seminars were attended by two senior leaders from each school. At each session, a leading educationalist gave a talk about great practice in schools, followed by a question and answer session (the speakers were Tim Brighouse, Steve Munby, Gordon Stobart and Alistair Smith). In between seminars, the schools in each hub carried out visits to each other and colleagues from every school worked on producing a case study of an area of great practice in their school. These case studies were shared in draft form amongst the hub school members for feedback and suggestions for development. The schools' case studies were presented in the second G4G book, Glimpses of Greatness.

In the summer of 2011, all outstanding secondary schools in London were invited to submit expressions of interest to be part of the third G4G cohort. Six of the Year 2 schools became new hub leaders and they were joined by 18 new schools. The format of the G4G programme remained that of Year 2 in the programme's third year. The guest speakers, each of whom offered their interpretation and reflections on great schools, were Christine Gilbert, Bill Lucas, Chris Husbands and Anthony Seldon. The participating school leaders continued to learn a great deal from each other's practice through conducting learning walks in their colleagues' schools, networking and discussions at the seminars, and supporting their hub group schools in the drafting of their case studies. The summer 2012 publication was entitled Growing Greatness.

The 24 schools in the 4th G4G cohort (2012-2013) comprised a mixture of schools new to the programme and some who had been involved in previous years. They were addressed by Jon Coles (Chef Executive of United Learning), Amanda Spielman (Chair of OFQUAL and Research and Development Director of ARK Schools), Baroness Morris of Yardley (former Educational Secretary) and John Dunford (Chair of Whole Education and ex-General Secretary of ASCL). Their collection of case studies was entitled Generating Greatness.

The colleagues from the 24 schools making up cohort five (2013-2014) were perhaps the most collaborative and outward-looking yet, and a pleasure to work with and learn from. The speakers who shared their thoughts and reflections on great schools and world class education with the cohort were Chris Husbands (Director of the Institute of Education), Andy Buck (Managing Director – Academies, United Learning), Baroness Sally Morgan (Chair of Ofsted) and Kevan Collins (Chief Executive of the Education Endowment Foundation). We hope that you will find the collection case studies from the 24 schools interesting and thought-provoking.

Rachel Macfarlane.
August 2014.
Gathering Greatness

CHAPTER 2

GATHERING GREATNESS

DAVID WOODS

"If you do not raise your eyes, you will think that you are at the highest point."
Antonio Porchia

"Innovation is a change that creates a new dimension of performance."
Peter Drucker

"Great organisations create talented people."
Malcolm Gladwell

This is the fifth volume of case studies to be published by **The London Leaderships Strategy's** programme, **Going for Great**. Collections of case studies are excellent evidence of self-evaluation and help to demonstrate a school's reflective intelligence. The shared process of collective investigation and review builds stimulus and impetus in terms of analysing evidence and planning future developments. It also increases the store of intellectual activity amongst staff, releasing energy and creating a buzz of excitement around the best practice and making a real difference to school improvement.

Great schools often publish their own collections and the **Going for Great** programme has drawn upon London's secondary schools to publish some 100 case studies between 2010 and 2014. In 2010, the first book of case studies was entitled **Going for Great**, and a year later a second book was published, **Glimpses of Greatness**. In 2012, came **Growing Greatness** and in 2013 **Generating Greatness**. This is the latest volume, **Gathering Greatness**, containing 24 case studies of great practice. All the studies have been tightly structured around aims, rationale, purpose, the context, the story itself, reflections on lessons learnt and next steps. They have been peer-reviewed before final editing.

To provide a framework of understanding of the range of characteristics that define 'greatness', successive groups of schools have worked with the editors, establishing and refining the idea of '**9 Pillars of Greatness**' derived from reading, research and practice. In headline these are as follows:

The 9 Pillars of Greatness

1. A shared vision, values, culture and ethos, based on the highest expectations of all members of the school community.

2. Inspirational leadership at all levels throughout the school.

3. Exceptional teaching, learning, assessment and feedback to support the highest levels of attainment and achievement.

4. A relentless focus on engaging and involving students.

5. Personalised and highly effective continuous professional development within a learning community.

6. A stimulating and inclusive environment and climate for learning.

7. A rich and creative curriculum, within and beyond the classroom, fully meeting the needs of individuals and groups of students.

8. High quality partnerships, with parents, the community, other schools and networks, locally, nationally and internationally.

9. Robust and rigorous self-evaluation, data analysis and collective review.

See the Appendix for a full description. These 9 Pillars are also published in a separate London Leadership Strategy Going for Great pamphlet.

From the very beginning of this programme, there has been an emphasis on particular texts of great schooling, some of them written, or referenced by, visiting speakers to the Going for Great seminars. The first volume in the series drew upon **Good to Great** (Jim Collins), **What Makes a Great School?** (Andy Buck), **What Makes a Good School Now?** (Tim Brighouse and David Woods), **The Moral Imperative of School Leadership** (Michael Fullan), **Twelve Outstanding Secondary Schools** (Ofsted), as well as other Ofsted reports and publications from the National College, SSAT and other agencies.

Since the first publication, there have been a number of key texts for successive cohorts of schools to consider, such as **Engaging With Excellence** (George Berwick), **New Kinds of Smart** (Guy Claxton and Bill Lucas), **Bounce – The Myth of Talent And The Power of Practice** (Matthew Syed), **High Performers – The Secret of Successful Schools** (Alistair Smith) and **Visible Learning for Teachers** (John Hattie). In the last two years, there have been further influential texts such as **Leadership: All You Need To Know** (David Pendleton and Adrian Furnham), **Focus – The Hidden Driver of Excellence**, (Daniel Goleman), **The A-Z of School Improvement**, (Tim Brighouse and David Woods), and **The Principal – Three Keys To Maximising Impact** (Michael Fullan) along with key Ofsted reports on **Unseen Children, More Able Children and The Pupil Premium.**

"This is the common factor about leading successful schools – teachers grow in a collaborative culture through the establishment of feedback for growth and transparency about practice and results. Healthy pressure (high expectations) and support (both technical and emotional) helps peers to grow."

Michael Fullan

There are a number of case studies that are concerned with the development of a positive ethos and shared values engaging and involving students (Pillars 1 and 4).

Swanlea School has focused its study on **A Whole School Approach To Involving A Shared Values System**, with the aim of developing a school ethos of respect and building a values-centred school culture. The school was determined to challenge consistent patterns of prejudicial behaviour and, with extensive consultation, developed a deeper understanding of the key issues. Through powerful visionary exercises, they were able to motivate key groups to help drive change with training and awareness-raising for staff and students. An agreed set of Swanlea Shared Values was introduced with the School Council and a team of peer mediators leading, embedding and reviewing the impact. A new behaviour policy was developed together with a reviewed PSHEE curriculum which embedded the idea of shared values, challenging prejudice and discrimination.

The impact of all this has been considerable in terms of whole school collaboration, a developed student voice and student leadership, an increased consistency of approach, high standards of behaviour and a welcoming and supportive ethos. Staff and student surveys reveal a significant reduction in the number of incidents of prejudicial behaviour and the values-driven approach is being sustained through key equalities events and training, the work of peer mediators, and as part of whole school planning. The school is now being used as a model to share good practice elsewhere.

At **Grey Court School**, the study entitled **From Conflict To Resolution – Embedding A Positive Ethos**, looks at the introduction of restorative approaches and the impact this has had on the school ethos. The aim was to become a school where restorative approaches are understood and used by students and staff to enable them to work 'with' each other. This was exemplified by rewriting the school behaviour policy in consultation with all stakeholders, so that all behaviour incidents were dealt with using restorative principles. The journey to becoming a truly restorative school has taken five years, incorporating tutor group circle time, year activity days, student-teacher conferences and action plans.

In 2013, the Grey Court Relationship Policy was written by students and staff, setting out the vision and principles of a restorative school. There is now an ethos with an emphasis on high-quality relationships, respect for one another and a high emphasis on SMSC within a calm, orderly learning environment. The school as a whole has flourished with this approach leading not only to improved behaviour but also improved attendance and academic outcomes.

King Solomon Academy has introduced a highly innovative approach towards positive behaviour management with its study entitled **Have You Earned It?** Based upon the experience of some charter schools in the USA, a 'payslip' was introduced enabling the school to track each good and poor behaviour choice every pupil makes on a weekly basis. The 'bank' of King Solomon Academy pays its 'employees' for attending school every day in KSA pounds and also rewards in pounds a range of merits for producing exceptional classwork or homework, positive behaviour, or for some sort of service. Pupils can also earn an AWOPR (act worthy of public recognition). Likewise when pupils make a poor behaviour choice, pounds are deducted from the payslip.

All pupils receive a payslip every week which goes towards earning a range of enrichment activities and associated privileges and rewards. Payslip also feeds into the fundamental mission of the school which is to prepare all pupils for success at university and beyond. As such there is an end of year residential every year for every year group, focused mainly on university experiences, but attendance on the trips has to be earned through the payslip. The system has now run for four years in this new academy and is well embedded in the culture of the school. It works because it is transparent, sending a powerful message to pupils that every choice does count. Behaviour conversations have shifted dramatically, with teachers and pupils having a common language which reinforces a strong ethos.

There are two studies specifically on the role of the form tutor (Pillars 4 & 7). **What Does A Great Form Tutor Look Like?**, the study from **Loxford School**, focuses on research into the form tutor role and the vital part that tutors play in the lives of young people. Loxford is part of a partnership of schools that work together in pastoral, subject and leadership networks and the role of the tutor was decided upon as a matter for joint investigation and research.

Using an online questionnaire, students were asked to evaluate and reflect upon the quality of support they received from their tutor. Loxford initially reviewed Year 7, where they found that tutors have a significant impact. Findings from Year 7-9, 10-11, and 12-13 were also analysed by the group of schools, focusing on tutors who scored highly. The researchers drew out what behaviour, attitudes and practices gave rise to such good results. Six key factors were identified in determining what a great for tutor looks like.

First the tutor's attitude (welcoming, caring, conscientious, friendly and personal), then the tutor as motivator (belief in the student, aspiration, ambition of their future lives), giving accurate and timely information (making tutees feel cared about and making sure they are secure about what is happening, the quality of relationships (two-way communication, reciprocity of openness, trust and reliability), facilitating relationships with other students in a group (enabling the group to become mutually supportive and creating a team spirit), and detecting and solving problems. All these factors have been used to challenge the perceptions of tutor teams and as a focus for improved tutoring. Having a great tutor is regarded as a gift of great value by all students and this research has enabled a more consistent approach to delivering significant elements of social and personal education.

The study from **Wren Academy, Coding The Tutorial Matrix**, explores how the experience of students in tutorial time has developed over the last three years from a mainly didactic approach, to a student-led model. Wren is a Church of England Academy and the pastoral system is run as a vertical one. It places great emphasis upon high quality, stimulating and impactful tutor time. The academy decided to improve its provision by introducing a new format incorporating the principle of students as Leaders of Learning. Each week, tutor groups followed a menu of activities – spiritual assembly, theme presentation, TRIAD activity, class forum and debate and a topical quiz. Learning walks and observations revealed the need for a greater standardisation in provision, training for students and staff, and a better monitoring and evaluation process. This was introduced along with the standardisation of materials and resources.

Using three standards (Statutory Inspection for Anglican Schools, Ofsted, with particular reference to SMSC and Wren-specific routines), a central document was produced, pulling these together into one evaluation tool. This was introduced in autumn 2013 and assessed through learning walks and feedback sessions. The impact data shows a clear upward movement towards a better standard of tutorial provision and very good feedback from staff and students related to the development of attitudes, competences and skills. Next steps will include the development of a Wren Tutorial Evaluation feedback pro forma to sustain further improvements and share best practice.

There are a number of case studies related to assessment and the Pupil Premium (Pillar 3). One, from **Sir John Cass's Foundation And Red Coat Church Of England School**, is concerned with **Maximising The Benefits Of Assessment To Ensure Pupil Progress**. This has played a pivotal role in improving standards of teaching and learning and pupil achievement. The school decided to reform its existing assessment system to better address three key strands for improvement – to provide the SLT and middle leaders with a rich source of data to monitor, to evaluate and implement interventions and to raise awareness as to the nature of outstanding assessment as part of every teacher's practice – and to devise assessment patterns that foster independent learning.

An assessment working party and staff consultation led to particular changes within the three key strands. On the first strand, the assessment cycle was shortened to three weeks and a detailed evaluation form was constructed with all criteria having grade descriptors. On the second, assessment-focused CPD sessions were introduced concerning whole school interventions and personalised interventions with reference to such issues as quality, consistency, expectations and the dissemination of best practice. On the third strand, there was a renewed focus on feedback as a stimulus to independent learning and encouraging students to more actively respond to their targets. There is some excellent evidence from both teachers and students as to the successful impact of the new system. The outcomes of the assessment scrutinies demonstrate much outstanding practice. Accountability has been balanced with support with sustained improvement in performance.

At **Walthamstow School for Girls**, the case study **Mind The Gap** focuses on the gap in performance and progress between Free School Meals students and other students, which was 28% in 2010. In terms of point scores, attendance, and participation in extracurricular activities, there are also similar gaps. The school decided to tackle this issue front-on through robust self-evaluation well before the introduction of the Pupil Premium in September 2011 and the 'ever six' category which would double the FSM figure to some 40% across the school.

A number of interventions were introduced – Student Progress Leaders were required to have the performance of FSM students as a standing item on all pastoral meeting agendas, FSM students were highlighted in bold on all student lists, records and mark books, and take-up of extracurricular activities by FSM students was encouraged via a range of strategies. There was an extra effort to link with the parents of FSM children and after Year 11 mocks, FSM students were prioritised to have members of the Leadership Team as academic mentors. The profile of all FSM students was raised and within all faculties a range of different strategies were introduced to raise attainment and progress with English, ICT and RE being particularly successful at closing the gap.

By 2013, the gap had narrowed to 8%, with FSM students achieving a value-added score greater than other students – a significant achievement. There is still some variability between subjects, but 11 GCSE subject areas have an attainment gap for Pupil Premium students of less than 10%. Lessons learnt include the simple principle of making these students highly visible rather than 'unseen', better tracking, targeting and interventions, and improved access to all curricular opportunities.

A similar theme is explored through **Uxbridge High School's City Year: Minding The Gap**, which focuses upon the impact of City Year working with the school on closing the gap for white British students, with a particular focus on improving behaviour, attendance and literacy. City Year is one of the UK's leading education charities, serving schools in socially-deprived areas with staff acting as tutors, mentors and role models. At Uxbridge, there was a City Year team of 11 young adults, many of whom were university graduates on a gap year. Each City Year tutor focuses on the literacy needs of targeted students by attending English classes, teaching literacy progress units, working on paired reading schemes and extracurricular writing clubs. They also take on a wider role in the school, mentoring challenging students and engaging with them before and after school and at break and lunch. They work closely with existing pastoral, inclusion and SEN teams, aiming to supplement activities that are already in place to increase student engagement and access to learning.

Their impact has been evaluated across English point scores, behaviour and attendance rates. The anecdotal data is stronger at this point in time than the hard quantitative data: there are three case studies from a student, a City Year participant and an English teacher which all give vivid insights into the experience and impact. This has been the first year of the programme and lessons have been learnt as to how to get the best out of this extra resource, but the school is in no doubt as to the excellent value for money in employing such a flexible, pro-active group of people.

Continuing on the theme of progress and closing gaps, **Core Kick-start** was launched by **Ruislip High School** in June 2013. The aim was to support underachieving, incoming Year 7 students in Maths and English through the transition period of the summer and autumn terms by providing evening sessions every week. The first wave in June/July ran with a total of 30 students and their parents regularly attending and resulted in a notable shift in the median attainment from 3cs and 3bs, to 4bs, which was the benchmark level allowing students to 'graduate' from the programme.

The second wave ran from September to October with 18 students and also made gains. The programmes were taught by the school's Maths and English teachers who were paid for their teaching and planning time. In summary, significant sustained gains were made by the majority of students and evidence from the student interviews suggested that not only were there academic gains, but also improvements in confidence and attitudes to learning. Parents also reflected on how their children had benefited from the programme and their presence in the classroom was a powerful strategy for enhancing the learning experience for everyone. Restoring the confidence of both parents and students in their competence in English and Maths appears to have led to an improvement in the cohort's progress in Year 7. **Core Kick-start** has succeeded on many levels and the scheme is now being run again, with evening sessions starting earlier in the summer term and the introduction of some family support worker assistance.

There are a number of studies around the themes of continuous professional development (Pillar 5) to improve teaching and learning (Pillar 3). The case study from **Nower Hill High School** on **Establishing Research Practitioners** examines the way the school, following research into evidence-based practice, has endeavoured to create research practitioners through the development and embedding of a school-based Masters programme. The school believed that through such a programme, 'home-grown' practitioners would benefit considerably in their understanding and application of different aspects of pedagogy and leadership. The first cohort of 10 participants was established in May 2010 in partnership with Middlesex University and was partly subsidised by the school in return for a commitment to stay at Nower Hill over the three-year period. A second cohort was established in May 2012. Participants undertook a different small scale action research project each year of their two/three-year Masters study. The result is that research has informed practice at both subject and whole school levels and the study contains some very good examples of this.

An unexpected benefit of the collaborative nature of the taught Masters sessions in the school was the professional bonding that took place between the research practitioners, resulting in joint training delivered to the wider school community. One challenge is to communicate research results more widely and more systematically within the school community and another is the continual funding of the scheme. However, the development over time of collective enquiry and evidence-based practice has added significantly to the depth and breadth of CPD and to the best practice in teaching and learning.

At **Hall Mead School**, the study reflects how **Appraisal + CPD = Outstanding Teaching**. After extensive consultation a new performance management policy was developed in 2010-2011 with learning at the very core of policy and practice, and a process to help teachers to develop their knowledge and skills to learn and teach better. The process begins with an annual self-appraisal and targets are set under three headings – pupil progress, leading learning and professional development – linking to the school development plan. Staff are now in the driving seat, linking their own professional practice to Professional Standards for Teachers. At the same time, the CPD programme became more focused, linking much better to performance outcomes and needs. For example, a bespoke Masters programme in literacy was offered and taught on site in partnership with the University of East London.

Further adjustments were made to performance management with the new regulations of 2012, ensuring a tighter link to Professional Standards. This was achieved through a very large task group working through a detailed, differential set of criteria, with teachers grouped into three different career phases and pay bands. There was also a distinct emphasis on training staff in the new procedures. This carefully planned approach has resulted in complete buy-in from the staff and, importantly, the targets linked to Pupil Progress and Leading Learning have kept teaching and learning at the fore, leading to improved outcomes for students.

There are a number of case studies concerned directly with teaching and learning. The study from **Haydon School** entitled **A Virtuous Circle: Sharing Good Practice In Independent Learning,** reflects on the drive to increase students' independence in their learning (Pillars 1 and 3). The idea behind the virtuous circle is that staff at Haydon are continually learning and sharing their expertise in helping students become more independent learners and this is represented visually around a shared vision. There are different activities that feed into the cycle including Teaching and Learning Committee Meetings, results of a learning review with the Teaching and Learning organisation, the professional development programme, specific training sessions on growth mind-sets, 'making them work harder than you do' and 'getting everyone on board', a training weekend for new staff and whole school and faculty learning walks. The impact has been that teachers have gained many ideas for their lessons from other colleagues who have in turn led training sessions, continuing the cycle of positive change. Attendance at after-school training sessions has been high and feedback has been very positive. There is now a concerted drive in all Faculties to foster independent learning, such as students teaching themselves and each other, consulting resources/people before the teacher, and planning their own work. A total of 22 colleagues have taken part in short case studies looking at the impact of different techniques.

Bentley Wood High School's case study is on **Inclusive Leadership: Teachers As Innovative Leaders of Teaching And Learning**. This explores how the school has further developed the concept of distributed leadership by creating 'innovative leaders'. The school's model of innovative leadership is composed of five areas – school improvement groups, the use of honoraria, strategic leaders, student leaders and innovative leaders. Innovative leaders currently focus on students with physical impairment, specific groups within the lower attainers and EAL students.

The key purpose of this role is to share expertise on innovative and creative teaching with teachers and support staff so that outcomes for these students can be improved. Innovative leaders lead specialist professional development for colleagues in the school. This case study focuses particularly on two innovative leaders – one who works with students with physical impairment (particularly visual impairment) and another who focuses on with low-attaining pupils. They both demonstrate the most effective use of resources and innovative teaching methods and the study contains detailed examples of their work and its impact on student learning and progress. Crucially the different teaching and learning strategies are shared during school improvement group meetings and on INSET days for colleagues to implement the same strategies. The school will continue to create and develop innovative leaders as part of its inclusive leadership strategy.

At **Newstead Wood School**, the case study entitled **The Power Of Perception: A Collaborative School Evaluation Of Teaching And Learning**, (Pillars 3 and 5) focuses on how the school has developed a collaborative process for Subject Review, ensuring that the school's co-constructive approach to leadership is reflected in the drive for school improvement. The aim of the review process was to both build the capacity of middle leaders and to change the perception of lesson observations from being 'done to' to 'done with', with the emphasis on the sharing of good practice.

In 2012, a Teaching and Learning group was established, open to all, which gave the group a rich mixture of experiences and viewpoints. Over two terms, including an INSET day for the whole staff, they defined and articulated what outstanding teaching and learning looked, felt and sounded like at Newstead Wood. The product was a new pro forma to be used in lesson observations with a list of ten criteria and 'observable indicators'. Ofsted language was avoided, although there was a striking similarity between the two sets of indicators. In terms of process, it was essential to move towards co-observation and collaboration so each subject review would include a 'Guest Head of Department', and each observation would be a joint one between a member of the Leadership group and a member of the department under review.

The first wave of observations began in autumn 2012 and by the end of the academic year had involved everybody. It was clear that both a significant shift in attitudes and a sharpening of middle leaders understanding was taking place, although several adjustments were required to get the best out of the process. The departments have now undergone a second year of reviews with an increase in the number of lessons described as 'Top Level' (outstanding) and a significant increase in the capacity for reflection and drive to improve teaching and learning even further.

The study from **Little Ilford School, Learning To Be Resilient And Brilliant**, outlines the strategies that have been developed to cater for the most able students so that they can reach the highest rates in the academic world and beyond. The school developed a new identification process for more able learners based on a wider application of KS2 data as well as talented students being identified at the end of their first term in Year 7. Altogether, this cohort amounted to 20-25% of the students and their target was to be four levels of progress by the end of Year 11.

To accelerate the progress of the most able learners, all departments would have to stretch and challenge these students in every lesson. This meant re-examining learning objectives and success criteria in planning before lessons, with particular reference to the development of higher order skills, differentiated questioning, collaborative tasks and independent learning during the lesson, and challenging homework tasks after the lesson. To achieve this, consistently bespoke CPD and staff training was organised. Deep learning weeks were also organised for two weeks a year to allow more able learners to immerse themselves in a topic demanding rigorous learning in depth.

Alongside all this, it was recognised that parents and students needed to be inspired to target entry to Russell Group universities. The school bought in the Brilliant Club to work with the primary cluster and Year 6 students to train students to write short dissertations and participate in summer schools, mentored by PhD students. The impact has been a significant number of students achieving A/A* grades at GCSE. Both the student and the parent voice have been very positive and the programme will continue to be developed and refined to get the best out of everyone.

At **Gumley House Convent School** the case study concerns **Preparing Students For The Commercial And Globalised World Through A Broad Curriculum**, based on competency-led learning (Pillar 7). In order to do this, a leadership position was created to drive the vision – a Director of Specialisms was required with significant managerial, business and commercial skills. Apart from the Business and Enterprise and Language Specialism, the role expanded to develop work-related competencies and to involve programme strategies across all curriculum subjects. A massive consultation exercise was necessary with staff, students and external parties to frame a comprehensive strategy that everybody could support and then various organisations were approached to lead bespoke programmes to shape the skills and competences learning that were required.

There was also a focus on local and international communities as the school was fully committed to developing a global citizenship agenda and this headed the initial stages of the student development programme. Further, work placements were essential for sixth form students as well as KS4, building self-belief and moving mind-sets for girls to achieve. The school has established and sustained an impressive range of business partners who provide a wide variety of opportunities. In terms of impact, Gumley has twice achieved the International School Award, as well as a range of Prince's Teaching Institute awards. There are strong partnerships and regional visits across the globe, including the organisation of a Global Conference for sixth formers in 2013, and participation in The Global Young Leaders Conference in New York and Washington. The development of competency-led engagement has resulted in students gaining rich and creative opportunities to develop their skills and attitudes in a broad curriculum.

The study from **Oaks Park High School**, entitled **Aspiring Higher**, is a unique initiative for Years 10 to 13, inspiring all students to get the best out of the opportunities that are available, inside and outside school, to prepare them for future success (Pillar 7). It was initially designed by the Head of Year 13 who wanted the students to have the same range of opportunities as those from independent schools and to aim really high. Working with the sixth form team, she developed a platform on Fronter describing particular pathways to success. All students had to log onto the page and choose a pathway with complete freedom to explore, although with appropriate guidance to match their effort and attainment to date. Aspire Higher gives each student the tools and direction to enable them to start differentiating between themselves and everyone else by building a particular profile. It gives them a portal to a huge wealth of resources but the students must take advantage of this, encouraging them to be independent learners. The aim is to help each student get to where they really want to go with high aspirations and wide horizons. There are a variety of support strategies to assist them on their learning journey, with review meetings along the way. The initiative is having a great impact on helping students to prepare for their future and the next step is to roll this out to Key Stage 3 students.

There is one study from **St Michael's Catholic College** that examines partnership work with primary schools (Pillars 8 & 7), **Learning To Love Language**. This particular project builds expertise in MFL teaching within primary schools using modelling, team teaching and team planning to increase confidence and subject-specific pedagogy. This began originally in 2008 as part of a government initiative but has been given new impetus with the introduction of a compulsory language at KS2 and the need to improve uptake and standards at KS3 and KS4, as part of new curriculum reforms.

The school works with five partner primary schools on a termly, bespoke programme led by a lead practitioner from St Michael's. The focus of the teaching is on speaking and listening with learning songs and playing games a prominent feature. Staff and student feedback is very positive, with considerable engagement and enjoyment. Over the course of the project, 11 primary teachers and 12 teaching assistants have been trained in planning lessons and teaching French. INSET training sessions for primary staff have been provided along with schemes of work. The secondary school has benefited from the increased confidence of its intake in MFL, with increased take-up of modern languages generally. Work continues to fine tune the partnership and make sure that there is adequate planning and feedback time.

The study from **Bishop Ramsey Church of England School, Rooted In Stewardship,** (Pillars 6 and 7) shows how the school community has used the school environment in creative ways to improve student experience and also to motivate and mobilise staff. A big impetus for this was the creation of a new post entitled Head of Environmental Sustainability to ensure that students had experience of environmental sustainability through the taught curriculum, pastoral and extracurricular activities.

Over the last four years, the school has developed an impressive range of environmental projects involving students, staff, parents and governors. It has developed links with outside agencies such as Groundwork, an Environmental Charity which helps students make a positive contribution to their local community and environment. An example of this was a voluntary group working with local residents to create a community garden. The 'Big Dig' was an original environment project that created an outside classroom, am important resource now used by many faculties. Curriculum enrichment days are used for everybody to participate in environmental projects, such as creating a school vegetable garden. Students get the opportunity to lead projects as members of the Eco Champions Club and there is an Eco Council to plan and drive projects such as the 'Zero Waste Challenge' and 'Switch off Fortnight'. Through focusing on environmental sustainability, the school has achieved cumulative benefits in terms of the growth of student awareness and skills, staff development and the physical and aesthetic improvement of the school grounds. The various projects have also encouraged parental and community engagement and have demonstrated 'stewardship in practice'.

The most original and innovative case study comes from **Heathfield Community School**, entitled **Cafe Parano – You Can Taste The Justice**. From 2007-2013 the school bought, marketed and sold the entire coffee harvest of a co-operative in Ecuador, with all profits going to support the schools at which the farm workers' children were educated. The project had three clear aims – students learning from a real-world business context, broadening the scope of international partnerships, and providing experiences to give students confidence and independence. By 2011, there was a defined company structure in which the students took on specific roles such as finance, marketing, design and international links with a managerial board.

Over the years, some 300 students and many staff have been involved and Cafe Parano has become a whole school project with links to many areas of the curriculum. Students have given presentations at many prestigious events, and there has been a strong link to the school's Comenius projects fostering other international links, with the project now moving on to the Dominican Republic. The case study provides an excellent range of comments and evidence from students and staff about the impact of the project, including the development of confidence, skills, promoting intercultural understanding and providing real-life learning experiences. It links very well to Pillar 8 and high-quality partnerships, together with Pillar 4, with a strong focus on engaging and involving students and Pillar 7, relating to a rich and creative curriculum.

Another original study is that from **Lampton School**, a case study in the power of sport to be transformative, **What Can We Do To Be Better?** The study examines the power of sports leadership to motivate students to develop behaviours and attitudes towards school and education. This is within the context of a Basketball Academy developed over the last four years with elite athletes who learn to exercise responsible leadership. There is an emphasis upon 'grit' and character development, resilience and self-discipline and a sense of pride and belonging. The ambition was also to break patterns of under-achievement among some students and provide alternative pathways to success. It involves some 70 students and the success of the academy reflects the research done on extensive hard work and practice, rather than just natural talent, allied to the impact of praise and motivation.

There has been a significant impact on the attendance and behaviour and academic progress of the students across the curriculum, with the development of real 'growth mind-sets'. This study demonstrates the power of sport to transform lives, breaking through social disadvantage whilst providing students with the structure and discipline to achieve their potential. This study relates very well to Pillar 7, providing a creative curriculum within and beyond the classroom to fully meet the needs of groups of students so that all are able to participate, progress and achieve.

The study from **JFS School, Succeeding With Succession**, (Pillar 2) focuses on the leadership and management strand of the school's overall enrichment programme for staff aiming to equip teachers with the skills to lead and manage their sections and teams in an effective and motivating way. The programme has run from 2008-2009, but each year is further developed in response to feedback. Crucially, the programme is facilitated by external consultants who specialise in training and coaching for leadership and team development. All staff are allowed to participate in the programme regardless of role, responsibility or experience. Over the years, a suite of eight programmes has been developed, suitably differentiated, with colleagues encouraged to opt for the courses they feel are most suitable for them.

Aspiring Middle Leaders 1 is 'Preparing for leadership', and Aspiring Middle Leaders 2 is 'Preparing yourself for a future leadership role' which includes an INSIGHTS model on personal behaviour and leadership styles. Middle Leaders 3 concerns 'Towards outstanding leadership', and Middle Leaders 4 'Getting the best from your team'. For new leaders there are two explorations of issues for those in the first years of their role, and for those with 3+ years of experience. There are two further programmes 'Coaching and Mentoring' and '360 degree bespoke coaching'. All of these are delivered in a series of four two-hour workshops after school over three months, concluding with a key note speaker. Participation rates are high and feedback has been highly positive. The programme has inspired many staff to consider, develop and realise their leadership abilities and of the over 100 different participants, more than half have already gone on to promoted posts within the school. This is an excellent study on how to build leadership capacity in a school which in turn drives success.

At **Plashet School**, the case study **Mentoring Matters – Here's How,** (Pillar 6) focuses on the work of the learning mentor team and how their intervention has made a significant impact upon the achievement of students, their progress and attainment. The Learning Support Unit at Plashet consists of three learning mentors, a learning support teacher and a Head of Department who have developed a highly structured and formal system of working with staff and students linked to aspects of the school development plan.

Learning mentor intervention includes the referral process, baseline assessment, a mentoring action plan devised with the student, reviews and re-assessment. The team is also closely involved with whole school pastoral provision through being attached to Year Teams and attending assemblies, parents' evenings and Year Group events, and being involved in pastoral plans, SEN and attendance meetings. The team members contribute to school newsletters, internal bulletins and lead a variety of events such as Anti-Bullying Week. The study references What's Different Now? in terms of provision and impact. Crucially, having a transparent criteria shared with all staff, termly monitoring, the development of a rich, range of resources based on student self-assessments with precise action plans, and specific assessment and accredited qualifications, have made a significant impact on the achievements and attitudes of students.

Along with AQA, the school has developed the first National Award for assessing progress made by students when working with learning mentors, and three more awards have followed. The Learning Support Team has developed and published a range of resources and in July 2013 they won the Times Educational Supplement Award for Support Team of the Year.

The study from **Clapton Girls' Academy, A Taste of Vocational Learning**, (Pillar 7) focuses on the establishment of an alternative vocational programme for a small number of Key Stage 3 students who were becoming disaffected and disengaged because the curriculum did not meet their needs. The aims of the programme were to improve student motivation, engagement, behaviour, relationships, emotional well-being and academic attainment and to establish pathways to KS4 alternative provision.

A pilot programme with four girls working with outside providers had yielded encouraging results and by September 2012, the Tuesday programme was launched for nine students in Year 9, followed by 10 students in 2013. This was a one day, weekly project run in partnership with INSPIRE, a vocational provider. The girls were provided with a comprehensive programme at various venues including catering, film making, fashion and textiles, hair styling, sports and leisure, construction and mechanics. There was a 'contract' that both students and parents signed and expectations were clearly explained.

The results have been impressive, leading to a marked reduction in the need for alternative places at KS4. There is a good range of evidence about the effectiveness of the programme from staff, students, parents and facilitators. Attendance has improved dramatically and grade levels have been maintained or improved in English and Maths, with the girls also achieving a Key Skills Level 3 qualification. Behaviour, engagement and emotional well-being have also been transformed so that these students will be much more successful at Key Stage 4. Now, in 2014, the programme is fully embedded as part of the Year 9 curriculum and each year disengaged students are re-engaged with the students' achievements publicly recognised during the end of year Achievement Assembly.

"The route to greatness lies in moral purpose: the determination, brought to reality that all members of the school community – teachers, support staff and students – should behave in a way that is mindful of each other. They will know what it is to feel grief and experience doubt, as well as great joy and success. Above all they will know, because they are the living examples of it, that fairness lies at the heart of any civilised society, and they will see that reflected in the everyday actions of their school."

Tim Brighouse and David Woods

CHAPTER 3

A WHOLE SCHOOL APPROACH TO INTRODUCING A SHARED VALUES SYSTEM

GERRY ROBINSON, SWANLEA SCHOOL

FOCUS AREA

This case study describes actions taken at Swanlea School to challenge prejudicial attitudes and behaviours amongst some students, and to establish a shared set of values that would result in a values-centred school ethos.

AIMS

The key aims of the initiative were to:

- Develop a school ethos of respect and to build a values-centered school culture

- Reduce incidents of prejudice and discrimination.

RATIONALE

Swanlea is an average-sized secondary school in Whitechapel, Tower Hamlets. The overwhelming majority of students are Bangladeshi. Somali pupils are the second largest ethnic group. A well-above average proportion of pupils speak English as an additional language.

In September 2012, it was identified that the number of incidents of poor behaviour relating to discriminatory behaviour (racism, homophobia, sexism) was of concern and that there was a need to tackle these issues across the school.

THE STORY

In September 2012 we identified consistent patterns of incidents of prejudicial behaviour. Concerns were also raised about the recording and addressing of these incidents and, as a result, a project of improvement was devised.

We ensured, in presentations to all stakeholders – including governors, parents, students and staff – that the key issues were outlined with clarity and transparency. Through extensive consultation, including whole school student and staff surveys, we developed a deeper understanding of the key issues, as well as initially raising the school's awareness. It became clear that attitudes towards women and girls and homophobia were real concerns that had not yet been spoken about or addressed explicitly in the school.

Having identified the problems, we then sought to outline the vision. As a result of powerful visioning exercises, we were able to motivate groups of key individuals to help drive and sustain change. For example, we ensured that every single member of the Senior Leadership Team was aware of the depth of the problem and that we were consistent in how we addressed it. This meant reviewing and updating our current systems, strategies and being absolutely consistent in how we addressed and spoke about the problem. We also, for example, garnered the support of governors and parents, through developing a working party with invited governors and presenting at both full governing body and committee meetings.

A fundamental principle was that any change should be inclusive. We conducted training with all staff, including premises staff, office staff, kitchen staff and all teaching and support staff – on how to challenge discrimination and prejudice. Students have benefited from rigorous, consistent and robust approaches to challenging unacceptable behaviour and all staff are now aware of their responsibilities and are held to account for them. The impact has been considerable.

In collaboration with the School Council, and in consultation with all of the school staff and governors, we created an agreed set of Swanlea Shared Values. These have further driven consistency and high expectations and have underpinned improvements in behaviour and students' treatment of each other. We exploited every possible opportunity to promote and reinforce the Swanlea Shared Values, through assemblies, the school magazine, the website, the student planner, the home-school agreement and at every public meeting.

Through this process, we further deepened our awareness of the importance of dispersed leadership in driving and sustaining change. The School Council and a team of Peer Mediators were key in leading, embedding and reviewing the impact of Swanlea Shared Values. These student leaders took real ownership of the project and ensured its success. We learnt that leadership is not about going it alone, but about developing teams of people coalesced around common goals and working towards a common vision. This vision was supported by good strategic planning and we ensured that at each stage change was manageable, success criteria clearly identified, and that when we reached each milestone, each success was celebrated publically. This kept a groundswell of support and ensured that the development of Swanlea Shared Values and its ethos were at the centre of everything that we did.

We think that all schools that seek real and sustained change should look externally. Part of the transformation of Swanlea's ethos and value system was for Swanlea students to see themselves as global citizens, not just citizens of Tower Hamlets. Throughout the process, we worked collaboratively with a range of national and international groups. These included Stonewall, Diversity Role Models and various high profile leaders. The involvement of these organisations and people was celebrated and shared throughout the school and local media.

All change requires evaluation and this is something that schools are not always good at. We therefore ensured that the impact of the work that we were doing was thoroughly evaluated at each stage. These evaluations exposed the need for further change and an improvement in consistency in the way that the unacceptable behaviour was dealt with. As a result, we led the radical overhaul of our whole school's behaviour systems and the created a new behaviour policy. Our new whole school consequences and reward system was built very firmly on the foundation of the Swanlea Shared Values.

The impact of that has been felt across the school and Ofsted commented: "The school fully embraces equality of opportunity for all its pupils. It is welcoming, supportive and based very strongly on a shared understanding of the importance of mutual respect."

Throughout this change, we developed our own understanding of leadership. What started out as a seemingly small project, grew to one that was significant and transformational for the whole school. We learned that resilience is not an innate, but a developed quality. We took each challenge or setback as an opportunity to re-evaluate and to exploit new possibilities. It was through these challenges and setbacks that the real need for the change was exposed and that new areas to be developed were highlighted.

HOW WE DID IT:

- We identified the issue and developed a vision with the Senior Leadership Team.

- A whole school survey of all staff (including support staff) and students about equality and diversity was carried out to identify the issues and areas for development.

- A focus group of staff looking at the issues around equality and diversity was formed to develop an action plan.

- A focus group of students worked with outside agencies including Stonewall, Diversity Role Models and The Jewish Museum to develop a shared understanding of the issues.

- Student Council, governors, parents and staff worked together to come up with a set of 'shared values' to introduce to all stakeholders.

- A whole school INSET on diversity and equality was delivered by the staff focus group. A step-by-step guide on challenging prejudice and discrimination was produced.

- A whole school INSET on diversity and equality was delivered by the staff focus group.

- The launch of Swanlea Shared Values in National Anti-Bullying Week included assemblies, a poster campaign, publication in student planners and the school magazine.

- There was continual reference to the values and whole school events to celebrate the ideas of equality and diversity – Black History Month, LGBT History Month, Holocaust Memorial Day etc. Much of this work was student-led. We became a Stonewall School Champion School, began the process of seeking the Equalities Award and now sit on the steering committee for Diversity Role Models.

- We rewrote the whole school PSHEE and Citizenship programme (Years 7 to 11) to continually focus on these issues and to embed Swanlea Shared Values.

- We shared good practice within the local authority, through the Tower Hamlets Behaviour Support Team and in feeder primary schools.

- A new rewards and behaviour policy was introduced in September 2013, clearly linked to the shared values. The consequences of not respecting the Swanlea shared values are made explicit in the behaviour policy.

IMPACT

- Collaboration of the whole school in supporting the values system.

- An increased consistency in approach to dealing with prejudice and discrimination.

- High profile events celebrating diversity and equality.

- An initial increase in the reporting of and then a reduction in the number of racist, homophobic and sexist incidents.

OUR ACTION PLAN

Next steps following the introduction of Swanlea Shared Values and whole staff training:

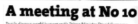

Refugee Week

BLACK HiSTORY MONTH 2013

One World Week

Schools news

A meeting at No 10

Pupils discuss world hunger with Prime Minister David Cameron

Story of Anne Frank brought to life

ACTION	WHEN?	WHO?
Priority 1: Developing a clear and consistent whole school behaviour policy.	Consultation with Learning Co-ordinators, Student Council and Senior Leadership Team beginning April 2013.	Senior Leadership Team, Learning Co-ordinators, Student Council.
Priority 2: Review/evaluate and then develop teaching and learning to embed equalities and diversity (&SMSC) in the curriculum – share good practice, focus in faculty meetings and CPD.	Audit/review in September 2014.	Heads of Year, Senior Leadership Team.
Priority 3: Develop PSHEE curriculum which embeds ideas of shared values and challenges prejudice and discrimination.	Planning ongoing delivery from September 2013.	Deputy Learning Co-ordinators, Senior Leadership Team.
Shared Values in planners, visible around school and promoted in assemblies.	Ongoing planners, September 2013.	Senior Leadership Team, Learning Co-ordinators.
Celebrate focus weeks/months – Black History Month, Beat Bullying Week, LGBT History Month, and Disability Awareness Month. Develop curriculum links.	Calendar for academic year beginning September 2013.	Senior Leadership Team, Learning Co-ordinators, Heads of Year.
Peer mentors – trained by LEAP – make these visible and useful.	Trained, now need to be promoted – May 2013.	Senior Leadership Team.
Create email address studentsupport@swanlea.towerhamlets.sch.uk	Done – needs to be promoted through planners, etc.	Senior Leadership Team.
Student interest groups – Oxfam Youth Group, Amnesty Youth Group.	Ongoing.	Senior Leadership Team.
Repeat whole school survey on equalities and diversity to monitor progress.	Spring 2014.	Senior Leadership Team.

RESULTS

- Collaboration of the whole school in supporting the values system.

- Increased student voice and leadership. The number of students who are actively involved in Student Voice activities (School Council, committees etc.) rose from 5% to 46% within the academic year. Students saw that being on the School Council or a Student Leader has real impact.

- Student and staff ownership of the Swanlea Shared Values.

- An increased consistency in our approach to dealing with and reporting incidents of prejudice and discrimination.

- Regular, high profile events celebrating diversity and equality.

- An initial spike in the reporting, and then a reduction in the number of racist, homophobic and sexist incidents.

- Extremely positive feedback from Ofsted (July 2013) about the culture of mutual respect evident in the school.

"The school fully embraces equality of opportunity for all its pupils. It is welcoming, supportive and based very strongly on mutual respect."

Ofsted 2013

"Students' behaviour around school is outstanding. They are very friendly, welcoming and courteous."

Ofsted 2013

"The school's very welcoming and supportive ethos and vision based on respect for all means that all students are valued."

Ofsted 2013

EVALUATION

The introduction of Swanlea Shared Values and the focus on mutual respect has had a noticeable impact on the behaviour of students. Prejudiced and discriminatory comments and issues of prejudice-related bullying are becoming less frequent. A Year 9 tutor and MFL teacher emailed us following the February 2014 LGBT History Month assembly to say:

"Really great assembly again this morning, it has made such a difference since the ones you did on the Shared Values and LGBT History Month last year."

"I haven't heard kids use the word 'gay' in a derogatory way for ages... it's having a definite effect. The impact of the work you do has been huge. There has been a noticeable shift in attitudes of staff and students."

To make a quantitative evaluation, we looked at the difference in responses to the whole school surveys from 2013 and 2014. In all questions regarding sexism, racism and prejudice there has been a significant reduction in the number of incidents. Staff have also reported that they are more confident and consistent in dealing with incidents of prejudice and discrimination.

STUDENT SURVEY

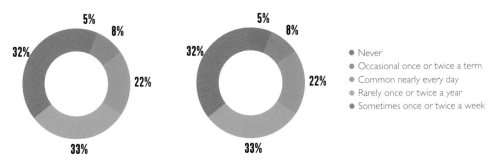

- Never
- Occasional once or twice a term
- Common nearly every day
- Rarely once or twice a year
- Sometimes once or twice a week

CONNECTING LIVES

This workshop was really interesting and fun. It made me realise how little I know about Jewish people. I was really surprised to learn about how many similarities there are between Islam and Judaism and many words in Hebrew and Arabic sound similar.

Mohammed, 6.6
ASSISTANT HEADTEACHER

During half-term all of Year 8 took part in workshops held held at my the Jewish Museum. This was part of a London-wide project called 'Connecting Lives'. Students met two Jewish women from the museum who talked to them and answered questions about their lives, culture and faith.

Students were given the opportunity to handle artifacts from the museum including a Kippah (skull cap), shofar (ram's horn) and a replica Torah scroll.

The workshops really challenged students' perceptions and allowed them to develop an understanding of the similarities between Judaism and Islam.

LEADING BY EXAMPLE:

are you aware of your own use of language and perceived judgements?

If we are ever to achieve equality in the school we must look first to ourselves; often, we make judgements on the students without even realising it. Have a look at this sheet below and ask yourself how many of these comments or judgements, or similar ones, you have made.

HAVE YOU EVER SAID SOMETHING LIKE THIS:

"That's not very ladylike."

"That is not a book for boys."

"Are you mental?"

"That is so gay."

"Idiot"

"That is a boys' subject, not for girls"

"What is wrong with you?"

HAVE YOU EVER MADE JUDGEMENTS LIKE THIS:

If boys are having physical contact, made a joke about them needing privacy.

Remarked that "boys will be boys"

Questioned the boys' masculinity.

Referred to the students of the school as if they are all Bengali.

Commented on the way girls look, dress or behave.

FINALLY, ASK YOURSELF HOW MANY OPPORTUNITIES TO CHALLENGE THESE KIND OF COMMENTS HAVE YOU MISSED?

LEAP INTO LEADERSHIP

Participating in this programme has my own voice and self-esteem. I also learnt have challenged my own prejudices and developed my leadership potential. I've really gained a lot of what I have achieved.

Jaleel Hussein, Year 9

A WOMAN'S PLACE IS IN THE HOME... (& THE CLASSROOM & THE BOARDROOM & THE NEWSROOM & PARLIAMENT)

ONE BILLION WOMEN ON THE PLANET WILL EXPERIENCE VIOLENCE IN THEIR LIFETIME

ALL FEMALE STUDENTS AND STAFF WELCOME.

BLACK HISTORY MONTH

NEXT STEPS

Equality remains a focus on the Whole School Development Plan for 2013/14. It continues to be a priority for the Headteacher and the Senior Leadership Team.

We will ensure that key equality-related events are formally included in the whole school calendar (e.g. LGBT History month, International Women's Day). These events will be linked to the School Development Plan, the SLT assembly rota and the PSHEE curriculum.

We will develop the school's programme on gender equality and look to increase the number of high profile women visiting the school to talk about careers and aspirations. To ensure that this issue is brought to the fore-front, a whole school CPD session will be delivered following consultation and feedback from focus groups on how to embed gender equality within teaching and learning. The school will continue its partnership work with external organisations. A member of the SLT will sit on the education steering groups for Diversity Role Models and The Jewish Museum.

The role of Peer Mediators within the school will be refined and further formalised through a more streamlined application/interview process, with focused training for students, and a clearer, more explicit role within the school's student leadership system. The school council will also be working with local feeder primary schools to share the Swanlea School Values and anti-bullying messages.

Equality awareness will be included as a prompt within internal school evaluation forms, from lesson plan pro formas, reward/trip request forms, faculty reports to governors, applications for funding for additional projects, to lesson observation forms. The impact on teaching and learning will be monitored and appraised regularly.

The school's electronic behaviour monitoring system has undergone a radical overhaul since September 2013 to explicitly include homophobia, racism and sexism within its parameters. This system is still a work in progress and through feedback from users, it has been refined and adjusted over time. The school maintains a close watch on the monitoring system to ensure that consistent and accurate recording of incidents is maintained. Regular training sessions are scheduled for new members of staff, as are as top-up sessions for existing staff who may need a refresher course.

Swanlea School is being used as a model to share good practice within the London Borough of Tower Hamlets. The Tower Hamlets Behaviour Support Team is working with Swanlea to disseminate the model to other schools and the school will work towards achieving the Equalities Award to celebrate and formalise the work the school is currently doing.

CHAPTER 4

FROM CONFLICT TO RESOLUTION – EMBEDDING A POSITIVE ETHOS

SHARON MERCER WITH VICKI PRICE AND MAGGIE BAILEY, GREY COURT SCHOOL

"If a window is broken and left unrepaired, people walking by will conclude that no one cares and no one is in charge. Soon, more windows will be broken, and the sense of anarchy will spread from the building to the street on which it faces, sending a signal that anything goes."

The 'Broken Windows Theory, James Q. Wilson and George Kelling in Malcolm Gladwell: The Tipping Point, 2002.

"If we change ourselves we can change the world, and changing ourselves begins with changing our language and methods of communication."

A. Gandhi in Nonviolent Communication, M.B. Rosenberg 2003

FOCUS AREA

This case study looks at the introduction of restorative approaches (RA) at Grey Court School and the positive contribution it has made to the school's development over a five-year period. In particular, it focuses on the improved behaviour and relationships between students, staff, and the local community as well as the positive impact this has had on the school ethos.

RATIONALE

Our aim was to become a school where restorative approaches are understood and used by students and staff to enable them to work with each other. In doing so, everyone in the school community would share a common language and have a greater appreciation of each other's feelings and needs, so that an ethos of mutual respect, care and understanding was fostered.

In its simplest form, restorative approaches can be used as a way of resolving problems when things go wrong. They involve a dialogue between two or more people who sit together with a facilitator to discuss the five key restorative questions so that they can move forward in a positive way and prevent future conflict.

THE 5 KEY RESTORATIVE QUESTIONS ARE AS FOLLOWS:

- What happened?

- What were you thinking and feeling?

- Who has been affected by this and how?

- What needs to happen now to put things right?

- What do you need to move on from this?

BACKGROUND CONTEXT

In 2003, Grey Court School went into special measures. After a succession of six Headteachers in five years, a new Headteacher joined in January 2007. The Headteacher set about winning the hearts and minds of the major stakeholders by adopting an 'open door' policy. She made herself visible and available to listen to the concerns of students, staff, parents, governors, local residents, community police and bus companies and discussing their ideas about possible solutions.

In 2008, a small group of Year 9 students went to speak to the Headteacher about their concerns regarding their year group, which included gossiping, bullying, disruption of lessons and the negative impact it was having on their learning and wellbeing. This was a turning point when restorative approaches became more than simple conflict resolution. RA became a student-led initiative, which would ultimately have a lasting impact on the culture and ethos of the school.

"*The students have come to be proud of their school. That pride came from two things: the realisation that the old standards weren't good enough (as with everything, growth and development is the key), and a revived sense of community which stemmed from our restorative attempts.*"

A Year 9 student, 2008

THE STORY

BEGINNING THE RESTORATIVE JOURNEY

In 2008, the Student Support Officers (SSOs) – non-teaching Heads of Year – were trained in restorative approaches. The aim was that there would be less disruption of lessons if conflicts could be resolved by the SSOs supporting the students. They would achieve this by talking things through in a nonviolent manner, in a safe environment where those involved were able to express how they were feeling and what they needed in order to be able to repair the harm done and move on in a safe and positive way.

Similarly, teachers would be able to meet with challenging students and discuss a way forward so that this behaviour was not repeated lesson after lesson. By providing the time to talk and to listen, a process of healing could take place, trust could build and importantly teachers could teach and students were able to learn.

"*It puts the emphasis on the student to make the right choice and it encourages them to take ownership of their behaviour. It also minimises conflict.*"

Grey Court School teacher

OVERCOMING EARLY PRACTICAL ISSUES:

FINDING TIME

In the initial stages, working restoratively was very time-consuming. Some restorative meetings were relatively straightforward but others were more complex and required several meetings before the matter was resolved. To cope with the volume of incidents that SSOs had to deal with, an enquiry sheet was devised.

A clear message was sent to students that what they had to say was important and they would be given the opportunity to put things right. After a while, there was a noticeable cultural shift. Students began to approach SSOs to help them to resolve problems by talking things through before they reached a critical point.

> **"**To take restorative approaches on board, there has to be a complete wholesale change in mind-set within the school and that's every single member of staff and with the students as well.**"**

Grey Court School Associate Headteacher

CULTURAL SHIFT

Developing a shared restorative vision was not easy – it required a paradigm shift about discipline and managing behaviour. Some staff, who were used to a more traditional way of dealing with behaviour, felt uncomfortable working restoratively. They believed it was the right of the teacher to expect compliance from students and that where school rules were violated, wrongdoers should be punished. We encouraged a culture shift through staff training.

In 2009, the Headteacher, Senior Leadership Team members and Middle Managers were trained in RA, closely followed by the rest of the staff. As leaders, the actions of SLT sent a strong message to others about what was expected when dealing with behaviour issues and what was important around school. They began to use restorative language and 'walk the talk'.

OUR BEHAVIOUR POLICY:

The school endeavours to involve students in the disciplinary process and apply, wherever possible, restorative approaches as the first step to repairing the harm done to the school or others. Restorative approaches aim to resolve conflict in a calm and positive way. They involve everyone who has been involved in a conflict or difficult situation together to find a way forward.

Developing a whole school approach by rewriting the school behaviour policy in 2010 meant that all staff were required to deal with behaviour incidents by using restorative approaches. Importantly, the policy was rewritten in consultation with staff, students, parents and governors and it has become the way we do things at Grey Court.

BECOMING A RESTORATIVE SCHOOL

THE POWER OF GROUPS

The shift from being a school that practises restorative approaches, to a school that is truly restorative has taken five years but its acceleration came as a result of the group of Year 9 students in 2008.

In September 2008, tutor group circle time conferences were organised to build trust. Students were encouraged to discuss their concerns, take responsibility for some of the negative issues raised, and to make amends where appropriate. Having heard how their behaviour had affected the learning and wellbeing of others, students publicly apologised to each other for the harm they had caused and pledged to change. The ideas that came from the students at the conferences were used as a starting point to create an action plan.

In October 2008, a Year 9 Activity Day brought the whole year together to get to know each other. Students followed a carousel of activities designed to encourage teamwork and bonding. At the heart of the day was a survival activity, which enabled the students to understand that they needed each other in order to succeed. Importantly, the Activity Day had identified leaders within the year group who would be able to take the action plan forward.

That December, a student-teacher conference took place to progress the action plan. Student group leaders guided each group through the activities, with a teacher attached to each. They agreed the priorities, the actions needed and a timescale. At the end of the conference, the group leaders presented the action plan to the students and teachers. What was clear was that the students and staff wanted to achieve the same goals – they had worked together and shared the vision.

In March 2009, the students presented the action plan at a full governors meeting and it was approved. The students recognised the need to improve student behaviour and engagement in the classroom. They also recognised that creating a positive ethos was not just dependant on the students. They expressed a desire for improved teaching and learning styles and positive relationships with teachers, as well as the need for an improved reward system to motivate students. See a short extract below.

In July 2009, as a reward, Year 9s were taken on their first residential trip. This has become an annual event along with restorative conferencing.

EXTRACT FROM A YEAR 9 ACTION PLAN – RESULTS, IMPACT AND OUTCOMES

BEHAVIOUR	HOW WE WILL ACHIEVE THIS	TIMESCALE
We need to be polite, show good manners and have mutual respect, including the way we speak to each other and the language we use, student-to-student and student-to-teacher. We all need to smile more and be kinder.	Put up posters, reward good behaviour – people could be nominated for prizes. We could use positive peer pressure and have student panels (with training) for consistent consequences – everyone to model. More group work. Use RA more often.	Immediately and ongoing.

TEACHING & LEARNING	HOW WE WILL ACHIEVE THIS	TIMESCALE
We would like the behaviour policy reviewed so that we have different punishments for poor behaviour. Detentions and exclusions do not always work. We would also like teachers not to send students out of class for too long – three strikes, phone calls home and report work better when students misbehave.	Discuss in collegium meetings, student reps could work with teachers to review the policy. Discuss sanctions – add community work, isolation, warning systems and parental input. Review classroom consequences, teachers to communicate more clearly what will happen. Use RA with teachers and students. All staff need to be consistent otherwise this will not work.	Summer term and ongoing.

REWARDS & MOTIVATORS	HOW WE WILL ACHIEVE THIS	TIMESCALE
Students should be rewarded for all the positive things they do, such as work, good behaviour, helping others, and kindness.	Reward more. Give more merits or vouchers that could be spent in a school rewards shop. Trips could also be used as rewards. There could be nominations for student of the week and good cards sent home. Introduce a House system.	Immediate and plan for autumn term.

IMPACT

The introduction of restorative approaches has had a powerful and positive impact on the school ethos and we have continued to embed it into everything we do. In 2013, the Grey Court Relationship Policy was written by students and staff and sums up our restorative philosophy.

Our vision of a restorative school is one in which:

- Everyone understands and uses restorative approaches, and staff and students use it to help resolve issues.

- We understand that we are not perfect, but we are patient and try our best to work together to resolve problems.

- Members of the community respect and care about each other and recognise that we are a nonviolent, anti-bullying school.

- We are reassured that everyone will be listened to and issues will be dealt with fairly.

- We are a positive community and are optimistic that relationships can be repaired.

- We learn from our mistakes and change our future behaviour.

- We trust one another to be honest and show compassion.

- We are a school where everyone is equal and people can feel safe.

OTHER INDICATORS OF SUCCESS ARE:

- Improved academic attainment: In 2008, 66% of students gained 5 A*-C grades compared to 99% in 2013. Combined English and Maths in 2010 was 54% A*-C compared to 77% in 2013.

- Improved attendance: In 2008, overall attendance was 91% compared to 95% in 2013.

- Improved behaviour: During a five-year period, the school has had no permanent exclusions and has had the lowest exclusion rate in the borough.

- As a school that practises nonviolent communication, aggression in and around school is rare as students seek resolution through talking, listening, understanding and repairing.

- Student voice has been strengthened and has brought about positive change by the introduction of a House system to further promote community spirit.

- A high emphasis is placed on SMSC, the spiritual, moral, social and cultural aspects of learning through annual restorative conferences, whole school CPSHE days, activity days and Resilience Programmes.

- A student mentoring system has been created to help with the transition from Year 6 to Year 7. Student mentors have also been trained as peer mediators and are able to help students to resolve smaller incidents of conflict using RA.

- The school has an improved reputation within the local community.

- Throughout 2011-13, we have trained schools in restorative approaches locally and abroad. We have been part of a British Council project, invited to Finland to train schools in Helsinki. We have also produced a restorative training DVD, recommended by the Restorative Justice Council.

- In 2013, Grey Court was awarded Outstanding in all areas by Ofsted:

"The school is committed to a restorative justice approach to resolving conflict and improving students' behaviour and relationships. This is highly valued by the students, who feel the system is very fair and has really improved behaviour in the school."

Ofsted 2013

"It is a lot easier to sort things out because you can talk about it calmly and not flip out and get angry."

A Year 9 student

"It helps me with my learning more because I am comfortable in my surroundings and I know that I can trust everyone and I can talk to them easily."

A Year 10 student

REFLECTIONS/EVALUATION

POSITIVE OUTCOMES

Restorative approaches are now part of our culture. RA has played a major role in our journey to becoming an outstanding school. We now have an ethos with an emphasis on high quality relationships, a calm orderly learning environment, respect for one another and high standards of personal appearance and manners. Increasingly, we are placing responsibility for learning with our students.

"As a new teacher to Grey Court, one aspect of the school that particularly stands out to me as different from my experience working at other schools is that the relationships between staff and pupils are grounded in a mutual respect.

*This is because, instead of simply being told when their behaviour is right or wrong, the pupils are asked to reflect upon it, leading them to a far deeper level of understanding of how they behave, and allowing them to make positive changes far more quickly.***"**

Grey Court School teacher

ONGOING CHALLENGES

It can take some staff longer to change their thinking about behaviour management and feel comfortable using restorative processes and language. Not all students find working restoratively easy; some AEN students find it difficult to sit and listen in order to resolve a situation, and may forget what has been agreed and go on to cause further upset. When students with challenging behaviour join our school in the upper years, they can be less responsive to RA as it is unfamiliar.

We continue to use RA in the belief that the benefits of working restoratively, such as increasing levels of empathy, improving emotional understanding, motivation and social and communication skills, will trickle thorough and enable our students to be better citizens.

NEXT STEPS

To ensure sustainability and enhancement of restorative approaches, we must maintain its existing high profile and develop fresh ways of delivering this through the introduction of a new sixth form, training pupils in additional feeder primary schools so that students are familiar with this process before they join our school, training parents and using restorative practises to enhance student and staff wellbeing.

CHAPTER 5

HAVE YOU EARNED IT? POSITIVE BEHAVIOUR MANAGEMENT

BETH HUMPHREYS, KING SOLOMON ACADEMY

FOCUS AREA

This case study describes the 'payslip' rewards and sanctions system introduced at a newly-established academy in West London, and evaluates its impact.

RATIONALE

Every school in the world is trying to teach its pupils how to be the best people they can be, both academically and in terms of character. Schools invest a great deal into managing and developing their pupils' behaviours. Whilst some schools leave it up to individual teachers or departments to design a system of rewards and sanctions, best practice suggests that the most effective schools have a centralised system. At King Solomon Academy, a payslip enables us to track every good and poor behaviour choice the pupils in our school make, on a weekly basis. In addition, it enables our pupils to manage their own behaviour and learn that they have an inner locus of control: their choices decide what their lives look like from one day to the next and from one week to the next, as well as in the long term. If they work hard and do the right thing, they will earn the rewards. If they choose not to, they will face the consequences.

BACKGROUND CONTEXT

Max Haimendorf was appointed as Designate Headteacher of King Solomon Academy Secondary in 2008, and opened the doors of the school to its first cohort of Year 7 pupils in September 2009. Max had spent a year planning the school, designing its culture and curriculum and visiting some of the best charter schools in the United States to observe the best practice he could find. The first year of any start-up is challenging and, while the pupils made a lot of progress and there were many, many successes, Max knew that there had been too much focus on the consequences of pupils' poor behaviour choices and not enough personalised, specific rewards for the vast majority of pupils who were making good behaviour choices. King Solomon Academy made the mistake that many new-start schools do, of prioritising strictness for its own sake. As a result, too many conversations about pupils' behaviour were negative: pupils didn't have concrete outcomes to aim for, other than to avoid punitive consequences such as detention. The school didn't have a common language to praise pupils who were consistently making better choices about their behaviour and limited systems for rewarding them.

THE STORY

Approaching the end of the first year, Max visited another round of high performing charter schools in the United States to reflect and build on the outcomes of the first year of King Solomon Academy and to plan further innovations and approaches which would change the school for the better. Having read and been inspired by Rafe Esquith's classroom-based payslip model (outlined in his book Teach Like Your Hair Is On Fire), he observed a whole school 'payslip' at one of the highest performing middle schools in the US, Excel Academy, Boston. He decided to bring it home.

Payslip works in the same way as an employee's payslip does. The 'bank' of King Solomon Academy pays its 'employees' for attending school every day: 15 KSA pounds a day for their work. Praising attendance has to be the foundation of a school's reward system – if pupils aren't in school, they can't progress.

After that, payslip rewards everything the school cares about. Narrating what's important to pupils' success both academically and in terms of their character development in a clear, formulaic way is very powerful. As such, pupils can earn merits (each with a value of two KSA pounds) for producing exceptional classwork or homework, for SLANTing well in class (SLANT = Sit Up Straight, Listen Hard, Ask and Answer Questions, Nod and Track the Speaker) or for some sort of service or going out of their way to do something nice for a team member, a teacher or another member of our community. Pupils can earn an AWOPR (Act Worthy of Public Recognition) worth ten KSA pounds for going above and beyond, and for making the most progress in a subject or being the highest attainer in the class each half term. We also recognise the massive impact homework has on pupils' success, so if pupils hand in all their homework, completed and on time, they earn a ten-KSA-pound homework bonus.

Likewise, every time a pupil makes a poor behaviour choice, it matters. Whilst one demerit wouldn't get you sent out of a classroom (three demerits in one lesson would), it matters because that's a two-pound deduction on your payslip. In exactly the same way as we reward positive behaviour choices, payslip mirrors the sanction for negative behaviours. Demerits are issued for disruption to learning, disrespect to staff, disrespect to pupils, disrespect to property, lack of effort in the classroom, deliberate non-SLANTing, missing equipment and poor corridor behaviour. An automatic detention (for bringing electronic equipment or food to school, unsafe behaviour in a science lab, more serious disrespect) carries a deduction of five KSA pounds. When one piece of homework is not handed in, four pounds are deducted. If it's handed in incomplete, it's a deduction of two pounds (thus illustrating that it's always better to try and hand something in rather than just give up).

Each week, a physical payslip is generated and printed for every pupil in the school. The weekly short-term goal is to earn enrichment, which is valued at 85 KSA pounds in a week. On Enrichment afternoon, the whole school is off-timetable and pupils choose an enriching activity they enjoy (sports, film club, art, drama and fun times) to participate in. If pupils have a low payslip total, they do not earn enrichment; instead they spend the afternoon catching up on work and reflecting on their choices.

This weekly target gives pupils a constant, near-term focus. Pupils with the highest payslips are celebrated in weekly assemblies, are given the first choice for going on trips and other randomly allocated rewards. With a half-term average of over 110, a pupil qualifies for a silver wristband and a series of associated privileges, while over 120 qualifies a pupil for a gold wristband. This visibly highlights pupils who consistently make excellent choices about how to act in our school community: how to 'work hard and be nice'.

Payslip also feeds into the fundamental mission of the school, which is to prepare all our pupils for success at university and beyond. Academic success is vital for our pupils to achieve this goal, but good grades alone are not sufficient preparation for life after school. The backgrounds of many of our pupils mean that university is an alien concept when they join the school aged eleven and for us to be able to change that for them, they need to visit universities and experience wider life as much as possible. As such, there is an end-of-year residential available to every child in our school. These are transformational life experiences; a week at Warwick University living in halls in Year 7, an overnight stay in Paris and a week at a farm, including visits to Bath and Bristol universities in Year 8, three days at Oxford University in Year 9 and an outward bounds camping trip to celebrate the end of KS3 exams.

In KS4, pupils are going on a Battlefields tour in Ypres this year, and have previously visited Cambridge and Imperial universities. King Solomon Academy pupils are told about these brilliant trips at the start of the year;

they are trips worth working hard for. An invitation is earned by a year average of 100 KSA pounds. As such, pupils who make poor choices earlier in the year can turn it around as the trip approaches. Each week, payslip tells pupils how much is needed to 'make the trip.' Heads of Year use this data in weekly assemblies to motivate and inspire pupils. Last year, the Head of Year 9 had a huge poster campaign about who had their 'seat on the bus' to Oxford – each week he'd update it with who had secured their place. It also makes for a great sense of team work: if a pupil knows their friend isn't making it, they will help them make better decisions, come to school more often, do some extra work, so that they can come on the trip too.

In September 2010, payslip was launched with the founding Year 8 students and the brand new cohort of pupils arriving in Year 7. Behaviour conversations shifted dramatically. Every teacher in the school now had a common language, and pupils soon learnt this same language and used it to communicate, too. Praising positive choices became easier, as they were more tangible: you've clearly worked exceptionally hard to complete all the extension work on the homework task, so you've earned two pounds on your payslip – well done! You don't get merits, you earn them. Similarly, negative behaviours were transformed into poor choices, where there was an alternate positive choice that could be taken next time. If you have a great day today, you can get on track to earn the trip. This shift to narrating the positive had a huge impact on the school's culture. Teachers aren't heard shouting in our school, nor will you encounter children not knowing why they are in trouble.

Merits and demerits are tracked on a class clipboard and the visibility of the choices is crucial, particularly to younger pupils. Conversations in form time turn to who has the fewest demerits to how pupils are earning merits and are on track for success. The conversations quickly move onto how that success is achieved. Pupils who have made negative choices are encouraged to learn from their more mindful peers.

The short-term goal of a weekly reward works well as an extrinsic motivation whilst the long-term goal of earning the end of year trip teaches the deeper fulfilment, which comes from sustained hard work and long-term reward. Financial literacy is also taught meaningfully: pupils learn to keep their own personal accounts through the week of what their payslip will be and how they can ensure they earn enrichment or a wristband. Each term, at the auction, pupils can spend their KSA pounds. Costs fluctuate, as you would expect in an auction, but what's important is the basic premise that the more money in the bank, the more opportunities you've got.

Some students choose to save their pounds over a series of terms, or even over the whole three years of Middle School, to be able to buy something of significant value that they really want – one of the governors has a VIP season ticket at Arsenal and he loans it to us twice a year for the auction as a top, much-coveted prize.

IMPACT

Payslip has been running in Middle School for four years now and it is well embedded into the culture of the academy. Each week, there are between four and twenty pupils out of over 180 who do not earn enrichment and spend the afternoon in enrichment detention. Some of these are pupils who have missed school, so took a hit on their attendance. This is a vital lesson to learn – if you are absent, you catch up. Others have made poor behaviour choices throughout the week and need the time to reflect. The vast majority of children earn enrichment every week and earn the end of year residential. Last year, only five children in Year 7 did not earn the Warwick residential, only two didn't make it to Jamie's Farm and we only left three in school when the Year 9s went to Oxford.

Most importantly, there is a strong correlation between those pupils who make the most progress and those who achieve the highest payslips, and this is exactly the point we need to teach – hard work does equal success.

REFLECTIONS

Payslip works because it is transparent. It sends a powerful message to pupils that every choice does count, in its own small way, and making more positive choices than negative ones will be better in the long run. Parents have a visible record of everything their child has achieved each week, and can track each poor choice to a day, a subject and the teacher involved. Payslip has to be signed by a parent every weekend and returned the next school day.

The school invests a huge amount of time and energy into ensuring the administration behind payslip works. It is not a system for the faint hearted. Merits and demerits have to be accurately recorded, in good time, by the teachers awarding them. The school runs a centralised homework system which means that we know by 9am each morning which pupils have and have not handed in their homework and whether or not it has been completed to TANC standard (TANC = On Time, Accurate, Neat, Complete). Without that rigid system, it would be extremely difficult to make payslip work. As soon as there are regular errors, inconsistencies or points of contention, its power diminishes.

Furthermore, as with any behaviour system, staff training is vital. The school invests in training staff, in detail, on how and when to award merits and demerits. If one teacher is over or under rewarding, the currency is devalued and the system becomes extremely unfair. It is important to be as explicit as possible about what constitutes a merit or demerit but there are always grey areas, which we work through in drop-ins, observations and coaching conversations. The totals and teacher merit: demerit ratios are circulated each week and discussed in line management and team meetings. The more regularly and informally we calibrate, the more consistent we become.

NEXT STEPS

When the frontier cohort of pupils moved into Upper School in Year 10, a new behaviour management system was implemented in an attempt to lengthen the reward/consequence feedback loop, and to build trust and responsibility in older pupils. This was a mistake that was learned from. The reintroduction of payslip for this year group and its consistent use across the whole school has re-established the clarity and consistency, which is a hallmark of the payslip system. As the frontier year group moved into Year 11, new rewards and privileges were introduced, including 'Dress like a sixth former' on Fridays for Year 11s with gold wristbands.

Now, looking ahead to the opening of the sixth form, the school is debating how best to reward pupils as they transition into young adulthood. The major discussion point is how to ensure that sixth formers are provided with in-school rewards, and see the relevance of rewards to their transition to university life. Whilst some may consider the concept of merits and demerits too childish for sixth formers, we are keen to ensure we have a payslip, which is genuinely meaningful for young adults, in preparation for the 'real' payslips they will be earning in the less distant future.

CHAPTER 6

WHAT DOES A GREAT FORM TUTOR LOOK LIKE?

ANDREW BAINBRIDGE, LOXFORD SCHOOL OF SCIENCE AND TECHNOLOGY

FOCUS AREA

It is a long-held perception that a great form tutor can play an enormously significant role in the life of a young person as they go through school. The quality and consistency of tutoring for all pupils is a hugely worthwhile focus. All pupils have the right to receive care and attention in order to succeed in secondary education. This case study examines research conducted by staff at Loxford School into the qualities of great tutors, as part of a drive to ensure consistently high standards of tutoring.

BACKGROUND CONTEXT

In autumn 2011, staff at Loxford, and a number of other local secondary schools, verbalised a desire to improve the quality and consistency of tutoring in our schools. We were part of a collaborative group known as the Leadership Improvement Group. This is a group of schools from Redbridge who have worked together in a series of subject, pastoral and leadership networks for over eight years. Staff from Loxford, together with colleagues at Beal, Oaks Park, Seven Kings and Wanstead High Schools met termly to share good practice, identify future needs, and to support the achievement of over 13,000 students. The research we conducted was resourced with additional funding from the Redbridge Learning Community.

AIMS

The aims of our work were:

- To identify the crucial aspects of high quality tutorial support at KS3, 4 and 5, as perceived by the students.

- To describe and document the actions and determining features of tutors whose care is particularly successful in the eyes of students.

- To disseminate the findings of this study in a way that empowers schools to manage the quality of tutoring for all students and thus raise achievement and well-being of students

- To create a core group of highly-trained staff who are able to carry this work forward in a sustainable manner.

THE STORY

We polled a large number of students in five schools to determine who had tutors that could be described as outstanding in pupils' eyes. We asked students from several year groups in each school to complete an online questionnaire in which they rated their tutor on a 1-5 scale according to various qualities. We then analysed the results. From this, we found one or two outstanding tutors in each school. Our next step was to carry out focus groups with randomly selected pupils from the tutor groups of the tutors who scored highly.

The aim was to identify what it was that these tutors did to make them so outstanding in the eyes of their students. An online questionnaire was created using Google Docs, as it is a platform which is freely accessible and it gave the opportunity for an unlimited number of participants. Our first network meeting focussed on creating, refining and sharing the questionnaire. Initially, two focus groups were run in order to test questions, check the direction of the project with students, and to test the online model. It was agreed that we would use the following questions:

1. How helpful is your tutor in giving you advice on progression through school and beyond, GCSE Options/A-Levels/sixth form, etc.?

2. How does your tutor respond to difficult situations?

3. How useful do you find tutor time at the moment?

4. How much support/advice do you get from your tutor if you are not making good progress in your subjects?

5. How effective is your tutor at teambuilding in your tutor group?

6. Do you think you have a good relationship with your tutor?

7. How approachable is your tutor?

8. Does your tutor give you what you need to have a successful day? (Check you have your planner, equipment, good mood!)

9. How important is it to you that you have a good relationship with your tutor?

10. How would you rate your tutor?

11. Do you feel free from emotional/physical harm in school?

12. If you didn't feel safe, how happy would you feel in speaking to your tutor about this?

13. How often does your tutor allow you to lead on activities?

14. How important is the above to you?

15. How effectively is bad behaviour dealt with when it occurs in your tutor group?

16. How often does your tutor engage in extra-curricular activities with your tutor group?

17. What would you like to spend more time on during Tutor time?

18. List the most important characteristics that you feel are needed to be a good tutor.

We agreed to gather feedback from a cross-section of ages. Within Loxford we initially reviewed the 215 results from Year 7. It was clear that the Year 7 tutors made a significant impact on the pupils who value them and the role they play; tutor time useful/very useful (78%), effective in developing team building (73%), helpful/very helpful in giving advice on progressing through school and beyond (79%), important/very important to have good relationship with their tutor (87%), established a good/very good relationship (78%), 76% also felt that their tutor was approachable/very approachable.

helpful

friendly good

intelligent   patience   approachable   **caring**   punctual open

respectful respect   calmness EVER situations   welcoming

nice handling   **polite** fairness   TRUST   engaging   reliable   control communication

FUN natured   shout   givetime awkward   listener

personality justified   skills

supportive   **understanding**

commitment   loyalty

kind

Pupils showed the desire to lead more on form-time activities, while some commented that they would like to see their tutor involved with them in extracurricular activities outside the form room. Some pupils requested more words of encouragement from the tutor. Form time was used to focus on activities that students suggested as most beneficial.

The image above shows a summary of the most important characteristics identified by 660 students from Years 7-13. From this, our initial conclusions were as follows:

1. There is no real difference between the year groups in terms of what they want and need.

2. The major theme/need is 'being set up for the day ahead'. This might be 'today', issues from the previous day, or long term information.

3. The students place a high value on the role of tutor and question whether the teachers place a similar value on it. Do tutors underestimate the impact they might have?

4. The tutor must not be a 'stranger' and must have a relationship with them.

5. The tutor must develop the relationship within the group and across individuals.
   A common ethos needs to evolve.

6. There is definitely more than one way to be a good tutor.

7. Students need to see their tutor as a real person, talking about their experiences, life, and modelling good relationships.

8. The relationship with parents is key. Students want this and value the 'comfort blanket'.

9. Some schools with rotating tutors were now questioning the lack of accountability of tutors over time.

Next, we identified tutors who scored highly and drew out what behaviour, attitudes and practices gave rise to such good results. To secure impartial results, focus groups were led by teachers from other schools.

Findings from Years 7-9: The tutor was seen as someone they could go to talk to, who would listen and understand, an ordinary person with feelings and emotions, while the subject teachers can be withdrawn and almost robotic, helping to push and motivate the students to do well. The tutor had created a two-way relationship where issues were shared; supporting extracurricular activities further bonded them to the class.

Their role was seen as more important than subject teachers as the tutor sees the big picture, helping the pupils to continually move forward and progress. The fact that the tutor always gives out daily information made them reliable and trustworthy. Students felt the tutor allowed them to be themselves and this helped them get to know the form. The form group was seen as a second home where they felt welcomed and cared for, creating a real identity. A consistent approach enabled students to know what to expect. The tutor guided them through school: 'You can always fall back on your tutor who will help'.

Findings from Years 10-11: A tutor should be relaxed, approachable, trustworthy, warm and a person who wants to get to know them, willing to go the extra mile for the students – very important in building the relationship. Students need to be able to talk openly to them and feel listened to. A consistent tutor was highly valued as it really helps to make a bond, with the tutor's personality coming out effectively whether it be very quiet, laid back or very competitive. Form time is the start and end of the day so it reinforces the bond within the form. The students could not put their finger on how their tutor had created the bond or what exactly they did that made them an effective tutor except for: a consistent approach, clear boundaries, listening and trusting the tutees.

A very important role was helping the students with both academic and personal issues at school. Universally, students felt that they had a connection with their tutor and they valued their view more, and so acted on this immediately. The shared termly targets worked well to ensure that the tutor knew the whole picture of the student.

Findings from Years 12-13: Similar key themes emerged. Effective tutors were flexible, not too authoritative, not trying to control, to guide not to lead – a critical friend. A more relaxed informal tutor time was valued: "If students don't get to know each other in tutor time, they will do it in lessons, causing disruptive behaviour." A good tutor can bring a tutor group together, like a family, where the tutor is the 'head of the family', taking on a guiding, supportive role. The tutor must understand their tutees personally and they need to feel comfortable talking to them: "They give us confidence and through their support and help guide us on how to improve. It is important that I always have the same tutor as I develop trust and understanding, respect, personal friendship and it makes me feel valued and liked."

"At times, we did not always see where the tutor was taking us and the bigger picture, however, reflecting now it is clear what their aim was and we understood the reason why sir acted as he did." Trust is developed through a stable a familiar routine, clear consistent boundaries and implications of breaking them. The tutor creates a whole group ethos, without sub-groups. This prevents peer pressure, tension, fallings out and cliques. Students said that they knew and could identify who would be a good tutor through their behaviour and actions around the school.

In analysing what was really valuable to students in schools, we became aware that the role of tutor seemed to be underestimated by school leadership teams and by staff and that the really significant part it played in helping students achieve needed to be celebrated and recognised more widely.

RESULTS

From our research, we were able to identify six key factors in determining a great tutor.

1. The tutor's attitude:

   a. Welcoming – great tutors are successful in making their tutees feel welcome, and that the tutor wants to be with them. The effect of this is underestimated by tutors, but the consistency with which students reported how genuine they felt the tutor's desire to be with them was, and how important it was to them, was remarkable.

   b. Caring – great tutors care about their tutees doing well. Their tutees become convinced that the tutor really wants the best for them and really cares that they do well. This grows as the tutor's consistency of intention is portrayed through their actions, and their attitude to tutees.

   c. Conscientious – tutees report with visible pleasure how conscientiously their tutor looks out for them and shows attention to their needs in detail, giving pertinent information and grasping opportunities, noticing their individual needs and keeping an eye on them.

   d. Friendly – this was expressed in different ways depending on the tutor's personality. If keen on sport, it may be competitively based; if keen on nature, it may be based on sharing this. The common factor is enthusiasm.

   e. Personal – great tutors are able to share personal information in a way that is significantly different to normal teacher behaviour – a sense of connection/intimacy is established that marks out the tutor as someone special in the tutee's life. The key is a degree of interesting, appropriate disclosure not generally associated with a pupil/teacher relationship. The relationship is multidimensional – a combination of a teacher, friend and parent, each at the right time. A tough challenge!

2. The tutor as a motivator

Tutors have a significant impact on the motivation of pupils, both in the short term to deal with each day, and long term as they help to sustain their tutees' belief in their ability to succeed. Great tutors declare a consistent belief in pupils' ability, help students see the point of working and learning and, link this with their aspirations and visions of their future. They build competence in the small but important skills needed to succeed and connect with parents with an approachable manner. They notice if a student's motivation is enhanced or flagging, being ready to help even when students haven't asked for help.

3. Giving accurate and timely information

Reliably conveying timely information about what's going on in school is highly valued; it shows a tutor's commitment. Tutors who brief their tutees on immediate issues (what's happening today or this week (procedures, exams, assemblies etc.) and encourage their students to make use of opportunities by giving them specific information that fits their interests, such as extracurricular activities, are much appreciated. A tutor who makes their tutees feel cared about because they know more than others is valued highly. The feeling that you have a tutor who really looks after you and your needs is much appreciated. Students love to be secure that they know what's going on, and they conversely hate not knowing.

4. The quality of pupil/tutor relationship

Great tutors somehow know that their students needed to know more about them to be able to be open with their tutor; approachability is paramount. Many tutors leave quite a lot of space for conversations with individuals. Reciprocity of openness (personal information, as well as work) was remarked on continually by students; it marked out the difference in role that the tutor played. Great tutors know that it matters how they use information that is disclosed to them – they gain a reputation for being 'trustable' through word-of-mouth between students. Most importantly, tutees knew that their tutor was reliable when they got in trouble, even with another member of staff. Not that their tutor would side with them, but that they would be their supportive advocate and help make amends. This was valued by all students – even those who never got in trouble.

5. Facilitating relationships with other pupils in group

This was perhaps the most surprising result. Great tutors don't simply provide support – they enable the group to become mutually supportive and create a positive environment throughout the students' life at school. What was surprising, was that the value the students placed on this far surpassed other factors.

One student who remembered fearing secondary school and could see that she could have become isolated, said she 'couldn't believe how lucky she had been to be placed in her tutor group', knowing there was always someone who would be welcoming whenever she walked into the dining hall. This kind of story was repeated again and again; one group said that their tutor group was 'like a family, with the tutor as a kind of Dad who made sure everyone supported each other to succeed'. A striking feature of this result is the disproportionate effect that a good tutor can make in this way on the lives of vulnerable students who lack support at home.

Great tutors actively create good relationships and clear norms and values, giving space to share information about themselves and their interests early on in the life of the group. Each tutor acts in a way with which they are comfortable – there is no universal recipe!

6. Detecting and solving problems

Great tutors spot when students get into trouble or need help. They keep an eye on each student in their group and know what's going on. If they are not sure – they find out. They notice little things, and because they are trusted, they get to know if things are not going right for somebody. They have a firm but supportive approach, don't avoid a problem – but are committed to being helpful rather than 'taking over' or instructing.

These factors have been used to challenge the perceptions of our tutor teams. Tutors have discussed and reflected on what the results have shown. The value of this direct feedback has been a great motivator; tutors have been able to compare the findings with their own 'modus operandi'. The results obtained give us a clear way forward for developing and training better tutors. We have seen the motivation of tutors increase as they appreciate more the value of their pastoral work, alongside that of being a subject teacher.

REFLECTIONS

Even in an outstanding school, there can be large variation in the quality of tutoring offered to students. Having a great tutor is regarded as a gift of great value by all students. The tutor group, when well run, delivers significant elements of social and personal education in a non-formal way that seems far more effective than formal teaching methods. It acts as a family with significant impact where the tutee's family is less supportive. Measuring the quality of tutoring by employing online questionnaires for students was an effective way of demonstrating interest in the topic by the school leadership team. Its use could be extended to other aspects of our school, including measuring the effectiveness of subjects or whole school initiatives.

Being a good tutor should be seen less as a quality of personality, and more as a disciplined professional task which uses the personality of the teacher to best advantage. Where people have genuine difficulty with the tutoring role, the best support is coaching on relationships, and the switch to a more personal connection with students. Thanks go to all the pupils and staff who took part in this initiative.

NEXT STEPS

As a school, we are reviewing our communication systems so that information can be shared in a more effective manner. This will support the tutor in being the 'Team Manager'. We are interested in exploring the link between an effective tutor and the achievement and progress of the students in their group. We are convinced that there is a strong correlation. If proven, this will further underline the value of the form tutor. Finally, we are looking at the time a tutor group spends together, how can this be made highly-productive, and what activities should be part of this quality time.

CHAPTER 7

CODING THE TUTORIAL MATRIX – DRIVING UP STANDARDS IN TUTORIAL PROVISION AND DELIVERY

DAN BARTON, WREN ACADEMY

FOCUS AREA

This case study explores how the experience of students in tutorial time at Wren Academy has developed over the course of three years, from a somewhat didactic approach, to a student-led model with a more rigorous system for evaluation of, and feedback on, sessions. The study also examines how leadership of this change across the academy was distributed amongst a new and developing team of Heads of House.

BACKGROUND CONTEXT

Since its inception in 2008, Wren has provided students with interesting, thought-provoking activities, planned centrally and facilitated by the tutor. The resources, initially released according to a two-weekly theme, had a multimedia focus and very strong links/references to the Church of England lectionary and Christian Values for Schools website. In addition to the delivery of these materials, it is compulsory that a prayer, reading or reflection be part of each tutorial session, functioning as an act of collective worship daily.

The pastoral system in the academy is run as a vertical system. Vertical tutoring allows for excellent transition and induction procedures, as well as peer mentoring and anti-bullying to be embedded in the daily life of all students at the academy. We count vertical tutoring among the structural aspects of the academy day, which are responsible for the extremely low rates of bullying, and high levels of student satisfaction and happiness at school. Tutor groups comprise five students from each of the five year groups in the lower school, and are balanced in terms of gender and other characteristics as far as practically possible.

In 2011, the academy embraced a number of whole school initiatives focusing on increasing student engagement and involvement in teaching and learning, decisions and ideas, which resulted from a middle leadership conference that year. Of particular importance here was the notion of students as teachers – taking responsibility for the delivery and planning of in-lesson learning on a daily basis across subjects and year groups. This idea was extended into the delivery of tutorial resources and therefore obviated a change in the way that these resources were planned and disseminated.

RATIONALE

Despite the lack of quality substantive research in the area, it is inherently obvious that the provision of high-quality, stimulating and impactful tutor-time has obvious benefits in all schools (calm start to the day, Spiritual, Moral, Social and Cultural (SMSC) outcomes, students challenged and developed spiritually), and in a Church of England Academy it takes on a particular significance. It is the vehicle through which core values and the Christian ethos are underpinned and 'taught' explicitly, and is also a key setting in which our unique learning culture is laid out and prepared.

At this stage in the evolution of the academy, quality assurance of the delivery of tutorial sessions was carried out, but was subjective and qualitative in the absence of a clear and unambiguous system by which sessions could be evaluated (more on this later…).

In consultation with the Head of House and tutor team, a new format was planned, taking the best elements of the previous system, but incorporating the principle of students as leaders of learning as detailed above. Each week would give tutor groups the following menu of activities:

SPIRITUAL ASSEMBLY – delivered and planned by a member of the extended leadership team, and focusing on a two-weekly theme.

THEME PRESENTATION – a short 'lesson', planned and delivered by a TRIAD*, mirroring the weekly theme and giving all students the chance to interact with the theme and learn together through a variety of activities.

TRIAD ACTIVITY – directed activity, planned centrally and aimed at focusing on more intimate group work, engaging students in small groups and allowing for greater personalisation.

CLASS FORUM – a debate, chaired by a TRIAD group, asking questions about the theme and building on students' public speaking and debating skills.

QUIZ – a topical quiz in which the tutor draws out some key issues for discussion.

*Students in tutor groups are allocated to TRIAD groups, which comprise three students from different year groups. These groups are fixed and are used to develop smaller group work in tutor time. TRIAD groups also present or deliver some of the other elements on the timetable.

Themes would continue to be two-weekly, and learning walks were to be carried out termly.

Principal challenges were encountered in ensuring staff buy-in, and in quality assurance. Since there was no definition of what constituted an 'outstanding' tutorial according to our requirements, how could observers on learning walks make a call as to the grade accurately? At the time, we followed a traditional learning walk format in which walkers noted what they could see, hear and notice, before making a qualitative judgement after a conversation between walkers. Feedback was given in terms of WWW and EBI and the collated documentation was reviewed at a senior level.

Over the course of the year, learning walks took place and, whilst some teachers' grades improved, other tutorials gave rise to concerns. Qualitative data informed us that we needed to increase levels of consistency in terms of delivery and routines, and that sustaining improvement across the cohort of tutors should be a target. The need was identified, therefore, via consultation with staff as well as at the leadership level, for:

- Standardisation in provision of an accepted minimum in terms of tutor materials as produced centrally.

- Training for students.

- Tightening up of monitoring and evaluation processes.

- Training for staff on the role of the tutor at Wren.

THE STORY

Addressing the four identified areas for development was done in a variety of ways:

STUDENT TRAINING

Students were, and continue to be, trained in leading tutorial sessions. It was felt by tutors that students had a tendency to revert to 'safe' techniques when planning and delivering activities – predominated by the now ubiquitous Powerpoint presentation and associated question and answer sessions. These can be quite dull, and more choices/options were needed. The simple resolution was for tutors and Heads of House to discuss their preferred teaching techniques for ensuring variety, engagement and enjoyment. These ideas were collated and turned into a menu which is now used by tutors when facilitating planning with a TRIAD group.

MATERIALS STANDARDISATION

The pastoral team, who lead in the planning of materials, alongside the chaplain and Head of RE, met to discuss the minimum standard of tutorial materials. This was agreed and quality assured on a weekly basis by the Assistant Principal responsible. In addition to the activities outlined in the previous section, there would be a 'Header' page, explaining the theme, and a choice of prayer, reading or reflection for each day of the week. There have been subsequent small developments to these minimum requirements which are explained in the next section.

MONITORING AND EVALUATION

This element of the evolution the tutorial system was the area which required the most research and development. After some thought, the evaluation of a tutorial at Wren was separated into three strands, which can be thought of as assessment objectives as set out by:

- SIAS (Statutory Inspection for Anglican Schools – part of the National Society*)

- Ofsted (with particular reference to the provision of SMSC)

- Wren-specific routines (including reference to our Building Learning Power – focused Student Leadership outcomes)

*All Church of England dioceses and the Methodist Church use the National Society's framework for the **Statutory Inspection of Anglican and Methodist Schools (SIAMS)** under Section 48 of the Education Act 2005. The framework sets out the expectations for the conduct of the Statutory Inspection of Anglican, Methodist and Ecumenical schools under Section 48 of the Education Act 2005.

A central document was produced which pulled all of these strands together into one evaluation tool. Referencing the descriptors from the organisations above, but rationalised into a single-purpose observation framework, giving a single grade with three focus areas. A sample is included below.

The advantages of this system were manifold. Firstly, the element of subjectivity was removed, as far as possible, from the programme of quality assurance. There was the attendant opportunity, therefore, for a marked depersonalisation of feedback to tutors following learning walks, and the ability to signal clearly the areas for improvement.

CRITERION	OBSERVABLE INDICATORS	OUTSTANDING	GOOD	REQUIRES IMPROVEMENT	INADEQUATE
The quality and outcomes of routines in Tutorial Delivery	- Routines are well established - The atmosphere is encouraging, nourishing, challenging - Activities are delivered by students - The session starts promptly and with a sense of purpose. - Distinctive Christian character - Includes prayer, reading or reflection - Display is inclusive, personal, interesting and interactive - Tutorials have a clear impact on the spiritual and emotional lives of the students - Students flourish as individuals	Students clearly value the tutorial and are involved explicitly in the routines of the session. There is clear evidence of routines and embedded behaviours centring on students leading the learning. Act of collective worship is integral, routinised and promotes reflective, spiritual development. The session is defined by a sense of purpose, variety and pace. Display is dynamic, interactive, current and valued by learners. The impact on learners enables them to grow and has an effect on their access to a wider curriculum.	There is evidence that the students engage in the delivery of some if not all tutorial sessions. The tutor has a positive impact on the session, leading activities and supporting students. Display is colourful and interesting. An act of collective worship takes place. Students in the session are content, if not active.	Students' experiences in the session are good. The atmosphere is generally positive. Students leading learning does not appear to be a routine. Act of collective worship is either unplanned or does not have an impact on students spiritually. Students who are late are not disadvantaged by their absence. The session is not likely to inspire or enable students to grow spiritually.	There is little or no evidence of embedded routines. Little or no evidence or reference to or explicit use of distinctly Christian ethos. Routines are not clearly established. Tutorial session is led by the teacher in the most part. Students do not appear as active participants. Display is non-existent or uninspiring. The impact on the learners of the tutorial time is negligible
The importance of worship on the group and the individual	- Students' experiences are transformative, inspiring, engaging and relevant - Worship is enhanced by music, song, symbol, prayer - A range of leaders and stakeholders participate in the delivery and reception - Session are characterised by reflection and create a sense of awe and wonder - Christian Values motivate the relationships between the members of the form community - Worship is inclusive and affirmative - Students' personal spiritual growth is developed	The act of coworship and the tutorial as a whole challenge, engage and inspire the students. A variety of media are used during the session. Students contemplate and reflect upon issues beyond the classroom. Concern for one's fellow human., wider global and moral issues characterises the session. All stakeholders are clearly included and celebrated.	An act of worship is planned and delivered as part of a clear and observable routine. Students participate in the delivery of the prayer, reading or reflection. The session and act of worship mentions issues which affect the wider world.	Collective worship exists insofar as it is mentioned and part of the routine/ timing. There is little discernible benefit to students of taking part in or hearing the act of collective worship. The session may or may not encourage students to consider a world beyond their immediate reality.	An act of collective worship does not take place or is undertaken as part of a required regime. Students are unmotivated and unchallenged. The teacher leads or the majority of students are passive throughout. Little or no reference is made to current events or issues. Spirituality is underdeveloped or completely absent in the planning of the session.

CRITERION	OBSERVABLE INDICATORS	OUTSTANDING	GOOD	REQUIRES IMPROVEMENT	INADEQUATE
Development of students' Spiritual, Moral, Social and Cultural awareness and understanding. Students…	- acquire insights into personal experiences - value a non-material dimension of life - search for meaning and purpose - question the heart and root of existence - learn to understand emotions and feelings - develop identity and self-worth - are ready to challenge	Students are seekers Students are questioning Students understand emotions Students have a sense of self worth and of the worth of others Students develop a sense of the 'other'.	The tutor facilitates activities in which students contemplate spiritual questions and develop self worth.	Opportunities exist but do not impact upon or develop students' spiritual lives.	Little or no activity in the session enables students to consider their own spirituality or that of others either explicitly or implicitly.
	- learn to distinguish right and wrong - assimilate and develop a moral code	Students actively engage with a notion of morality which challenges and enriches their sense of right and wrong	Students are given the opportunity to think about varying approaches to morality.	Examples of different moral viewpoints are implicit at best, and not developed.	Students are not given the opportunity to capitalise to compare and comment upon questions of morality
	- participate responsibly and contribute their personal viewpoint or understanding - are sensitive to the values and opinions of others - show understanding and respect for diffence and diverse communities	Students take part, respect others point of view and explicitly consider and are sensitive to the fact that their own moral orientation may not match that of others	Students listen to others' point of view and accept that a different perspective is allowable and expected.	Students are sometimes exposed to traditions different from their own.	Others' point of view, different religions, different cultures, artistic endeavour or history is in no way alluded to or capitalised upon. Students do not take a lead.
	- appreciate diversity - understand influences on cultural heritage - respond to cultural or artistic enterprise - are ready to address discrimination	Students understand that their own narrative is not exclusive. Students interact with art, music, poetry, history, tradition in a way which widens their horizons and contributes	Students are given the forum to demonstrate their acceptance and understanding of others' background, culture and art.	Students are aware of the influences on their own lives of a cultural heritage.	Little or nothing is made of the potential learning relating to the diverse communities in and outside the academy.

STAFF TRAINING

In autumn 2013, following a whole-staff training session during which the new framework was presented and discussed, the new learning walk programme, using the framework, took place. Learning walk teams featured paired observers from the Head of House and Academy Leadership teams in order to ensure that standardisation of grading and feedback (which was also paired) took place from the outset.

After the first round of learning walks, during a feedback session, tutors and other attached staff were asked for their comments on the quality of the new system, and any teething problems they may have encountered. Staff members were universally in favour of having a matrix for evaluation which made explicit the criteria against which judgements would be made, comparing this to the previous method of unquantifiable, subjective judgements. Those using the matrix to inform their judgements of others were also pleased to have the decision-making process further depersonalised and more unambiguous. The main area of concern from tutors was that they felt it was difficult to achieve SMSC outcomes as referenced in the framework.

An addition was therefore added to the minimum requirements for staff tasked with planning tutorial materials – namely that opportunities for developing SMSC outcomes would be signalled and highlighted throughout the materials – so that tutors and students would be able to facilitate/plan their sessions to accommodate these.

The next round of walks took place in January 2014. Results of the walks are included below.

IMPACT

This study forms part of an ongoing monitoring process which will continue long after publication. Thus far, there have been two rounds of learning walks from which we can draw conclusions. As is evident from the data, the work done here marks the beginning, rather than the end of a process. After the second round of walks, the following summarises the picture in terms of session grades.

After Walk 1			Cumulative 1+2	
Number of 1	1		Number of 1	3
Number of 2	5		Number of 2	11
Number of 3	4		Number of 3	8
Number of 4	0		Number of 4	0
TOTAL	10		**TOTAL**	22
Percentage of 1	10		Percentage of 1	14
Percentage of 2	50		Percentage of 2	50
Percentage of 3	40		Percentage of 3	36
Percentage of 4	0		Percentage of 4	0

These tables illustrate the grades after the first and second rounds of learning walks.

Pleasingly there is a very clear upward movement towards the Outstanding category with a change of +4% coming from the 'Requires Improvement' category.

With only two rounds having taken place and no substantive historical data with which to compare, this cannot yet be called a trend and should be read as encouraging, rather than summative.

Teachers whose grades were evaluated as a '4' overall, received detailed feedback and support from the Head of House before being seen again. The figures above show the results post-intervention. There were two incidences (one in each half term) where this happened.

Tutor perception of the new system is positive, with staff members pleased to have guidance as to the criteria that are now used for evaluation, as well as being complementary about the outcomes.

A sample of comments from tutors demonstrates this:

> "...presenting the theme builds confidence and independence."

> "It's a really great way to start the day."

> "Having the observation matrix helps me to focus on what I should be doing."

> "The students enjoy the chance to debate issues and have discussions."

> "They become one school with no divisions. Year 7s are helped through their first year, which could have been more difficult."

> "...themes allow them to discuss and understand recent events and [...] express their independence and self-confidence."

Similarly, a sample of student feedback demonstrates their positivity:

> "I like being able to work with people from other year groups."

> "I guess I'm better at speaking out loud."

> "We talk about moral issues all the time."

> "I am prepared and informed about the wider world outside school. Public speaking is something you need."

NEXT STEPS

We plan to prepare a feedback pro forma sheet to standardise this process further. Each tutor will receive a typed document showing precisely the breakdown and allocation of scores against each of the three outlined criteria.

We intend to implement randomised student interviews to validate conclusions about habits/routines in observations. Students will be asked for their opinion on the quality of tutorials at Wren, specifically how they felt about leading sessions, and to what extent they felt that they had the opportunity to grow and develop spiritually, morally and socially.

We aim to more effectively signal SMSC outcomes. Where SMSC outcomes are likely to be achieved in resources planned centrally, the staff member responsible for the plan will add brief icon/single word signal to slides on the resources to highlight ways in which key outcomes can be reached. We also plan to gather qualitative feedback from staff and student surveys.

CHAPTER 8

MAXIMISING THE BENEFITS OF ASSESSMENT TO ENSURE PUPIL PROGRESS

PATRICK BALL AND LEENA HUSSAIN, SIR JOHN CASS'S FOUNDATION AND RED COAT CHURCH OF ENGLAND SECONDARY SCHOOL

FOCUS AREA

It is no secret that teachers spend a significant amount of their time marking books. Indeed, the most recent Teachers' Workload Survey from the Department for Education suggests a classroom teacher spends on average five hours per week marking. Other surveys estimate this figure to be nearer seven hours.

With this in consideration, a recurring question can be heard across staff rooms and in school meeting rooms around the country: How much impact does our marking actually have on pupil progress?

This case study documents the transformation of assessment routines at Sir John Cass's Foundation and Red Coat Church of England Secondary School. This has played a pivotal role in improving standards of teaching and learning and ultimately raising pupil achievement.

BACKGROUND CONTEXT

Despite the challenging social context, students at Sir John Cass achieve some of the highest levels of attainment in the country (83% 5 A*-C at GCSE including English and Maths in 2013). Of our total student population, 75% are Pupil Premium and 81% learn English as an additional language. Behaviour for learning is exceptional and visitors to the school invariably comment on the positive atmosphere in and around the corridors. The promotion of independent learning is embodied in all of our teaching and learning strategies. It is clear to all involved with the school that we do a lot of things very well, and this is celebrated. However, just as important to our way of working is our willingness to acknowledge when there is a need to reform.

In previous years, there had been an assessment scrutiny routine whereby members of senior leadership would monitor teachers' marking on a half-termly basis. This would then be judged against the school's Assessment Policy, and the teacher would either pass or fail the assessment scrutiny. In terms of monitoring the degree of assessment being undertaken, this method worked.

However, it became clear from lesson observations, senior and middle leader meetings, teacher working parties and even student council meetings that there was room for considerable improvement in the school's approach to assessment scrutiny. Although the current way of working allowed for effective monitoring, there was little scope for measuring the impact this assessment was having and shaping interventions where necessary. At this point, the need for reform was acknowledged, and a commitment to change was made.

AIMS

The fundamental aim of the reform was to create a rigorous and robust assessment routine that would ultimately contribute to raising pupil attainment. It emerged in discussions that in order for this to be the case, the new system would have to address the following key strands for improvement:

1. Provide the Senior Leadership Team and Middle Leaders with a rich pool of data to monitor, evaluate and implement interventions.

2. Raise awareness of the nature of outstanding assessment to ensure that it is at the core of every teacher's practice.

3. Devise assessment patterns that foster independent learning.

THE STORY

To get the ball rolling, an assessment working party was established. A newly appointed Deputy Headteacher, offering the benefit of fresh insight, led the working party. The rest of the working party was comprised of a stratified cross-section of staff: one Assistant Headteacher, two Middle Leaders, and four teachers. Within this sample, there was a mixture of levels of experience and representation from a range of departments.

The initial meetings centred on determining what the Assessment Policy should be in terms of frequency of diagnostic marking and levelled assessments. There were also discussions regarding what information was required in progress tracking pro formas in student exercise books. These issues were largely negotiated without much debate, and any changes were consulted on and fine-tuned at senior leadership and middle leadership meetings.

The real steps to reform were then made in the subsequent meetings when the agenda progressed to the actual mechanisms we would use to monitor assessment. At this stage, some key outcomes emerged:

- The information gathered during assessment scrutinies should be recorded centrally and shared with Heads of Department in order to highlight and share outstanding practice.

- In terms of raising the quality of assessment, it is important to use detailed feedback letters to staff which highlight the key strengths and specific areas for improvement in their marking.

- Greater emphasis must be placed on evaluating the quality of diagnostic comments, as opposed to just the frequency of them.

- School-wide and departmental inset should be incorporated in the assessment routines so all staff have the capacity and confidence to improve their assessment practices.

- Exercise books or assessment folders should display evidence that students have used their diagnostic comments to improve the quality of their work.

The assessment cycle should foster independent learning and students should have the capacity and desire to use diagnostic feedback as a means to ensure their own progress.

These outcomes, amongst others, led to the establishment of the three key strands for improvement, as set out in the Aims section above. How these strands for improvement were addressed is outlined below.

Strand 1: Provide the Senior Leadership Team and Middle Leaders with a rich pool of data to monitor, evaluate and implement interventions

In order to ensure targeted and meaningful intervention, there needs to be regular, detailed and consistent monitoring across the school. With this in mind, the Senior Leadership Team decided that the assessment scrutiny cycle should be shortened to three weeks. In addition to this, rather than simply evaluating whether teachers had passed or failed in relation to the Assessment Policy, a much more detailed evaluation form was constructed and agreed at the assessment working party. One major change was that each of the criteria had a graded descriptor, ranging from Outstanding to Inadequate.

Criteria	Grade
Frequency and quality of diagnostic comments in last three weeks	
Evidence of students using comments to improve work already completed or subsequent pieces of work	
Students' awareness of their targets to improve and how to implement them	
Completeness of departmental pro forma	
Correction of spelling, punctuation and grammar	
Frequency and amount of time spent on homework	

Under the new system, Heads of Department were given greater responsibility to lead on the assessment scrutiny for their subject area, therefore empowering them to shape and implement departmental interventions.

The data from each scrutiny was collated on a central system by the Deputy Headteacher and shared with Heads of Department. This regular and forensic evaluation was crucial in providing the direction on how assessment could be improved in the school. An example of this is provided in the Impact section below.

Strand 2: Raise awareness of the nature of outstanding assessment to ensure that it is at the core of every teacher's practice

Under new Ofsted guidelines, assessment is more important than ever, not just as means to demonstrate pupil progress – but also with regards to the specific reference in the School Inspection Handbook that pupils understand how to improve their work. Integral to the new assessment routine is the fact that teachers are fully aware of what outstanding assessment looks like and are equipped to get there.

OUTSTANDING GRADE DESCRIPTOR:

There is clear evidence that students regularly use the diagnostic comments to return to and improve pieces of work. Furthermore, it is clear that diagnostic comments are used to improve future pieces of work and this is assisting in pupil progress.

The first of the assessment-focused CPD sessions was rolled out in the first week of the academic year. Some of the key activities of these CPD sessions included:

- Presentation on the importance of assessment for new Ofsted framework.

- Clarification of the school's new enhanced expectations as set out in the Assessment Policy.

- An opportunity for departments to discuss and make a judgment on the quality and consistency of their current assessment practice, as well as set out a plan to adapt to new expectations.

- Time for cross-departmental discussion, in order to enable diffusion of best practice.

Following the initial CPD sessions, data from the assessment scrutinies was used throughout the year to improve teaching and learning in two distinct yet complimentary ways:

1. Whole school interventions	2. Personalised interventions
Identifying areas for improvement across the board This top-down approach involved members of Senior Leadership and Middle Managers identifying, in a general sense, the areas of greatest need for improvement. From this, whole school INSET was delivered through Advanced Skills Teachers.	*Formal feedback to teachers* The use of graded feedback (rather than just pass or fail) letters has increased the level of awareness that teachers have relating to their performance in this area. Crucially, the feedback letters use the grade descriptors to highlight the key strengths and areas of improvement following each scrutiny.
Sharing outstanding practice As a consequence of the more regular and thorough assessment scrutinies, an increasing number of discussions were taking place across the school relating to examples of outstanding assessment practices. Opportunities for teachers from across different subjects to share their methods were provided through various CPD sessions and cross-departmental meetings.	*Head of Department support* Heads of Department are now more equipped to provide the one-to-one support needed to develop the assessment practices of team members. The more detailed breakdown involved in the assessment scrutiny allows for support to be provided in the specific area of need, whilst the graded judgements offer the ability to set measureable targets.

Strand 3: Devise assessment patterns that foster independent learning

As mentioned above, independent learning is central to the ethos at Sir John Cass. So much so, that it is highlighted in the school mission statement: Everyone is enabled to be confident and independent in their learning.

As a consequence of the assessment reform, independence has been improved in a variety of ways. For example, in lower year groups, students have developed the habits of returning to their work and responding directly to teachers' comments. Additionally, many older students have developed their own routines to respond to feedback, allowing them to do so in a way that they are comfortable with, and that is effective for their own learning. Examples of this are highlighted in the Outcomes section below.

OUTCOMES

An obvious starting place to measure the impact of the new assessment routine, is to look at the outcomes of the assessment scrutinies themselves. The pie charts below show the improvements in the results of the assessment scrutiny under the new system.

FIRST ASSESSMENT SCRUTINY RESULTS UNDER NEW SYSTEM

ASSESSMENT SCRUTINY RESULTS AFTER TWO TERMS OF NEW SYSTEM

The whole school INSET that has been delivered to improve the quality of assessment also had overwhelmingly positive responses. Crucially, 78% of staff strongly agreed that 'attending this training will have a positive impact on the development of our learners'.

As mentioned above, increased involvement from Heads of Department has also been a key success of the new system. This was explored in a discussion with one Head of Department:

> *"The new system has allowed me to take greater ownership over the team's assessment performance and what needs to be done to improve it. The improvement in the practice of one team member of the team stands out in particular."*

> *"Under the old system, the teacher probably only just passed each assessment scrutiny. However, the teacher would have just read each letter they received simply as 'passed'. Under the new system, the Requires Improvement grading quickly highlighted the need for intervention. More significantly, the evaluation grid allowed me to discuss the specific areas for improvement that were needed and to use best practice from other team members in the department as a means to lift performance. Results from assessment scrutinies since the intervention have evidenced the improvements."*

Adapted from a discussion with our Head of Science

Some Heads of Department have used the assessment scrutiny data in more creative ways. The Modern Foreign Languages department has a system whereby those excelling in one area of assessment are buddied up with another team member who may require some peer-support in that given area. As well as improving assessment practice, such an approach has the added benefits of improving collaboration, empowering team members, and using resources effectively and efficiently.

A key outcome has been the varied methods that teachers have devised in order to encourage students to actively respond to their targets. One example of this (right) is how a MFL teacher develops reading skills with a Year 9 French class.

A further example is how the sixth form Social Science department has developed its own routines to ensure that students are maximising the detailed diagnostic feedback they are receiving (see below). The extract shows the targets that the student has set themselves following an essay in Sociology.

 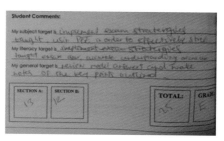 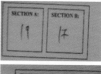 

Above is the feedback from the same essay, which was reworked using the targets. The progress is evident.

When putting this case study together, a number of teachers and students were spoken to regarding the changes outlined above. Perhaps the most telling piece of evidence that the reform has been successful, is the extent to which student reflections mirrored those of the teachers:

"Before, we just got our books back and were told to look through our comments and copy it into our grade tracker… now we actually get time to do something about and it helps us get better at that subject."

A KS3 student

"After each piece of major work I have marked I provide the students with Direct Improvement and Reflection Time (DIRT), which is something I picked up from the CPD. I am surprised about how much students thrive on the opportunity to improve a piece of work."

A Science teacher

"We are always marking each other's practice questions and using success criteria to give them a grade. But you know when it is an important assessment that Miss will mark it, and you always get a least three comments. Then she makes us correct our spellings – which we hate!"

A KS4 student, referring to History

"The new three-week cycle has added a little more balance to how I mark. I always ensure that one piece of work is marked in detail at Key Stage 3 with diagnostic comments which the students follow-up on. With other pieces of work I rely mostly on self and peer-assessment. This has actually made more time available for detailed diagnostic comments at Key Stage 4 and 5."

History teacher

A final remark, made by an RE teacher, captures perfectly how the new strategies have influenced teaching and learning in its broadest sense: "New assessment routines have actually made us focus more on assessment and progress when designing new schemes of work."

REFLECTIONS

The transformation of assessment at Sir John Cass has been underpinned by the three key strands for improvement identified after the early meetings of the assessment working party. Although these still very much represent the driving force of the reform, reflection has surfaced two more underlying factors that have contributed significantly to the overall impact.

Firstly, the reform was successful because there was a shared understanding amongst all involved as to why the changes were taking place. Senior and Middle Leadership, classroom teachers, and students, could all buy into the demands of the new system because everything can be clearly linked backed to the rationale of improving pupil progress.

Secondly, improvements in the use of assessment have been maximised through balancing accountability with support. The regular scrutiny and graded letters ensure that teachers are accountable for their performance in this area. When this is combined with support to improve, the outcome is sustained improvement in performance.

NEXT STEPS

The new system is undoubtedly extremely rigorous and this has led to some discussion relating to the marking load that is generated. This is especially the case for those who teach a large number of different classes in a literacy-based subject. The next steps in the process are to address the issue of how assessment workload can be balanced without the successes of the new system being compromised. Early discussions have centred on strategies to help place more onus on students increasing the level of ownership they have for their assessment outcomes. For instance, teachers across the humanities department are developing techniques for meaningful self and peer-assessment, which can be moderated (but not marked) by teachers. Another strategy being explored at post-16 is a requirement that students self-assess essays against a mark scheme prior to submitting them. The value of this is that the teacher can focus on where the discrepancy is between the student's judgement and the actual quality of the essay, ultimately helping the student to 'close the gap'.

The assessment reform has been an overwhelming success. As within any initiative, we expect continued improvement and now the foundations are in place, we believe the added value will come almost exclusively from teachers themselves, particularly in the shape of sharing good practice.

CHAPTER 9

MIND THE GAP – CLOSING THE ACHIEVEMENT GAP

DAVE SHACKSON AND GEMMA BUGDEN, WALTHAMSTOW SCHOOL FOR GIRLS

FOCUS AREA

In spring 2011, our Whole School Self Evaluation Activity focused on the gap in performance and progression between Free School Meal (FSM) students and other students. This was investigated because our previous year's results had seen a gap of 28% between FSM and non-FSM students in our headline KS4 figure. As a result of the report produced, the school made a range of changes that sought to close the gap.

AIMS/RATIONALE

The concept of 'The Observer Effect' exists in various areas of science, but the common principle is that the act of observation changes the outcome, or influences what is being observed. To some extent, it was this type of effect we tried to harness as a school in 2011 when it became apparent that, despite having achieved our best ever GCSE results in 2010, there was an embarrassing gap of 28 points between the percentage of our Free School Meal students achieving the key measure of five A*-Cs including English and Maths (at 46%) – and that achieved by our other students (at 74%.)

Our concerns predated this issue being raised by Her Majesty's Chief Inspector in his 2012 report Unseen Children: Access and Achievement 20 Years On. They also predated the direct linking of funding through the Pupil Premium with the expanded Free School Meal 'Ever Six' designation. With FSM students being a significant proportion of the school population (22% in 2011) and national data suggesting that FSM students are at a disadvantage in both achievement and further progression, such a gap was unacceptable. Our data also showed that our 2013 Year 11 cohort would reach a peak of Free School Meal students, at 23.5%.

Just as Michael Wilshaw would publically highlight the disadvantaged Children of the UK underachieving in 2012 as being characterised as 'unseen', in 2011 we hoped to highlight our own unseen children and spur action at all levels within the school that would hopefully create a positive observer effect.

BACKGROUND CONTEXT

In 2010, the startling statistic emerged that only 40 students entitled to FSM progressed to Oxbridge – this was fewer than the total number that gained entry to Oxbridge that year from Winchester College alone. In our school, in light of the clear achievement gap of 2010, our 2011 Spring leadership Self-Evaluation Activity involved all of the leadership team making a trawl of data in their respective areas of responsibility to see the extent to which the achievement gap was evident.

Our capped best eight subjects point score of 369.4 for FSM students was significantly higher than the national average but was 11 points below that of other students. The value-added figure for our FSM was also very high but considerably below that for other students. It was therefore apparent that as well as not matching other students in attainment, our FSM students were also not making as much progress. Data from KS2 indicated that our FSM students already had a significantly lower points score on entry than other students, but we had not successfully reduced that pre-existing gap.

In terms of attendance, there were clear disparities between FSM and non-FSM students' absences. For example, although FSM students made up 20% of the school population, 40% of the students with less than 85% attendance were FSM. In addition, half of our Educational Welfare Officer referrals were FSM students.

In terms of behaviour, we found a mixed picture. In the previous year, there had been twenty four fixed-term exclusions, but only two of them had been FSM students. However, with regards to referrals to our duty room for serious incidents in and outside lessons, nearly a third of those were for FSM students and they accounted for nearly half of our internal exclusions.

FSM students were also not participating in as many extracurricular activities as their peers. In fact, the data painted a picture of a group of students who were not always having the same rich and rewarding school experience as their peers. In some musical and dramatic activities, the FSM students were woefully underrepresented – only two FSM students participated in the school carol concert (against 65 in total) and of the 23 girls involved in a recent school play, only one was FSM eligible. Some other performing arts activities such as the steel pans ensemble were better balanced, as were many of the sporting teams. Somewhat unsurprisingly, only two of the 23 students attending the annual ski trip, which is by far the most expensive school enrichment opportunity for students, were FSM eligible.

In fact the only extracurricular areas where there were consistently high numbers of FSM students participating, were out-of-hours activities already targeted at disadvantaged and underachieving students such as the Saturday School programme.

In terms of post-16 education, we looked back at a survey we had conducted amongst our Year 11s during their final week of GCSE exams, asking them to indicate where they had applied to and what level of course they had applied for. Fewer FSM students indicated that they were applying for level three courses. FSM students were also underrepresented in STEM subjects and overrepresented in business courses, which seemed to indicate that their choice of post-16 education was possibly based on concepts and ideas about which subjects would improve their financial situation more immediately.

Clearly we had a responsibility to highlight this group of students to all staff and ensure that comprehensive efforts were made to make them less 'unseen'.

THE STORY

The Self Evaluation Activity of spring 2011 made sobering reading and led to a number of action points. Keeping in mind that Pupil Premium funding would not be introduced until September 2011, these were not made in order to spend specifically targeted funding, but rather to raise the profile of FSM students and improve their experiences at all levels. In the first instance, we had identified many areas of good practice and sought to emphasise and remind people of these. Teachers had been required to identify FSM students in their records and mark books for some time. Most subjects provided textbooks for home use free of charge and many subjects allowed equipment loans.

In some areas, there had already been a policy of prioritising FSM students for enrichment activities, such as for the Aim Higher trips to universities. Aware of the low numbers of FSM participation in extracurricular performing arts, the Head of Performing Arts was already looking at a new funding model to make instrumental lessons more affordable.

From the beginning of 2011, identifying the achievement of FSM students from the data collection for each year became part of the termly Student Progress Leaders' Reports. SPLs were expected to implement strategies where they identified underachievement. In Year 11, based on the underachievement amongst FSM students in the Year 11 mocks, FSM students were prioritised to be allocated members of the Leadership Team as academic mentors. The SPLs were also required to put the progress and attainment FSM students as a standing item on all Pastoral Faculty meetings. An additional focus identified for SPLs was to ensure they were making links with the 'hard to reach' parents, often parents of FSM students. The SPLs needed to ensure parental support and contact. This would allow them to support teaching staff needing to contact these parents.

Although FSM data was already included on student lists, we decided to emphasise this cohort of students even more. For any list generated, whether it be class registers, lists of attendees on trips – or lists as part of data analysis, we decided to have a general policy of FSM students always highlighted in bold. Another 'highlighting' initiative was to have a looping Powerpoint presentation on display at the start of all staff meetings featuring the photographs of FSM students most immediately relevant to the attendees of that meeting. For example, a meeting of Year 10 tutors would feature the pictures of the Year 10 FSM girls.

Given the fact that many of our FSM students lived in areas of Walthamstow with high levels of deprivation, we tried to improve the resources these students had at home. The school had an excess stock of older personal computers left over after the Building Schools For The Future rebuild and our transfer to a managed IT service. These were given to targeted FSM students on a permanent basis. All faculties were asked when reviewing and rewriting schemes of work to review and consider the type of home learning tasks that were set to account for access to resources, especially if asking students to do work that required access to computers and the internet.

It was also asked that faculties such as Performing Arts and Art, Design & Technology look at ways of subsidising and bringing down costs for FSM students. The Performing Arts faculty, as indicated earlier, had already been looking at this issue. The outcome of their review was to offer instrumental lessons in small groups rather one-to-one, so reducing the cost per student. We also discovered we could reduce the cost of practising and learning the more popular instruments by directly employing our own part-time instrumental teachers rather than using the borough musical service. These additional savings could then be passed on to parents in what were already subsidised lessons.

It was hoped that each of these small initiatives would promote marginal gains and would cumulatively lead to significant gains for our FSM cohort. It is hard to get a sense of every teacher who made an adjustment to the time and effort they spent supporting a student because their face was on display in a meeting. One example of a positive 'marginal gain' was the policy adopted by the Gifted and Talented co-ordinator, which saw any FSM student who applied given a place on aspirational trips to universities and activities about studying law and medicine.

To some extent, the most effective strategies amongst faculties were those that targeted underachievement in general and were then very much having an impact on the FSM students. Two faculties that have been very successful in closing any achievement gap are English and ICT.

English was the faculty with the lowest FSM gap in 2010, but the team was given an extra impetus to address underachievement after the 2012 results; they were partly affected by the WJEC board grade boundary change. The new Head of English introduced a targeted approach to improving the results for 2013 by ensuring that after the Controlled Assessments completed in Year 10, targeted students were given an additional opportunity to complete a fresh Controlled Assessment. This involved much extra work for students and English teachers but allowed a large number of students to improve their grades. Regular fine grading was also used to identify students that needed to be targeted on account of the fact that they had an insecure C grade. As well as reviewing students' grades every six weeks, it was a requirement that the books of these students had additional marking above the regular marking for all students. Workshop sessions that were well publicised were offered to targeted groups with the clear message that the sessions could deliver the few extra marks they would need to get the higher grade. The English Faculty was determined to maintain mixed-ability teaching throughout Year 11, convinced that it was a proven method of expanding achievement for all. But, given the different demands of the tiered paper, they did change class groups for the last six weeks before the exam to allow a tier focus.

The ICT faculty, until 2013, offered a DIDA ICT course. Again, their sessions and additional workshops were targeted at underachieving students in general, but resulted in many FSM students benefitting. They also made very effective use of the Fronter intranet to provide support materials that modelled exemplars and made grading very clear to students. Tracking data was used effectively to highlight underachievement and communication of this to students and parents was effective.

The RE teachers adopted a different approach. Most GCSE students at Walthamstow School for Girls sit the short course – which is studied as part of the GCSE timetable – but students are given the option of doing full course if they are willing to study for an extra paper in their own time. Each year, around one third of the students take this option and in 2013 90% of FSM students achieved A*-C compared with 96% of other students. Material to study was made available on the school virtual learning area and there was a single scheduled weekend revision session – but otherwise, the content for the entire paper had to be studied in the student's own time.

This success was most likely achieved because of the range of papers that the students could choose from. The teachers supported students in their choice of whether to sit the Christianity, Islam or Religion and Society paper. This choice of papers suited our school community. Nearly all the FSM students who chose to do the full course option were of Pakistani ethnicity and their own personal knowledge of their home religion was strong. The strategy demonstrated the value in tailoring a curriculum and offering choice to reflect and suit a particular community, especially if a significant number of your disadvantaged students are from that community.

IMPACT

Tracking the impact of this initiative has been complicated somewhat by the fact that the focus has changed nationally to encompass a larger range of disadvantaged students as identified by the 'Ever Six' category which defines any student who has been in receipt of a Free School Meal in the last six years as being eligible for the Pupil Premium funding, as well as any looked-after children. This group is double our straight FSM figure: 40% across the school.

In terms of the points gap on our headline GCSE figure, changes were initially slow, and identifying any trend has been furt her complicated by a general dip in results in 2012 (see table on next page).

Four-Year FSM (pre-2012 measure) comparison for 5 A*-C including English and Maths

	2010	2011	2012	2013
FSM	46%	49%	54%	63%
Other	74%	74%	56%	71%

In 2012, we had successfully narrowed the gap to only two points. However, it was hardly worth any self-congratulation as it was due to a significant drop in the performance of our other students. The silver lining in that year was that FSM attainment did not seem to suffer from our exam board woes and was still improving.

The 2013 results provide better evidence of where our gap stands. Overall, we are pleased that a 28-point gap has been reduced so far to eight. The overall positive trend here is that each year FSM attainment has increased.

The data and evidence now being tracked at a school and national level is based on the Pupil Premium. Given that there is an overlap of around half the students in this group, it would be expected that our 2011 focus should have some impact on the Pupil Premium comparison (see table below).

Three-year Pupil Premium comparison for 5 A*-C including English and Maths

	2011	2012	2013
PP & CLA	52%	52%	64%
Other	79%	60%	73%

Again, the 2012 rapid reduction in the gap is hardly indicative of success given our overall results and the fact that we only reduced the gap from a 27-point margin to eight through the other students doing worse. However, as with the old measure, we feel that 2013 more accurately reflects the impact of our focus. Our 2013 results also showed that our value-added score for FSM students was higher than that for other students, which gave us a greater sense that FSM students were making more progress than their peers and thus were closing a pre-existing gap.

NEXT STEPS

In terms of analysing the Pupil Premium gap across subjects in 2013, it is very pleasing to see that 11 GCSE subject areas have an attainment gap of less than 10%, including English and Drama where Pupil Premium students outperform the rest. However, there are six subjects where it exceeds 10%. This in-school variance needs to be addressed, especially as it is repeated when looking at the average point differences in some subject areas.

As a school, we need to use our data and learn from the success of our focus in 2011 to apply the same principles on a larger scale to encompass all the PP students. This is particularly important given that all schools need to be ensuring that the Pupil Premium funding is targeted at the students for which it is intended. Currently we are reviewing our collection and use of data to ensure that our monitoring of Pupil Premium students across all year groups is smarter and more efficient. We also need to have a new data focus that looks more sharply at progress and addresses any progress gap given the new measures to be implemented by the DfE.

Already we have started a process by which faculties make bids for Pupil Premium money for interventions that they can show will raise progress and attainment amongst PP students. The English Faculty's initiative of 2013, for example, is being repeated but with PP money being used to pay for additional marking that the intervention generates. Other faculties have also put in bids for specific intervention strategies that seek to support raising achievement amongst Pupil Premium students.

There are a few lessons we can take away from our success in closing the FSM gap to support our next steps in seeking to close the Pupil Premium gap.

Firstly, there is the simple principle of not allowing these students to become 'invisible'. It is perhaps unsurprising that the Pupil Premium gap is usually worse in schools and areas of the country where they are less represented and their underachievement has less impact on the overall results of a school. By making PP students a focus at all levels, and in all areas, marginal gains can be maximised.

Secondly, targeting and tackling underachievement as a whole will always help. There is an understandable concern about the legitimacy of offering extra classes and interventions that exclude students that are not Pupil Premium. However, if Pupil Premium students are significantly underachieving then any strategy that targets underachievement will have an impact and should ultimately narrow the gap.

Finally, taking account of the particular circumstances of a school community can always offer ways to improve access and outcomes for Pupil Premium students. A curriculum tailored to suit a particular culture or group and take advantage of their strengths can help the Pupil Premium students in that group in terms of accessibility and prior knowledge. Additionally, subjects and areas of the school with specific access issues (such as access to musical instruments and instrumental lessons) need to find ways to subsidise or bring down those costs.

Ultimately, we are confident that our ongoing focus will continue to see improvements in this area and we are glad that we had a focus on this in advance of the DfE specifically raising the issue as a national education concern with the attached Pupil Premium funding.

CHAPTER 10

CITY YEAR – MINDING THE GAP

ROWLAND WELLER AND KATH CORRIGALL, UXBRIDGE HIGH SCHOOL

FOCUS AREA

This case study evaluates the impact of an initiative called 'City Year' on efforts to narrow the gap between the performance of white British students at Uxbridge High School and that of students from other ethnic groups.

AIMS/RATIONALE

The introduction of the innovative City Year programme was designed to have a significant impact on the literacy levels, attendance and behaviour of the target group.

BACKGROUND CONTEXT

Uxbridge High School is a larger than average 11-18 mixed comprehensive school in West London. While 45% of students are of white British heritage, the school serves students from a very wide range of minority ethnic backgrounds. The school faces challenges from issues relating to the high proportion of students who come from backgrounds of social deprivation. This is most evident in low literacy levels, particularly among white British students. Last year's English GCSE pass rate was 48%, compared to 69% in Maths. It is a similar story with progress, where 47% of students achieved their expected progress from KS2-4 for English compared to 70% in Maths. Furthermore, the attendance rate and behaviour of white British students is significantly worse than for the school population overall. The recent downshift in exam pass rates and a movement towards a more academic curriculum have put additional pressure on this group of students, for whom the controlled assessment and speaking and listening components added value to their overall grade.

THE STORY

Literacy has become a key priority for the school. The school has employed a range of literacy strategies including the Ruth Miskin literacy catch up, Drop Everything And Read (DEAR), whole school extended writing, a new literacy marking policy, a literacy working party, library events, a boys' reading clubs, the Get Caught Reading campaign, library lessons for KS3, across year setting at KS3, a focus on core skills at all levels (English Language GCSE for all students), the use of learning support for targeted interventions, extracurricular activities, English Week, World Book Week and Hillingdon Book of the Year.

While these interventions have had some impact, particularly at KS3, they have not stemmed the downward trend in GCSE results in English.

City Year is one of the UK's leading education charities. They serve schools in socially deprived areas, providing staff who act as tutors, mentors and role models. A team of 11 young adults, many of whom are university graduates taking a gap year, were introduced to UHS in September 2013, funded by pupil premium money. UHS is currently one of only 10 secondary schools in London to employ City Year staff.

The team is in addition to our existing pastoral, inclusion and SEN teams. They have been employed to supplement activities that are already in place in school, to increase student engagement and access to learning. Each City Year student focuses on the literacy needs of targeted students by attending English classes, teaching literacy progress units and engaging in paired reading schemes, extracurricular writing clubs and breakfast clubs. Each City Year participant is attached to an English teacher and supports the students in that teacher's classes. They have specific students to work with and keep up-to-date tracking records to monitor and demonstrate progress.

City Year supports literacy in particular through the use of literacy progress units, created by the DfE and distributed to English departments. These units are taught to small groups and focus on particular literacy skills such as spelling, sentence and text level. Once a unit has been taught, the student is tested in the writing skill to check that it has been embedded. This process can then be repeated, if required. At UHS City Year employees are working with Year 7, 8 and 10 students.

City Year students have also taken a wider role in the school mentoring systems, challenging and engaging with students before and after school and at break and lunch.

IMPACT

City Year had been working at UHS for a term when we started to analyse some of our school data to try to quantify the impact they were having. Whilst it is hard to ascribe any individual change directly to City Year on a cause and effect basis, by looking at a broad and balanced range of measures, we hope to paint an overall picture of their impact. There were four main information sources we looked at; progress in English, behaviour point score, attendance, and anecdotal evidence/case studies.

English point score: It was important to see if the support from City Year was accelerating the progress made by those students who were receiving it. Evidence particularly from the Education Endowment Foundation Teaching and Learning Toolkit suggests that in-class support is not always an effective intervention. The data in term of progress for the lesson intervention strategy is not strong and conflicts with all the other indicators. We see some deceleration of progress in Year 9, which is hard to explain, but in relative terms those pupils supported by City Year staff have performed better.

BEHAVIOUR: The school operates a behaviour system where students are sanctioned with behaviour points on a 1 to 5 scale. The data indicates a slight fall in points overall but a significant drop in points from the target group of students, with less than half as many white British students involved in behaviour incidents compared to last year. Further analysis and break down shows that many of these students fall into a category of students who are not our most challenging, but whose behaviour is often adversely influenced by the most difficult to manage students.

The data also shows a stronger impact on in-lesson behaviour where City Year staff are working. City Year staff often work in the quiet margins of school life, they are always 'out and about' at lunch, break, before and after school, they make little interventions with students – the things that you can't quantify and often go unnoticed – but as a result, the incidence of fights and aggressive behaviour during these times has fallen and school feels a calmer and safer place. For example, City Year staff play in the football games with the students, they subtly lead them and intervene before an aggressive tackle escalates.

Our annual bullying survey shows by far the lowest levels of bullying since we started it eight years ago, with a 7% drop in the number of students experiencing bullying.

First term	Points	No. on roll	Points per student
2013	1007	1271	0.792
2012	947	1179	0.803

First term	No. of incidents	No. of White British students
2013	901	63
2012	855	155

ATTENDANCE: The tables below show attendance for the first term of the year, broken down by year group for two consecutive years before and during City Year's intervention. The data allows a comparison between similar terms and shows a positive impact particularly with Years 8, 9 and 10, where City Year has been focussing. The Persistent Non Attenders (PNA) rate has also reduced and this is where impact from City Year with white British students has been felt most, as this is the group where most of our PNA students come from.

2013

Group	Presents	Approved educational activity	Authorised absences	Unauthorised absences	Possible	Attend
Year 07	94.8	1.1	3.4	0.7	100.0	95.9
Year 08	92.9	2.1	4.0	1.0	100.0	95.0
Year 09	93.0	1.6	4.0	1.5	100.0	94.6
Year 10	90.5	3.1	4.3	2.0	100.0	93.6
Year 11	89.0	4.8	4.8	1.3	100.0	93.8
Totals	92.1	2.5	4.1	1.3	100.0	94.6

2012

Group	Presents	AEA	Authorised absences	Unauthorised absences	Possible	Attend
Year 07	95.4	0.8	3.4	0.4	100.0	96.2
Year 08	93.4	1.7	4.3	0.6	100.0	95.1
Year 09	91.1	2.7	5.1	1.1	100.0	93.8
Year 10	89.9	3.0	4.7	2.5	100.0	92.9
Year 11	89.8	3.7	4.3	2.2	100.0	93.5
Totals	92.0	2.4	4.4	1.3	100.0	94.3

Case Studies: Case studies bring a human element to this report and are, in some ways, the most powerful form of evidence, given the early stage of the programme.

STUDENT A

Student A is a white British Year 7 boy who was demonstrating attention-seeking behaviour and finding it difficult to form positive relationships with his peers. As a result, he regularly engaged in low-level disruption of lessons, which was affecting his learning. The current pastoral support structure was responding to the symptoms but not dealing with the underlying causes. His behaviour point score was rising and with a poor balance between positive and negative interactions with staff and few friends. He was at risk of becoming disengaged.

He became involved with the City Year programme in late September. The City Year staff have given him a significant amount of support and input. He has joined the Young Hero Programme, a community citizenship based project run by the City Year volunteers, a citizenship workshop focusing on teamwork and social skills. He also attends breakfast club, which is run by City Year before school, where he is able to play board games with others and receives a hot drink and some toast.

This simple act of playing games and nurturing his basic needs has developed his social skills beyond all recognition. He has subsequently engaged in other activities such as becoming a library monitor, a bookworm and he has taken part in numerous competitions – for example, languages and scrabble quiz. His behaviour point score has stopped rising and since mid-November he hasn't had a single behaviour point.

CITY YEAR PARTICIPANT

"During my time at Uxbridge High School, I have been assigned to one teacher's classes in English. In particular, I have been most present in her Year 9 lessons. At first, I was working with a select few students, checking their spelling and grammar, taking a small group out to read, but as time went on I started to get to other students and in time built a relationship with most of them."

"Now, although I do focus on certain students who need a little more attention, I do my best to move around the room for general in-class support, just re-explaining the tasks set or stimulating thought, just so it is easier for Miss James to teach the rest of the class. I feel like I have made an impact,

especially behaviour-wise, as my relationship with a lot of the students has made it possible for me to keep them focused and engaged in the lesson, which I hope has somewhere along the line made an effect on their learning."

ENGLISH TEACHER

"I have found it hugely beneficial to have a City Year Participant working alongside my classes. She is able to connect with the students in a way that, as a teacher, I am unable to. She is a very positive role model to some of the less-engaged students and shares her enthusiasm. Having her in the room has enabled me to be more creative with my teaching and to take more risks when trying to engage students in challenging work. A small group of students in particular have benefitted from her interventions, and they miss her when she is not there — becoming less motivated and engaged. As a result of her work, these students enjoy English more and I feel confident this will be reflected in their end-of-year performance."

REFLECTIONS

This report has been generated at the start of the project and it is too early to draw any direct cause and effect conclusions. However, it is fair to say that the impact of City Year has been 'felt' across the school in a positive way, and we can say that the City Year staff have added value, ethos and impact to the outcomes at UHS.

The integration of City Year to UHS has not been without its challenges. The City Year team members are not contractually 'tied in' in the way that teachers are and a number of those that started have left. Of the 11 staff, only six of the original team remain. Some City Year staff would appear to have used the programme as a stop gap after graduating whilst they sought more permanent employment. One of the keys to their success is the relationships they build with our students, particularly those challenging students whom they mentor, and we would like to be able to manage this aspect better next year.

The model has its origins in the primary sector: some of the initial activities City Year introduced transferred well and others were less successful. For example, the before school 'brain gym' did not work well — our students were too self-conscious to engage with this. City Year was flexible and proactive in trying to develop it, but on reflection we should have acted more decisively to stop this earlier rather than to try to coerce students into participating.

As we reflect on the roles we have given City Year staff, we are reminded that providing effective intervention in a specific subject is a highly skilled and challenging task, requiring expertise in subject knowledge and pedagogy. To succeed, it may require a greater investment in training the core members before they start in-class support.

City Year is a flexible, proactive group of people. They have integrated well into the fabric of the school and are benefitting students in all sorts of ways. They without doubt represent excellent value for money and fill a niche within our school's staffing structure.

NEXT STEPS

The programme is very much a work in progress. We need to develop the activities and the role that City Year staff provide, being more ruthless when filtering out those elements that are not working so well. The monitoring of the intervention data needs to continue, with a careful analysis of the variables, to establish the most effective deployment of the team.

CHAPTER 11

CORE KICK-START – HOW TO DEVELOP STRONGER RELATIONSHIPS WITH 'HARD TO REACH' (HTR) FAMILIES

MARTINA LECKY, DAVID RICH AND DAN STENT, RUISLIP HIGH SCHOOL

FOCUS AREA

Core Kick-start (CKS) was launched in June 2013. Its purpose was to support underachieving incoming Year 7 students in Maths and English through the transition period. Weekly workshops, in both subjects, were delivered to Year 6 students by staff at RHS. Students were targeted using the most recent summative assessment data collected from their primary school. All students who attained a 4c or below in Maths and/or English were invited to attend. To engage parents with the learning of their son/daughter, and to improve communication between school and home, parents were encouraged to attend the workshops with the students.

RATIONALE/BACKGROUND CONTEXT

Ruislip High school opened in 2006. Since then, the percentage of Free School Meals (FSM) and Pupil Premium (PP) students has increased significantly. All the permanent exclusions of students in the school's short history have been from HTR families. The school appointed Key Stage 3 and Key Stage 4 Pupil Premium co-ordinators in 2013.

When the Year 7 catch up funding was first introduced, several staff at Ruislip High School discussed establishing a summer school, based around sporting, behaviour/pastoral or subject themes for Year 6 students intending to join RHS in September. The idea of a summer school was rejected on the grounds that the target students (those who were finding literacy and numeracy particularly challenging) were unlikely to welcome the additional lessons during their long-awaited summer holiday.

Moreover, as many parents/guardians of the target group work during the day, it would have been difficult to engage them in their children's work, which was felt to be vital. The final reason for rejecting this approach was that the school values a very formal start to Year 7. This is seen as a strength of the school, which is annually established through a carefully phased induction for all new students to the school. It was felt that to offer a more informal summer school would not provide the appropriate establishment of ethos.

Therefore, it was decided to offer an evening school during the summer and autumn terms respectively, aimed primarily at students unlikely to reach the expected level of 4b or above in English and Mathematics. From this, Core Kick-start was to evolve.

THE STORY

Initially, some members of the English and Mathematics teams were sceptical – one of the main objections was that staff and students would be too tired to work effectively in the evening. After several discussions with the Deputy Headteacher and the KS3 PP co-ordinator, subject teachers began to see a whole school perspective, which encouraged early parental engagement. The ability to sustain this was seen as particularly attractive.

Also, as exam courses were finishing in late May, subject teachers would have capacity to take on extra provision in the latter part of the summer term. Two English and Mathematics teachers respectively agreed to run the course and were paid for their teaching and planning time.

The English and Mathematics teachers included the Head of English and a combination of experienced and newly qualified teachers. They were paid for their teaching and planning time. The sessions ran each Wednesday from 5:30-7:45pm, with two separate one-hour lessons in English and Mathematics. The scheme of work was developed in-house. The English workshops focused primarily on key literacy skills, inference and deduction, and spelling, punctuation and grammar. The Mathematics workshops covered basic number work, fractions, shape, space and measure and sequences. The workshops were tailored to the needs of the individuals and were planned with those students in mind. Parents sat with their children and were encouraged to work with their child on the tasks set, participate in plenary activities and work with their child on homework tasks.

The Assistant Pastoral Manager and the newly appointed CKS co-ordinator assumed the pastoral responsibility for the scheme. They developed rapport with the students and their families on arrival, and during the fifteen-minute break, where healthy refreshments were provided between each literacy and numeracy hour. Based on feedback, however, parents did not value this informal time and so refreshments were removed and break time was reduced to just a five-minute movement time. Other more effective ways of strengthening the relationship between families and school staff are being considered for 2014-15 (see 'Next steps').

IMPACT

June – July 2013

The first wave of CKS ran from June – July 2013 with a total of thirty students regularly attending workshops held at school. A baseline assessment was administered in the first session and a breakdown of the results can be seen in Figure 1. To provide the school with comparative data, a summative assessment was administered in the final session of the course. Unfortunately, six students were unable to complete the assessment due to other commitments, the results of which can be seen in Figure 2.

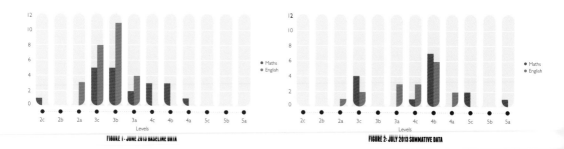

FIGURE 1 - JUNE 2013 BASELINE DATA   FIGURE 2: JULY 2013 SUMMATIVE DATA

These figures show that the CKS workshops supported the majority of the thirty students to attain higher levels in Maths and English. There is a notable shift in the median attainment of the students from 3cs and 3bs, to 4bs, which is a significant increase. A 4b was the benchmark level that allowed students to 'graduate' from the programme. In July 2013, 66% of students graduated from Maths and 47% graduated from English.

The second wave of CKS ran from September – October 2013 with a total of eighteen students regularly attending. Using information gained from a Parent Focus group, the workshops were condensed into two groups instead of four. The co-ordinator used the available data from June and July 2013 as the baseline (Figure 3) and administered a final summative assessment in October 2013, the results of which can be seen in Figure 4.

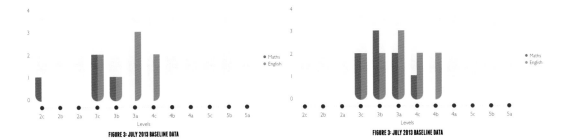

FIGURE 3: JULY 2013 BASELINE DATA

FIGURE 3: JULY 2013 BASELINE DATA

Figures 3 and 4 show that the autumn workshops further supported those eighteen students who were at serious risk of underachieving in the core subjects. The students who attended the autumn programme were most in need of support, and it was the commitment and expert planning of the workshop leaders that helped these students to access the curriculum.

Quantitative analysis results: students' fine-graded levels in English and Maths from June to November

To determine whether the gains in students' attainment were sustained, the autumn tracking data (November) was analysed for English and Maths. For the students who studied both English and Maths, the mean increase for Maths was 1.17 – this equates to students making, on average, one sub level gain, which had been sustained from the summer term.

Two students made sustained gains of four sub-levels, which was comparable to their progress in English. In English the gains were greater, with a mean increase of 2.58 – this equates to students improving, on average, by two and half sub-levels. For the students who took only Maths or English, the increase in sub levels was 3 and 2.67 respectively.

In summary, significant sustained gains were made by the majority of students who participated in the programme. It is worth noting that the data indicates that the students' progress in Maths was reduced if they took English as well, which was not the case for the latter.

Qualitative analysis

The quantitative data, collected through summative assessment, indicates the positive impact that CKS had on students' attainment. The initiative was also scrutinised through qualitative means to inform future planning and processes. In addition, evidence was collected to ascertain the more subjective ways in which CKS had impacted upon the learning and attitudinal outlook of the participants.

Focus groups and interviews were held with students, parents, and teachers of CKS during the evaluation part of the programme. The findings from student interviews are illustrated through the following two case studies.

CASE STUDY B

Nathan

| 4B | MATHS | 5A |
| 3B | ENGLISH | 4B |

"Core Kick-start made me interested again in Maths and English and gave me confidence."

CASE STUDY B

Ellie

| 3A | MATHS | 5C |
| 3A | ENGLISH | 4B |

"I thought I was going to be behind and I was worried about that, but Core Kick-start has helped me to be more confident and get on track."

Evidence from the student interviews suggested that the programme not only impacted positively upon the attainment of the students, but also upon the perception of their own competencies and abilities, thus improving their attitude towards learning.

Parents also recognised the transformation enjoyed by their sons/daughters as a direct result of the CKS programme. During a focus group held in the final session of the programme, parents reflected on how the tutorials had:

- Identified weaknesses in their child's subject knowledge that they could then work on at home with them.

- Encouraged students to learn together and help each other to understand content that they may have "given up on."

- Helped to ease any anxieties about joining Ruislip High School.

- Reinvigorated their son/daughter's love for learning.

Evidence from the focus group confirms the school's assertion that a parental presence in the classroom is a powerful strategy for enhancing the learning experience of the students, as well as strengthening the relationship between home and school. This strategy was integral to students' academic success.

Interviews with the teachers of the CKS programme highlighted the impact of the initiative on both the students and the parents. An English tutor suggested the following:

"*Many of the students struggled at English because their parents struggled at it. The challenge I found most often was assuring the parents that their child could do the work. I often had parents saying 'Oh he can't use capital letters, he's never been able to do that and neither can I'. As parents were involved in the work, they were building up their own skills in English and their confidence.*"

Restoring the confidence of both parents and students in their academic competency appears to have led to an improvement in students' progress. This may indicate that an increase in parental engagement in their child's learning may encourage family learning as a regular activity at home. A Maths tutor affirms this assertion, stating that:

> "Parents were all really positive about Core Kick-start. I think it boosted their confidence in using skills that they might not have had to use in over a decade. I think the importance of them learning alongside their children is paramount because it means they can cement the knowledge with them at home when completing home tasks."

Parental engagement with the tutorials and home tasks served to demonstrate the commitment of the parents to the learning of their son/daughter. This further strengthened the motivation of the students and encouraged them to succeed. Whilst the inclusion of parents added another tier to the programme, the school believes that their engagement was one of the main reasons for the success of the programme.

These qualitative studies support the school's conjecture that CKS was a success on many levels. The programme provided a positive environment for learning that engaged students with weaknesses in their subject knowledge so that they could work toward bridging these gaps with the support of their parents/guardians.

NEXT STEPS

Clearly the school will want to build on the success of CKS in the future. It intends to run the scheme again throughout the summer and autumn of 2014, but with a number of changes to enhance the programme:

- The school will endeavour to start the evening sessions earlier in the summer term. This is dependent on the willingness of the local authority to provide the school with student data at an earlier stage.

- The formally taught English scheme of work will draw partly on material from a major West End production; the conclusion of the programme will be a fully-funded visit to central London for the students and their parent/guardian to watch the production. This will seek to build cultural capital as well as provide a fitting end to the formal scheme.

- In order to capitalise further on the positive relationships, which the school establishes through CKS, it will formally introduce some family-support worker roles. These staff, themselves members of the local community, will provide regular contact for families, ensuring that parents continue to be engaged with the school to support both the educational attainment and wider social development of their children.

Additionally, once the formal CKS evening school comes to an end in the autumn, English and Mathematics teachers will continue to work with the families remotely, providing one evening per week of electronic/telephone communication support, on the night that English and Mathematics homework is to be set. Teachers will be able to help students directly in solving any homework issues, but will also continue the dialogue with the parents/guardians in order to embed the notion of families working together to secure the best educational outcomes for their children.

CHAPTER 12

ESTABLISHING RESEARCH PRACTITIONERS

JULIE WILKINSON, NOWER HILL HIGH SCHOOL

FOCUS AREA

Ben Goldacre in his paper Building Evidence Into Education (March 2013) argued that education needs to mirror medicine by becoming an evidence-based profession. He reminded his readers of the many medical advances that have taken place as a consequence of the culture change brought about through the introduction of randomised controlled trials. Embedding research into everyday practice, Goldacre suggested, would not only enable teachers to make informed decisions, but could even eradicate government interventions and innovations if teachers themselves showed them to be politically rather than evidence based.

Marc Smith in his Guardian article Evidence-Based Education: Is It Really That Straightforward? (26th March, 2013) was encouraged by much of Goldacre's paper and furthermore recommended "the creation of research practitioners, teachers not only skilled in the art and science of teaching but also with the skills and aptitude of a researcher; teachers who are able to identify the problem, formulate a hypothesis and test that hypothesis using scientific methods, if such methods are deemed appropriate for the problem under investigation".

This case study examines the way Nower Hill High School has endeavoured to create such research practitioners through its establishment, development and embedding of a school-based Masters programme.

BACKGROUND CONTEXT

As a consequence of the 2007 McKinsey report How The World's Best Performing School Systems Come Out On Top, the DCSF (Department For Children, Schools And Families) was promoting teaching as an all-Masters profession – not only to help in the recruitment and retention of teachers, and to have a direct impact on pupil outcome – but also to bring the profession in line with the highest performing countries in the world (DCSF, Being The Best For Our Children 2008).

To help achieve this goal, in 2009 a government-funded three-year classroom-based Masters in Teaching and Learning (MTL) was launched by the Training and Development Agency for Schools (TDA) initially for NQTs in the north-west, as well as those in schools across the country facing challenging circumstances. The original aim had been to roll out the programme nationally in 2012. Furthermore, roughly £100m was provided by the government to part-fund Masters programmes for teachers with QTS.

At Nower Hill High School, the time now seemed right to investigate the introduction of a school-based Masters programme. There was much media coverage of the government's funding proposals and there was talk of career progression becoming linked to further academic qualifications. The Headteacher believed that a school-based Masters programme would provide access to recent academic research to underpin training. Moreover, it would have the added benefit of providing 'home-grown' practitioners with the necessary tools to be more forensic about their understanding and application of different aspects of pedagogy and leadership.

"It provides an excellent platform for self-reflection, a good critique about current views on teaching."

Nower Hill Science teacher

AIMS/RATIONALE

Recently appointed NQTs and early-years teachers with an 'M' level PGCE wanting to complete a Masters part-time with that same university, before their credits ran out, were already part-funded on an individual basis. However, the 'ad hoc' nature of these studies prevented effective support of their authors from systematically converting their findings into whole school improvement.

In a few cases, these universities were some distance away from the school. Travel time was exacerbating the pressure felt by teachers through their additional studies. We wished to discourage the pursuit of a further academic qualification during new recruits' NQT year itself, offering an alternative pathway just a year or two later into a teacher's professional career.

Practice and benefit from research undertaken through this route was already beginning to develop. For example, at the start of their induction programme, NQTs are annually provided with the critical reflections of a colleague's induction year written up as part of her MA research.

As a consequence of the government's rhetoric around Masters level qualifications, growing numbers of potential recruits enquired about Masters' level provision at interview. An in-house programme would have the benefits of providing local, bespoke, academically rigorous and cost-effective training to help develop current staff, which would in turn support recruitment and retention.

"*It certainly benefits their own professional and personal development. It however involves sacrifices and hard work! I would recommend it but I would warn teachers they have to be able to embrace added responsibilities and commitments.***"**

TA Strand Manager

THE STORY

Several different universities contacted the school around this time to offer their services as 'partners' in this new age of school/HEI collaboration; some seemed more equal than others. In the spring term of 2009, we responded to an initial contact made by an Assistant Headteacher at a school in the next authority to our own – a part-time lecturer at Middlesex University. His suggested model seemed to be the most flexible and best suited to our needs.

The initiative was first raised with staff through an item in the weekly bulletin inviting them to a twilight meeting in April. It was felt that meeting and starting to build a rapport with the course tutor would encourage staff to visualise themselves on the programme. A whole staff email was sent out, as well as notices at twice-weekly briefings. This regular and frequent awareness raising was fundamental in generating as much interest as possible in this meeting. The meeting was very well attended. The tutor's professional presentation as well as representation from SMT showed staff that the school was giving the programme its full support.

Further prompts at briefings and one-to-one conversations to reassure staff then took place. Although time-consuming, these did much to reassure doubting staff and to overcome the psychological barriers that were dissuading some from embarking on further academic study. Regular email and telephone communication between the tutor and school at this time was also vital in providing swift and accurate feedback to colleagues before the university's deadline.

"*Quite simply I couldn't have done it if it had not been put on at school. Getting from school to uni and then home would have been a nightmare in transportation and time. I had time before meetings to get work done and was able to balance after-school interventions (part of my trial) with all other aspects of my job and studying.*"

Nower Hill Art teacher

We asked applicants the following five questions:

1. Why do you want to follow a degree at Masters level?

2. How do you think it will improve your role at Nower Hill High School?

3. How do you think you will manage the extra time involved in this postgraduate degree course?

4. If we have a minimum of 10 people from Nower Hill who join this programme, we will be able to host it at Nower Hill itself. We would prefer a 5pm or 6pm start for the fortnightly two-hour twilight workshops. Do you have a preference for a day? Is there a day you wouldn't be able to attend these?

5. We will commit to paying a minimum of £375 and a maximum of £450 towards the £750 each year of the three-year Masters programme. However, in return we ask that you commit to staying at Nower Hill for this time. We would ask you to return this subsidy if you left either the school or the Masters programme within these three years. Do you accept these conditions?

The first cohort of 10 participants (all members of teaching staff) was established in May 2010. On the eve of the university deadline, only nine had signed up, so the AHT Development enrolled to ensure the programme was viable. Of course, as a participant, she gained first-hand experience of the programme, which could be conveyed when reporting on developments to SMT and governors, as well as at the introductory awareness-raising session for the next cohort. This second cohort of 15, including two members of the Educational Support Staff (ESS), both Teaching Assistants, was established in May 2012. (It had been decided the previous year to offer the programme only in alternate years to keep the costs down).

Participants undertook a different small-scale action research project each year of their two/three-year Masters study. Unlike in many other schools, there was no expectation that the focus of their projects had to link with any whole school development area. In fact, the school's expectation was the opposite, as we believed that aspects of future school development would be informed by the outcomes of very recent evidence-based research. However, annually completed portfolios were handed over to the relevant senior leader to review and use in consultation with the researcher when devising or amending policy and procedures for the following year.

Governors committed an annual subsidy of £5,000 towards this staff development programme. This sum has been added to the central CPD 'pot' within the school's training budget. For teaching staff, the school has paid approximately 50% of participants' fees. The school delegates a portion of the school's training budget to each Head of Faculty. The Head of one faculty chose to allocate a part of this budget one year to subsidise further one member of his team – as the focus of the research 'How Can Year 12 Students Be Supported To Avoid Underachievement In Social Studies Subjects?' was deemed central to the faculty's improvement.

As there was no government subsidy for ESS who did not have QTS, their fees were double those of teachers'. However, to show the school's commitment towards the development of the whole school workforce, it was decided also to subsidise 50% of ESS fees, even though this was considerably higher. In any one year if the £5,000 did not cover the cost of the subsidies, the remaining money would be taken from the central CPD budget. There was also commitment to providing short-term loans to any members of staff who were unable to pay their contribution to the fees in full at the start of each year.

"*The flexibility of the dissertation topics was very appealing.***"**

Nower Hill Classics teacher in charge of KS3

IMPACT

Research has informed practice at both a subject and a whole school level. The displays and practice in the music department, for example, are testament to the research done on Assessment for Learning (AfL) as part of one research project. Moreover, the department is regularly visited by teachers who wish to observe the outstanding teaching with AfL strategies embedded in each scheme of work.

A classics teacher researched 'How To Promote Classics To The 21st Century Youth: A Critical Evaluation Into Strategies To Promote The Value, Wide Appeal And Relevance Of Classics In Schools' As a consequence of developments put in place, there was a significant increase in the number of students who opted to study classical subjects. In addition, the teachers in the department now deliver an annual twilight promotional programme on classical subjects, which is open to parents and staff. Delivering her findings to an annual national conference of classics teachers extended the scope of the project's impact; of course, this experience also enhanced the professional standing and confidence of the researcher herself.

The focus area of one study was a critical evaluation of strategies provided for NQTs in moving them towards becoming outstanding teachers. This research was carried out the year before the school workforce expanded considerably with the addition of a Year 7 cohort, so it was timed to enrich the provision for a much larger cohort of NQTs. Findings informed the selection and training of NQT mentors as well as the tailoring of the whole school NQT induction programme so that tasks and strategies that had secured minimal impact were removed. Furthermore, short and focused follow-up observations were added to half-termly observations to provide guidance on the successful implementation of targets set.

The author of another project had recently procured a role as Year Co-ordinator and wanted to use an academic focus in her first year in post to gain a greater depth of understanding of the upcoming pastoral issues. Her project *'A Critical Investigation Into How To Motivate Year 9 Students To Enjoy, To Achieve, And To Help Prepare Them Well For Aspects Of Adult Life'* highlighted the various ways that student voice could become a powerful motivational tool. These were subsequently implemented – not only within her own year group, but also the others. Student dissatisfaction with the rewards system, which emerged from this project, helped to precipitate the introduction of a new and much improved whole school one.

Sometimes, subject research has also had whole school impact. For example, 'A Critical Investigation Into The Impact Of Hand-Held Devices On Teaching And Learning' by a Geography teacher resulted not only in a significant increase in their departmental use, but also a greater understanding of best generic practice. In addition, this research helped to disseminate that good practice through further staff training when employed in other curriculum areas. Following an initial pilot scheme using iPads in 2012/2013, a further development has taken place in 2013/2014 using tablet technology in all subjects with one Year 7 form.

Another researcher, both a Science teacher and Year Co-ordinator, took a subject focus one year, and a student support one the next. Thus, she was able to enhance both aspects of her professional life. She referred in her first portfolio to the development of her understanding of different pedagogical techniques within her own faculty and her improved confidence as a teacher. This was shown most poignantly in her dissertation 'A Critical Examination Of The Different Ways To Engage Difficult Parents'.

It resulted in passionate and detailed awareness-raising presentations to SMT and the Student Support Leadership team. Her strategy provided the basis of training sessions for parents and staff, and revised procedures were rolled out across all year groups. For the colleague herself, came a much-deserved external promotion.

"*It made me into a better form tutor. I have a much better understanding of behaviour and helping students to cope with stress.***"**

Nower Hill Quote teacher in charge of KS5

REFLECTIONS/EVALUATION

Many schools have embarked upon their own research programmes. However, most impose a limited range of research opportunities to drive on whole school improvement in targeted areas. The desire for staff to develop areas of their own interest to foster and develop their intellectual curiosity remains. Of the three annual Performance Management targets, one should have a CPD focus. For those teachers participating in the Masters programme at Nower Hill, their target is the Masters focus area.

Several participants on the Masters programme left the school before completing the full qualification. However, despite an initial insistence to the contrary, the decision was made not to ask for the subsidy to be returned if the annual portfolio of evidence had been submitted. So, was the Masters programme really encouraging retention if participants were leaving for promotion, as a direct consequence of the enhanced skills and confidence they had gained – or was its introduction counter-productive? There will always be some staff who leave for promotion – if studying for a Masters had helped to give researchers the edge over others when applying, then their enhanced skills and understanding would now also benefit another school.

Colleagues have not been asked if the offer of our Masters programme encouraged them to apply to the school, so definitive quantitative data cannot be supplied to evaluate this aim. However, it is often recently appointed members of staff who express greatest interest in pursuing the programme. An unexpected benefit of the collaborative nature of the taught sessions was the professional bonding that took place between the researchers. Not only were research tips and evaluative methods exchanged during the projects themselves, but several have subsequently delivered joint training to the wider school community.

Furthermore, informal links set up with local schools to explore different educational practices have burgeoned as researchers have maintained and developed them into more formal networks.

Although many benefits to the introduction of the programme are evident, there is a need for several tweaks. Communicating research results more widely and more systematically within the school community is needed to maximise impact in both the short and long term, and to encourage others to participate in the future. The submission dates need consideration: the May deadline saved money at the outset, but an August deadline would take the pressure off staff at one of the busiest times of the year.

> **"I** decided to take on the MA to improve the quality of my teaching and enhance potential employment opportunities. I felt having a Masters degree would help me not only professionally to progress in my career, but also because it allows me to develop skills and knowledge in specific areas of education that would make me a more proficient and effective teacher.**"**

Nower Hill PE teacher with responsibility for BTEC

NEXT STEPS

Following the publication of the school's white paper, *The Importance of Teaching* in November 2010, the Secretary of State for Education, Michael Gove, announced that central funding restrictions meant that, in future, there would be no central Government funding for postgraduate study programmes, including MTL. Therefore, only teachers already studying for the MTL are now being funded to complete the programme. He went on to state that the Government is still keen for teachers to gain postgraduate qualifications – "but that teachers should decide for themselves which Masters level course is the right one for them". Furthermore, cuts in teaching grants have now removed the subsidy previously enjoyed by teachers with QTS to pursue a part-time Masters programme.

This resulting increase in fees at the same time as a tightening of the whole school budget makes the continuation of this project a much more challenging task. However, the development of collective enquiry and evidence-based practice as the bedrock of the school's in-house training programme has added significantly to its depth and breadth. Even if additional funding from governors is not possible in the future – allocating more of the central CPD budget into further subsidising the fees to make pursuing the qualification a more affordable option for prospective practitioners is possible.

Middlesex University was the school's initially preferred provider. It may well be that five years on another provider may be better suited to the school's needs. As a member of a Teaching Schools Alliance, the possibility of an alliance rather than school-based programme is being pursued if minimum numbers are not met. In the interim, the school has embarked upon a small Research And Development project with another high school within the Alliance, following a successful bid to the National College Of Teaching and Leadership. The aim to create a hub of research practitioners has been realised.

CHAPTER 13

APPRAISAL + CPD = OUTSTANDING TEACHING: A SIMPLE, EFFECTIVE FORMULA FOR RAISING STANDARDS

DANIEL LOCKWOOD, HALL MEAD SCHOOL

FOCUS AREA

This case study outlines the implementation of a revised staff appraisal system with dramatic effects, at Hall Mead School.

BACKGROUND AND CONTEXT

Hall Mead has a long history of being a good school. Dedicated, loyal, hardworking staff; very positive parental engagement, a family ethos and, most importantly, fantastic students who have all contributed to the creation of a strong learning community. The school's long-standing Head retired after more than 30 years of service. His successor was, unfortunately, taken ill early in his tenure and for two years, in the absence of a Head, the established SLT worked very hard to keep the school running, maintaining the school's positive reputation in the community and its 'good' Ofsted grading. A new Head was appointed in January 2008, determined to build on the school's successes and lead the school from good to outstanding.

In September 2009, the new Head made his first appointment to the SLT. One of the responsibilities of the new Assistant Head was to oversee the Performance Management system. In the academic year 2009-2010, the school continued with the Performance Management system as it had been running. It became clear that improvements needed to be made to the system if it was to have maximum impact on pupil progress, school improvement and staff development. During the year 2009-2010, just 65% of colleagues completed and returned their Performance Management paperwork. Along with automatic pay progression on the Main Pay Scale (MPS), a culture had begun to grow in which staff expected that progression onto and within Upper Pay Spine (UPS) would also be automatic. After all, we were a good school, with good staff and good examination results.

As an SLT, we asked ourselves: Are we coasting? Is this good enough? What is our strategic plan to make Performance Management meaningful?

THE STORY

To review the system, a working party was convened. This group would consult on proposed changes to policy and procedure. It consisted of over a quarter of the teaching staff. We met regularly throughout the year 2010-2011. Alongside colleagues, the SLT, the unions and governors were also consulted.

A new policy was designed and implemented, based on the following straightforward principles:

- Learning was to be at the very core of policy and practice.

- PM was to facilitate teachers in the ongoing development of both the knowledge and skill to discharge their professional duties in a way that supported the teacher as learner.

- All progression agreed and targets set were to be cross-referenced with the 'Professional Standards for Teachers'.

- Performance Management is not a passive activity. Teachers have a professional duty to actively participate in PM – it cannot be seen as something that is 'done to them'.

SMALL STEPS, BIG GAINS

In order to guide colleagues into self-reflection and into assuming responsibility for their own Performance Management, the new cycle was designed to begin each year with a 'Self-Appraisal', removing any passivity from the process. Prior to meeting with their appraiser to review the performance of the preceding year, all colleagues conducted a self-review against the previous year's targets and met their appraiser with proposed draft targets for the following period. These proposed targets formed the basis of a professional dialogue between the appraisee and their appraiser. SMART targets were now set under three headings:

- Pupil Progress

- Leading Learning

- Professional Development

It was expected that all would link to the school development plan. Suddenly, colleagues were in the driving seat. They had ownership of their Performance Management and were the architects of how their own professional practice would contribute to whole school development. Performance Management was linked to the Professional Standards For Teachers. Colleagues were already very familiar with these – as a school, we had long been the main hub for the Havering Teacher Training Partnership and colleagues were used to applying the Qualified Teacher Standards to trainees.

However, it seemed that once a colleague had demonstrated that they had met the standards and qualified as a teacher and once they had a seat in the staffroom, the relevance of the standards seemed to fade. They were forgotten. Establishing a clear link to Performance Management and the Professional Standards for Teachers, at both core and post-threshold level, refreshed colleagues' thinking about ways in which to demonstrate the expected professional standards in their day-to-day practice.

In the year 2010-2011, 84% of colleagues completed and returned their PM documentation, an increase of 19%, with long-term illness and maternity leave accounting for those colleagues who had not taken part in the process.

Two key drivers were responsible for this increased return. In accordance with the newly adopted policy, our Performance Management paperwork became the only documentation that colleagues were eligible to submit in support of an application to progress onto or within the Upper Pay Spine. With colleagues submitting their past two years' paperwork as evidence to support applications for pay progression, all colleagues between M4 and UPS2, which included most of our middle leaders, had to buy into the process if they wanted to be able to provide strong evidence for pay progression.

As well as developing a clear understanding of the process for their own pay progression, these Middle Leaders were also the appraisers of their departmental colleagues. The new policy and procedures were quickly rolled out and adopted by staff. At the same time, we reviewed the CPD offered via our twilight programme, initiated in the previous academic year. We moved from an open approach to running sessions that had seen colleagues choose to offer sessions ranging from Yoga For Relaxation to No Hands Up – An Approach To Including All

Students In Discussion And Questioning (guess which was the best attended session?!). We also adopted a more focussed approach, only offering sessions that linked directly to the Academy Improvement Plan.

A key strand of our Improvement Plan in 2010-2011 was to further raise levels of literacy across the curriculum. As part of this drive, we negotiated a deal to provide some bespoke training from the University Of East London, one of our Academy Partners. This training was open to both teaching and support staff alike. Upon conversion to academy status, we dedicated part of our LACSEG funding to facilitate a Masters in Education programme, taught on site as part of our twilight CPD. In 2013, nine colleagues, including a Librarian and an HLTA, graduated with an MA in Education (Literacy).

This holistic approach to improvement planning, appraisal and target setting, as well as the provision of high-quality CPD means that we now have a team of nine literacy experts in the school. These experts work in a range of subjects, with a variety of job roles. In May 2014, these colleagues will be leading literacy-based twilight CPD sessions for colleagues to disseminate the MA learning across the staff. These sessions will focus on: marking for literacy across the curriculum, addressing literacy in practical subjects, developing reading comprehension, moving beyond writing frames to developing extended writing, breaking down text to develop students' note making skills, and using literacy skills to unpack learning objectives to evoke assessment as learning.

A CHANGE IN THE LAW MEANT A FURTHER CHANGE IN PRACTICE

The changes that we had made to Performance Management in the academic year 2010-2011 meant that we were well placed to deal with the requirements of the Education School Teachers' Appraisal (England) Regulations, 2012. As a school, we were confident that our system was now robust. We had already grown a culture where Performance Management was important, relevant, and impacting on pupil progress. It was easy to change the name of the process to 'appraisal'. We wanted to maintain the principles upon which our policy and practice were built. Less easy, was getting to grips with the changes to the Professional Standards for Teachers that this legislation brought.

Until 2012, a teacher had to demonstrate thirty three 'qualified teacher' standards in order to attain QTS, a further forty one 'core' standards whilst on the Main Pay Spine, and an additional ten 'post-threshold' standards in order to access payment on the Upper Pay Spine. The 2012 legislation reduced the 84 professional standards required of teachers to just eight.

Whilst this simplification was much welcomed, the new Teachers' Standards did not differentiate. There were no post-threshold descriptors. How were colleagues to demonstrate that their practice was at the higher levels expected on the Upper Pay Spine? The expected standards of professional practice for UPS teachers had been woven into the ten new professional standards. Using the old post-threshold standards as a 'bolt-on' was too crude an option. We wanted something that both linked to the new teachers' standards but reflected the ethos and practice of Hall Mead.

DIFFERENTIATION, DIFFERENTIATION, DIFFERENTIATION

The working party was reconvened. This time, even bigger than before. Along with exploring ways to work within the new system, the working party also consulted on the revised pay policy that the new legislation required. Colleagues saw that being part of the steering group that liaised at all levels across the newly converted academy structure – and with all stakeholders including staff, unions and the Governing body – was a great opportunity to demonstrate Standard 8 of the new Teachers' Standards – Fulfil Wider Professional Responsibilities. Many were also concerned at the change in teachers' pay and conditions nationally, which made it clear that from September 2014, automatic pay progression on the main scale was a thing of the past.

We looked at the new Teachers' Standards and discussed how to differentiate them for career stage expectations. How would we expect standards to differ when demonstrated by a colleague on MPS1, compared to a colleague on UPS3, for example? The difference in pay is £15,316 a year. Inevitably, questions were raised. Were we getting the best value from our UPS staff? Was it possible that a colleague in the classroom next door was being paid £15,316 a year more than you, yet having less of an impact? Under the new system, could pay progression be accelerated? The answer was yes.

Working in sub-groups, the working party compiled a list of activities and practices that could potentially demonstrate when a colleague was meeting all eight of the Teachers' Standards. These were then sorted into examples of practice that you may expect to see from teachers with varying experience, and at various points on the pay scale, literally differentiating by career stage. It was clear that, as professionals, we would simply need to differentiate the all-encompassing eight Teachers' Standards to enable colleagues to work with them at the appropriate level. The whole process was, surprisingly, just like teaching!

We had been doing a great deal of work to improve learning outcomes in the classroom. Whilst we had no groups in Raise Online that were showing up as underachieving in our data, Raise had highlighted that some of our higher attaining boys had not been making the same excellent levels of progress that all other pupils had. This had led to an academy-wide focus on differentiation. The working party suggested that we take a similar approach to differentiating the Teachers' Standards. Breakout groups created various models for differentiating the standards. Unsurprisingly, we decided that the simplest was likely to be the most effective. Teachers became grouped into three distinct career phases and pay bands, linked to their position on the old pay scales:

Teacher	Accomplished Teacher	Expert Teacher
Old MPS1-3	Old MPS 4-6	Old UPS 1-3

We were aware that the changes that the 2012 act brought to teachers' pay meant that, theoretically, from September 2014 every teacher on MPS could apply to be paid on UPS. Political rhetoric was declaring that the best teachers could be paid more. This was something that the academy was in favour of – it is a useful tool for retaining high quality teaching staff. However, with finite funding, how could this be managed?

As a school with a long history of successfully training teachers, colleagues in the working party were acutely aware of the journey needed to turn even the most talented teacher into an expert teacher. Therefore, it was suggested that accelerated pay progression be possible within the three pay bands, but not across them. This suggestion was agreed by both SLT and the governors, becoming policy.

Career stages and pay bands had been differentiated, but how were we to support colleagues in demonstrating the difference in practice expected at each career stage? How could colleagues be clear that their appraisal targets, agreed in their appraisal meeting, were appropriate? There was, and still is, a great deal of change happening in education. Pensions were being reformed, pay and conditions were changing, and the standards required by the new Ofsted framework seemed to be updated almost daily. Colleagues were concerned. People began to ask, understandably, for examples of appraisal targets that would support pay progression. Colleagues simply wanted to know that they were on the right track.

The working party discussed this — we wanted to avoid taking an approach where colleagues would simply pick a target from a sample list in order to allay fears that future pay progression could be jeopardised if they got their targets 'wrong'. The working party had aimed to create a system that promoted professionalism, CPD and pay progression. However, the removal of automatic pay progression nationally had caused jitters in the staff room, as it surely did in staff rooms across the country.

TIME FOR TRAINING

We dedicated a morning of an INSET day to training staff in the new appraisal procedures. Staff were largely behind the principle of the differentiated career phases and pay bands as laid out in our policy, but colleagues were still unclear as to what kind of appraisal targets should be set at each career stage. The Assistant Headteacher had previously approached some colleagues from the working party to seek their permission to share their anonymised appraisal targets from the previous year with colleagues. They agreed. During the training session, colleagues were given colour coded, anonymised appraisal targets. They knew that they were real targets that had been set the previous year. In groups, they were then asked to sort them into career stage-appropriate targets. We had 'Teacher' targets in one colour, 'Accomplished Teacher' in another, and 'Expert Teachers' in the last.

There was much discussion among colleagues regarding what should be expected of teachers at different levels of experience and pay. It was interesting to note that colleagues were incredibly accurate at spotting the targets set for 'Accomplished Teachers'. However, the targets created by 'Teachers', our newest entrants to the profession, colleagues believed to be targets appropriate for 'Expert Teachers'!

As part of this training, each table group was asked to create three targets (pupil progress, leading learning, and professional development) that could demonstrate that an imaginary teacher was meeting the Teachers' Standards at the appropriate level at each of the three career phases ('Teacher', 'Accomplished Teacher' and 'Expert Teacher') on post-it notes. These were then stuck onto large pieces of paper with the appropriate heading around the room. Colleagues were asked to reflect and consider their own targets in light of the training. The ideas for targets were collated and distributed to all staff. Feedback made it clear that colleagues, particularly those at the 'Teacher' and 'Accomplished Teacher' career stages, are happy with our Pay Policy and understand the expectations at the differentiated career levels.

OUTCOMES

The appraisal procedures at Hall Mead are a success story. Since 2012, we have had a 100% return of completed appraisal documentation (three years ago, the return rate was just 65%). The Hall Mead policy has been adopted by two local secondary schools and a local primary. Our policy supports both pay and career progression, we have around four young teachers who are likely to be eligible for accelerated pay progression within their pay band in September 2014.

However, most importantly, our targets with Pupil Progress and Leading Learning foci, linked to academy development planning, have kept teaching and learning at the forefront of what we do. This has led to improved outcomes for students. Data suggests that we are expecting 85% of students to achieve 5 GCSEs at A*-C grades, including Maths and English this summer.

In February 2013, Ofsted commented:

"Annual target setting for teachers is based on the school priorities and is used to develop best practice... As a result, the academy provides excellent opportunities for all groups of pupils."

Using Appraisal to focus on Pupil Progress and Leading Learning along with CPD, linked to Academy Development Plans, played a key role in Hall Mead achieving an 'Outstanding' judgement in all areas in our Ofsted report. The consultative approach has meant that we have taken teachers with us on the journey from good to outstanding.

In March 2014, colleagues commented:

"Whilst coming to the end of my NQT year, I worked with my Induction Tutor to use my targets from my observations and meetings to produce appraisal targets that were realistic and practical for the following year. I have made clear professional progress from my NQT year to my NQT+1, due to the Hall Mead Appraisal System."

– Teacher on the Hall Mead pay scale.

"I found the CPD and the exemplar target bank a great help in setting targets that helped me become recognised as an accomplished teacher after only two years in the profession!"

– Accomplished Teacher on the Hall Mead pay scale.

"The new Appraisal system is more formal. Having calendared times during the year for targets to be reviewed is important in ensuring that staff are working towards their targets when they meet with their appraiser. The paperwork is easier to complete and clear targets are set. This is important for newer colleagues in the profession that have to provide evidence to progress within the pay scale."

– Expert Teacher on the Hall Mead pay scale.

NEXT STEPS

We need to consult the working party again to review the policy, now that it has run a full cycle and to explore any changes necessary to prepare for September 2014 when automatic pay progression for teachers in England ceases. We also need to explore with SLT and governors mechanisms and time frames for assessing all colleagues for pay progression.

We are considering whether the procedures that had been in place for assessing threshold applications in the autumn term with payments made in January, backdated to September, are now appropriate for all colleagues. If all colleagues' Appraisal paperwork is to be assessed, will the deadline for application for pay progression need to be brought forward to 31st September, from 31st October, to allow time for all applications to be properly assessed? Who will complete the assessments?

We plan to share work with colleagues in other schools and academies to disseminate how an appraisal system can be used to drive improvements. We will use the data from appraisal meetings and reviews to analyse and publish anonymised figures outlining the percentage of colleagues who have met, and the percentage of colleagues that have exceeded their targets, as a further indicator of the quality of teaching and rates of pupil progress alongside transition matrices and lesson observations.

CHAPTER 14

A VIRTUOUS CIRCLE: SHARING GOOD PRACTICE IN INDEPENDENT LEARNING

REBECCA SKERTCHLY, HAYDON SCHOOL

FOCUS AREA

This case study outlines aspects of Teaching and Learning at Haydon School that have helped to encourage students to be more independent. This initiative has been approached from a number of different angles in order to share good practice around school. These ideas feed into each other and are disseminated throughout the workplace by means of a virtuous circle.

AIMS/RATIONALE

The drive to increase students' independence has been a focus for several years at Haydon. In 2008, 22% of AS results were U grades. Although partly due to students taking a compulsory four A Level subjects, students' approaches to their own learning needed to be addressed. The Co-ordinator of Teaching and Learning Initiatives interviewed Heads of Faculty in the academic year 2011-2012 to establish the habits and characteristics of learners in their subjects. It was found that in general, students needed to use teachers more effectively, to take ownership of their own learning, to engage more with their subject content, and move away from being spoon-fed.

Working towards students becoming more independent is a target in the School Improvement Plan: "Increasing the percentage of good and outstanding lessons to 95% through improving independent learning habits." A target on the school's Strategic Vision 5 Year plan is to move towards 'personalised training and development by effective use of training days'.

Professor Chris Husbands, in his G4G presentation Great Teaching And How To Get It talked about schools as rich learning environments where each person is "A productive member of a highly skilled team, drawing on their expertise and contributing their own in a process of continuous learning". The idea behind the Virtuous Circle is that staff at Haydon are continuously learning and sharing their own expertise in helping students to become more independent through a process of identifying good practice, training, trying out ideas and feeding these back into the cycle.

BACKGROUND CONTEXT

Haydon School is an academy with 2007 students aged 11 to 18 on roll and 150 teachers, spread over a large site. Consistency of practice is crucial to ensure teachers know what independent learning looks like in the context of our own environment. External training courses are an unnecessary expense if there are already outstanding practitioners in school to deliver training. A system needs to exist to connect this knowledge as an archipelago of good practice, rather than islands of excellence. The Co-ordinator of Teaching and Learning Initiatives was asked to find volunteers to run training sessions to embed ideas across the school. These members of staff were identified through learning walks and learning reviews.

In June 2013, the school conducted a Learning Review using a group of teachers trained by a consultant from an educational advisory company called 'The Learning Organisation'. The group visited over 40 lessons, looking at students' learning, rather than what the teacher was doing. Feedback highlighted many positives about teaching in the school but also suggested that most classes needed to be given more opportunities to work independently: "The students' cognitive habits may be under-developed in some areas. Do teachers require students to think for themselves, or do they do too much of the thinking for them?"

THE STORY

The following diagram explains the Virtuous Circle process:

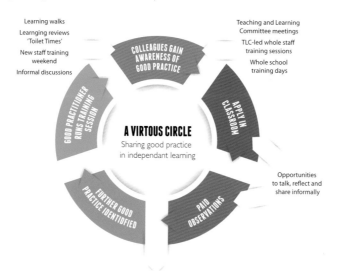

Learning walks
Learnging reviews
'Toilet Times'
New staff training
weekend
Informal discussions

Teaching and Learning
Committee meetings
TLC-led whole staff
training sessions
Whole school
training days

COLLEAGUES GAIN AWARENESS OF GOOD PRACTICE

GOOD PRACTITIONER RUNS TRAINING SESSION

APPLY IN CLASSROOM

A VIRTOUS CIRCLE
Sharing good practice
in independant learning

Opportunities
to talk, reflect and
share informally

FURTHER GOOD PRACTICE IDENTIDFIED

PAID OBSERVATIONS

1ST PILLAR OF GREATNESS: A SHARED VISION

The different areas that feed into the cycle are described below:

1. Teaching And Learning Committee (TLC) Meetings

There are currently 22 members of the TLC. These come from all 10 faculties within the school. They have regular breakfast meetings (with breakfast!) once a month to discuss teaching and learning, to try out ideas between meetings, and to disseminate these to their faculties.

2. Learning Review June 2013 With The Teaching And Learning Organisation

From this review, members of the TLC were able to identify good practice and also use the observations to reflect on their own teaching. Staff identified as strong practitioners of independent learning and those who observed good practice were invited to run sessions for other staff in the academic year 2013-2014.

3. Professional Development Programme

We are now in the second year of a new professional development programme. The Deputy Head responsible for the programme met with the Co-ordinator of Teaching and Learning Initiatives at the end of the academic year 2011-2012 to plan for the following year. Both felt that the training programme needed to be more closely aligned with the SIP and the vision for the school, and should contain more workshop-style sessions.

This change was also due to staff feedback that they would prefer more personalised practical sessions that they could opt into. One member of staff in the survey commented: "The type of training that is the most enjoyable

Haydon School Directory of Training 2013-14 (V2)

Day	Date	Session A	SIP and Teacher Standard	Time	Location	Facilitator	Session B	SIP and Teacher Standard	Time	Location	Facilitator
Tuesday	8 Oct	**Making them work harder than you do** How to turn teacher led lessons in to learner focused lessons. Ensuring you know *how* they are learning.	SIP TL1 TS 4	15.20	S03	TLC	**How to be an even more effective form tutor**	SIP BS1,5, 6 TS 8	15.20	S04	
Wednesday	9 Oct 13						MA in Leading Innovation and Change – MA Candidates only.			S03	
Wednesday	16 Oct 13						MA in Leading Innovation and Change – MA Candidates only.			S03	
Wednesday	23 October 13	**The science of reading** Most useful for teachers who want to develop effective literacy practices	TS 3	15.20	S03						
Tuesday	5 Nov 13	**Effective use of Fronter to support independent learning**	SIP TL2 TS 2	15.20	81		**Getting everyone on board** How to personalise learning to ensure that all learners are catered for	SIP TL1 TS 5	15.20	S03	TLC
Tuesday	5 Nov 13	**Smart target setting clinic** Bring you questions regarding target setting.	SIP LM3	15.20	S04						

and rewarding is the training that provides an opportunity to complete planning and development work whilst doing it. The Building Learning Power (meta-cognition) and Fronter (VLE) sessions are good examples of this as you went away feeling that you had made progress on something you wanted and needed to do." Another, said: "Too didactic sessions in the hall lead to little change in practice."

Three examples of these training sessions are described below:

- TLC Training Session Feedback For A Growth Mind-set (Assessment For Learning)

This session looked at getting students to be more independent through the use of Carol Dweck's concepts around 'mastery' over 'talent', thus helping students to focus on the next steps they need to take, such as 'level ladders' to assess their own work. Two colleagues identified as giving excellent feedback to students shared ideas in this workshop.

- TLC Training Session 'Making Them Work Harder Than You Do'

In this workshop, staff identified some of the areas where they work harder than students such as 'thinking for them' and even 'caring more than they do' sometimes! This session was developed to help teachers put the onus of learning onto the student.

- TLC Training Session 'Getting Everyone On Board'

Staff in this session reflected on themselves as learners, in addition to trying ideas that would benefit different students and get them to take a more active role in their own learning.

> Impact of TLC discussions and INSET training day
>
> BEFORE: "Teaching of this topic was mainly from the front with students copying code from the board. This wasn't developing their thinking and problem-solving skills."
>
> AFTER: "I came up with the idea of challenge cards with different levels of programming problems which students would choose. This approach encouraged them to work independently and they also really enjoyed it!"

4. New Staff Training Weekend

All new teachers are expected to attend this event where interactive workshops are run to ensure consistency of practice. Sessions on improving students' metacognitive skills and on outstanding lessons give teachers practical advice on how to make their students more independent.

5. Learning Walks

All members of staff are invited each summer term to take part in 'learning walks' into each other's lessons. In the summer term 2013, about 30 members of staff took up the opportunity to use the observation form developed by the TLC which moves the focus from the teacher to looking at how students are learning.

6. Faculty Learning Walks

In November 2013, members of the TLC took part in observing colleagues in the Science department to reflect on their own practice and to look at how students were learning. This showed that progress in getting students to be more independent had taken place. For example, in June 2013, the consultant said: "Students need the opportunity to collaborate. i.e. they cooperate and are interdependent but are not necessarily collaborating towards a common goal."

He also said that students needed more practice in employing more cognitive and strategic skills. In the November Learning Review, students in many Science lessons were found to be working collaboratively and teachers were providing many opportunities for students to think for themselves.

7. Staff Training Days

These have been used to introduce colleagues to teaching and learning ideas. This January, the training was reduced to a half-hour reminder of the content of various sessions and initiatives that people could be working on, and the rest of the day was set aside for faculties to develop ideas from these sessions.

8. Toilet Times

This initiative makes use of a captive audience, with many members of staff writing short case studies to be displayed on the back to toilet doors (see below). Many staff have used ideas from these.

What does "Less teacher talk" look like?

One of the EBIs from The Learning Review in June 2013 and the Mock Ofsted this term was that teachers need to get students to do more of the talking. Afterwards, colleagues involved and the TLC discussed what this means…

…General Ideas:

- Anything where you might do a demo, tell them something, say what to look out for etc. can be an opportunity to ask them what they think.
- Intervention is really important, so 'less talk' doesn't mean you can't give verbal feedback during a task to move students on with their learning.
- Visible Thinking Routines (Real life example: Mirror, signal manoeuvre). Google this for more teaching examples.
- Find opportunities to ask students where you would normally tell them what to do.
- APP lessons where students refine their work.
- Students re-capping on prior learning.
- Comment box for students who don't understand.
- Silent demonstration: students have to spot the deliberate mistake or comment on what the teacher or student is doing.

…Group activities:

- Sort phrases into the correct order.
- Peer (& self) assessment.
- Break up sentences into laminated words and put them in the correct order (e.g. Grammar in languages).
- Identifying the strengths and weaknesses in 2 different pieces of work.

…Level Ladders:

Students could:

- Use a level ladder to refine their work.
- Put the phrases of a level ladder in order.
- Fill in the blanks in a level ladder.
- Look at various outcomes and create a level ladder as a class.

…Student as the teacher:

- Students could vote on who does something well in the class and get them to teach everyone else.
- Student–led discussion. Scaffold this in first couple of lessons with a list of potential things to ask each other and then in future lessons allow students to come up with their own ideas.
- Nominating an 'expert' to go around the room (with a prompt sheet with suggestions for feedback on it).
- Question relay – a student asks another student a question who answers and then asks the next one a question etc.
- Students could revise a section of a topic and teach it to the rest of the class (e.g. a part of a cell).

Rebecca Skertchly November 2013

> Impact of Toilet Times
>
> *"I am finding the posters on What Does Less Teacher Talk Look Like? on the back of toilet doors extremely useful and I have tried various techniques already... sixth form classes expect me to give 'lecture-style presentations' and I'm trying to get away from this by giving them resources to respond to and teaching them more research and analysis skills that can be used in every subject."*

IMPACT OF THE VIRTUOUS CIRCLE:

The impact has been that teachers have gained ideas for their lessons from other colleagues, who have then in turn led training sessions, continuing the cycle of positive change. As a result of this, students are being giving more opportunities in lessons to work independently and take charge of their learning. At this point in the year, the number of good and outstanding lessons stands at 93%, very close to the target of 95%.

Attendance at the after-school training sessions was high, thus increasing their impact, with an average of 22 teachers taking part in each TLC-led session. Feedback was extremely positive, with 95% of staff rating the sessions four or five out of five for usefulness. One member of staff felt the session they attended was so useful, that the staff running it were invited to deliver it again to her whole faculty, thus disseminating ideas to a further 11 colleagues.

Members of the TLC discussed with colleagues in their faculties how they had used ideas from different sources in school. In all faculties, there is more of an emphasis on trying to help students to become more independent – such as students being given the opportunity to teach themselves or each other, students being encouraged to do 'C3B4ME' (to consult three different people or resources before the teacher), students planning their own work, using level ladders, students discussing their metacognition – and gaining awareness of what they need to do to be an independent learner.

For example, in BTEC Sport, *"Students are now more willing to try new activities without giving up. They are becoming more resilient… they challenge themselves to do more independent work whether that be resourcing information or extending their work further to meet Merit or Distinction."*

In addition to feedback from faculties, 22 colleagues took part in short case studies to look at the impact of different initiatives on their practice. The case studies showed that colleagues had developed a great variety of ideas for making students independent such as student-led plenaries and demonstrations, getting students to teach each other and student-led planning.

For example, one colleague who teaches Spanish, attended the session Making Students Work Harder Than You Do and developed different student-led lessons, which she called 'Group Work Fridays' with her Year 10 students. She said: *"Students are becoming more independent now, and even in the other two lessons of the week they ask each other for help or use resources instead of me, in other words they are getting good at 'C3B4ME'!"*

Another member of this faculty has been working on Harvard 'Visible Thinking Routines' after attending TLC training. These help students to synthesise knowledge and to work things out for themselves. He has rolled this out across the department and staff are beginning to see the benefits in terms of students' learning. He is now going on external training for this and will run a training session to disseminate ideas to the TLC.

In the Summer Term 2013, the art department trialled Year 12 student-led workshops. Students planned, resourced and delivered a half term's worth of workshops, which included setting each other homework.

One English teacher, in her case study, said that students in Year 13 "Tend to be very lazy and enjoy the concept of 'teacher talk'." She worked on putting the onus of the lesson onto the students and said: "This has enabled the students to understand what they are learning … they are also more able to identify gaps in their learning which they can address during their independent study."

REFLECTIONS/EVALUATION

This case study reflects pillars 1 and 3 of greatness: *A Shared Vision: Values, Culture And Ethos, Based On The Highest Expectations Of All Members Of The Community and Personalised And Highly Effective Continuous Professional Development Within A Learning Community.*

The short case studies completed by colleagues show that there can be huge impact in the classroom from drip-feeding ideas from different angles and ensuring that teachers have the opportunity to work on ideas and talk to each other. Through this process, collective values and beliefs are articulated. Teachers have discovered ideas through training, meetings, informal observations, or on posters – and have not only tried them out – but have also developed their own resources and shared these within their faculties.

NEXT STEPS

The most powerful tool for affecting change seems to be talk. Workshops and TLC meetings, where teachers can discuss teaching and learning informally in a supportive environment, have been extremely effective in helping colleagues to make changes in their practice. Having identified more good practitioners willing to run training sessions, through case studies and observations, the Virtuous Circle continues.

One development point from the Learning Review in June 2013 was to, 'encourage further joint observations of learning and teaching by creating triads of teachers from different curriculum areas'. This is currently being planned for the TLC in the Summer Term 2014.

The Virtuous Circle is a continuous cycle, rather than a project with a specific end date. There is no quick fix for enabling students to become more independent. In the training session *Making Students Work Harder Than You Do*, a member of staff commented: *"As we move to try and get students to become more independent, we need to deal with our own feelings of wanting to give up when it doesn't work as well"*. And of course, it would be interesting to survey students, as one teacher quoted students as saying: *"This independent learning is all very well, but we seem to be doing most of the work!"*

CHAPTER 15

INCLUSIVE LEADERSHIP: TEACHERS AS INNOVATIVE LEADERS OF TEACHING AND LEARNING

JONATHAN GUNZI AND JOHN FLANNAGAN, BENTLEY WOOD HIGH SCHOOL

FOCUS AREA

This case study explores how Bentley Wood High School has developed the concept of distributed leadership by creating 'Innovative Leaders' as part of the construct of inclusive leadership. Innovative Leaders are outstanding teachers in the early stages of their careers who lead on improving teaching and learning for a particular group of students. The focus area for this study will be on Innovative Leaders leading on supporting visually impaired students, and students with lower prior attainment, in their first GCSE year.

RATIONALE

Bentley Wood has continued to build on and develop beyond the model of distributed leadership set out in *Generating Greatness* (2013). The article describes the model of interactive shared leadership with teachers, support staff, students and governors, all actively focused on improving teaching and learning. The aim of this model is to improve outcomes for students by enabling talented teachers and Middle Leaders to lead on areas of whole school improvement.

The model is composed of five key areas:

SCHOOL IMPROVEMENT GROUPS: Each member of the school community – including governors, is part of a School Improvement Group (SIG). There are currently seven SIGS. Meetings are scheduled once every half term and take place during allocated meeting times.

HONORARIA: Annual honoraria are awarded to teachers and support colleagues who successfully meet the criteria and satisfy the appointment panel, to carry out action research on any of the key areas of whole school improvement to further strengthen the model.

STRATEGIC LEADERS: Strategic Leaders were introduced in 2011 as a new layer in the teaching staff structure, positioned between Senior and Middle Leaders. They each lead a School Improvement Group and lead whole school initiatives focused on pedagogy and student learning and progress.

STUDENT LEADERS: Student Leaders, such as the digital, numeracy, learning, media and STEM Leaders, contribute and impact positively effectively on many aspects of school improvement.

INNOVATIVE LEADERS: The current innovative leaders focus on students with physical impairment, specific groups within the lower prior attainment band, and EAL students. They share their innovative and creative teaching with others to improve outcomes for those students.

THE STORY

This case study focuses on two Innovative Leaders. GCA is in his third year of teaching and focuses on students with physical impairment (PI), and in particular visual impairment (VI). JF is in his second year of teaching and focuses on students with the lowest prior attainment.

The key purpose of the role of Innovative Leader is to share expertise to enable all teachers and support staff to take responsibility for all groups of students including those with very specific special educational needs and disabilities (SEND).

Innovative Leaders lead specialist professional development for colleagues in school. GCA co-chairs the meetings for the VI student's teachers with the Harrow Visual Impairment Specialist to demonstrate to teachers how to make best use of the VI student's iPad. GCA took a leading role in the Spring Term INSET day. The vision for the INSET day was to have eight teachers delivering outstanding lessons to small groups of staff.

Staff could choose which sessions to attend, and GCA delivered three lessons to enable all teachers to attend his session on effectively teaching students with VI. He also regularly delivers *Tuesday Teach Talk*, which is a 10-minute presentation to all staff every Tuesday morning, and contributes to the technology SIG which includes exploring ways to use iPads, provided for all teachers and TAs.

GCA shares his excellent classroom work beyond Bentley Wood. Bentley Wood hosts the half-termly Harrow Inclusion Meeting for all Secondary Inclusion Leads across the local authority. Inclusion Leads asked for a CPD afternoon for all schools to send a number of delegates to learn from his use of technology for the visually impaired. He teaches PGCE students effective use of the iPad at the Institute of Education each term. At the 2014 BETT conference, Bentley Wood was one of two schools to deliver a workshop. GCA had 70 teachers sign up to see his workshop, where he demonstrated the work he does with visually impaired students.

CASE STUDY OF A STUDENT WITH VISUAL IMPAIRMENT (NAME HAS BEEN CHANGED):

Mariam has a statement of SEN and is visually impaired. She is in Year 8, and will start her GCSEs next year. Her KS2 English, Maths and Science scores were all level 2. She has a CATS score of 86. She has dystrophy, nustagmus and a squint. Mariam's extremely poor vision impacts negatively on her learning. She is able to see at six metres what someone with full sight can see at 60 metres.

The school has provided Mariam with an iPad to enable her to have full access to the curriculum with targeted support and intervention by teachers and teaching assistants. GCA's creativity has centred on the use of technology to improve Mariam's access to the curriculum. GCA has created shortcuts for Mariam to have instant access to a personal folder that she can access in class and at home. Teachers upload Powerpoints and Word documents, of the appropriate font size, prior to the lesson and place them in the appropriate folder. GCA has also created a shortcut for Mariam to access what is on the Interactive Whiteboard (IWB) via her iPad. This is live, and enables Mariam to follow the lesson without needing a scribe or enlargements.

The impact on Mariam's progress can be demonstrated in a number of ways. As part of the annual review process, Mariam was asked about her progress in school. She explained that she felt the iPad had made a huge difference to her learning at school since her transition from Bentley Wood. She feels she can access her work when she needs to in order to make progress in class. The family made a point of thanking GCA for all his work with Mariam. In her careers interview, Mariam says she wants to be a chef and is keen to take on GCSE Food Technology. She also wants to take GCSE History.

Responses from teachers indicate that they greatly value the use of the iPad. Miriam's folder shows that teachers regularly upload work. The History teacher uses the folder for the interpretation of pictures and sources and feels Mariam will achieve a level 6c this year, which is a full level above her target. The Maths teacher uses the IWB projection effectively for Mariam to access writing on the board, while her English teacher makes good use of the personal folder for worksheets related to books that are currently studied.

The most recent assessment point shows Mariam has very clearly progressed from Year 7 to Year 8. She is on track to achieve her target level for nine of her 13 subjects. The other four subjects are ICT, Music, French and Art – where she is predicted to underachieve by two sub-levels. Mariam has average effort scores of 3.86 out of five, and she has been awarded 665 achievement points so far this year. Both figures are above average. She has an excellent attendance record (97.50%). All factors above indicate that GCA has enabled a level of access for Mariam that is enabling her to progress with confidence.

CASE STUDY ON LOW-ATTAINING STUDENTS:

JF is trialling innovative teaching methods in Year 9 Geography with a specific focus on a small group of seven students with lower prior attainment. All students bar one achieved negative residuals at Key Stage 3 (the one student who achieved a positive residual is the only one on target for all her subjects in Year 9). All students took one or two fewer languages in Key Stage 3 to receive extra literacy lessons. At Key Stage 4, they are all following a full curriculum. Therefore, there was a need to address their individual needs within the classroom to develop an integrated approach to inclusive learning and early Key Stage 4 intervention.

One of the most successful strategies was the introduction of student reflection grids. Students reflect and track their progress throughout the lesson, developing a critical understanding of what and how they learn best during the lesson. The example below clearly shows that pupils are directing the teacher to where they think the learning objective has been achieved. The grids have been successful in providing visual feedback in marking and informing the teacher of how the pupils are progressing.

An example of the student reflection grids in Geography:

 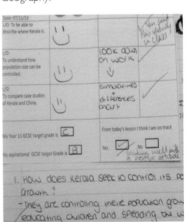

The different teaching and learning strategies implemented by JF have been shared during pedagogy school improvement group meetings (SIGs). JF has led and fed back to the whole school, findings from the pedagogy group during INSET days and twilight sessions. In the spring CPD day, JF was also one of the most popular choices. He 'taught' lessons on the importance of student reflection and feedback using examples on the previous page.

Colleagues then implemented those strategies in their teaching practice and fed back to JF their successes through discussion on the school's teacher networking site, Yammer. JF has been open to new teachers and trainee teachers observing him deliver innovative teaching and learning strategies. He has delivered, and will continue to deliver, Tuesday Teach Talk sessions during morning briefing. This has proved to be vital in keeping teachers up to date on the strategies he has been implementing.

The strategies were also used in another subject, to show the impact of the interventions – rather than the qualities – of JF as a teacher. A Health And social Care teacher volunteered to trial the same strategies with her Year 9 class, which included the same targeted pupils. This means those students are exposed to target strategies for almost a third of their time in school. Other strategies used included arranging the seating plan based on reading ages, teaching through pictures to help students visualise, and a planned build-up of the use of keywords and connectives to improve sentence structure.

Progress data shows that the target students have made significantly more progress in Year 9:

Student	Amount of subjects underachieved in Year 8	Percentage of subjects underachieved in Year 8	Amount of subjects underachieving in Year 9	Percentage of subjects underachieved in Year 9
1	10/12	83%	4/8	50%
2	5/12	41%	0/8	0%
3	8/12	67%	3/8	38%
4	9/12	75%	5/8	63%
5	11/12	92%	1/8	13%
6	6/12	50%	1/8	13%
7	9/12	75%	2/8	25%
Average	**8/12**	**66%**	**2/8**	**25%**

All students in the small focus group are on target for three subjects in Year 9; Geography, Health And Social Care, and PE. The targeted strategies being used in Geography and in Health And Social Care appear to have had an impact.

Student interviews revealed that in the beginning, they were reluctant to use the student reflection grids. However, once they saw examples from Year 11 classes, they soon realised the impact that they could have in their learning. This was clearly demonstrated in the responses during a Year 9 Geography departmental review focus group. The focus group was aimed at understanding the transition from KS3 to KS4. One of the targeted pupils stated: *"I like the student reflection grids, they help me to understand where I am during the lesson – they are clear, easy-to-use, and have helped me this year."*

This demonstrates that pupils are reflecting on their progress whilst understanding where they are heading in their learning. All of the pupils during the focus group stated that they think the student reflection grids have helped them this year.

NEXT STEPS

The development of inclusive leadership is a school priority. This leadership construct fully embraces the new code of practice for Special Educational Needs, which clearly emphasises that all members of staff are responsible for the progress of students with SEN. This reflects the deeply embedded ethos of the school where there is a shared responsibility for ensuring all groups of students make expected or better progress.

Bentley Wood High School is expanding in September 2014. An additional 24 students with Statements of SEN will join the school. The vision is to replace the notion of 'SEN' with 'barriers in learning and participation' and to continue with a focus on intervention in the classroom where the highest expectations are set for all groups of students. Innovative Leaders will continue to be the experts in overcoming specific learning barriers, and will be responsible for sharing their expertise to enable all classroom practitioners to effectively differentiate and effectively meet the needs of each individual student.

CHAPTER 16

THE POWER OF PERCEPTION – CHANGING ATTITUDES TO LESSON OBSERVATION THROUGH DEVELOPING COLLABORATIVE SCHOOL EVALUATION OF TEACHING AND LEARNING

ANDREA WRIGHT, NEWSTEAD WOOD SCHOOL

FOCUS AREA

This case study explores how Newstead Wood School has developed a collaborative process for Subject Review, ensuring that the school's co-constructive approach to leadership is reflected in the drive for school improvement.

AIMS/RATIONALE

The aim of a collaborative review process was two-fold. Firstly, we aimed to build capacity among Middle Leaders by improving their effectiveness in measuring the impact of teaching on students' learning. Successive subject reviews would help build a clear picture of the quality of Teaching and Learning over time and provide a narrative to describe the continuous forward motion of departments in line with Team Development Plans. Secondly, we aimed to change the perception of lesson observation to one where, rather than feeling 'done to' by Senior Leadership, teaching staff felt like an integral part of the improvement process. The collaborative nature of the review process would ensure that the focus was on the sharing of good practice, encouraging both individuals and departments to be more outward-facing in their approach to team development.

BACKGROUND CONTEXT

Newstead Wood is a selective state school for girls with a co-educational sixth form and just short of 1300 students on roll. Attainment in all subjects is consistently high and the school's last Ofsted report in 2010 praised the school's ethos, curriculum and teaching:

> "Students excel academically and socially and develop an impressive sense of mature and thoughtful communal responsibility... students enjoy their learning and, in most lessons, teachers engage students well by framing a variety of creative learning and assessment activities that facilitate high-quality acquisition of knowledge, understanding and new skills."

Ofsted report, 2010

Despite consistently high attainment, the Leadership Team was conscious that there was variance across lessons with regards to the quality of students' learning, which needed to be reduced. The 2010 Ofsted report indicated that a determining factor in this was inconsistency in the quality of middle leadership. The school needed to ensure that "leaders at all levels focus more sharply on improving the quality of students' learning and (that) any development points are followed up".

> "The role of middle managers is crucial to the steady and sustained improvement of schools. The Headteacher and Senior Managers provide the vision, but Middle Managers affect the long-term changes, which will raise standards and improve the quality of education."

Ofsted 2010

There was a need, therefore, to sharpen the school improvement and evaluation process to ensure that all leaders were fully equipped to effectively develop their teams, and know how to improve the quality of students' learning. It was paramount that this was done in a way that embraced distributed leadership, leading to active and shared school improvement. The school had long been inspired by David Hargreaves' research on peer-to-peer working across departments and had a strong history of colleagues working together on cross-curricular development projects.

However, despite some willingness to collaborate on specific projects, opening the classroom door to the Leadership team and other colleagues in order to evaluate the quality of Teaching and Learning remained an area of anxiety for staff. It was essential that this perception of lesson observation was challenged so that the sharing of best practice could be more wholly embedded into school improvement.

THE STORY

The action points from the May 2010 Ofsted Report were reflected in the School Development Plan that followed. In January 2011, there was a significant increase in Year 12 intake, which led to a series of drop-in observations to Year 12 lessons. This was an opportunity for the Leadership Team to engage in the constructive process of dialogue about lesson observation criteria with staff to ensure a shared understanding of effective Teaching and Learning.

Following this, and in response to the new Ofsted Framework of Sept 2012, an Ofsted inspection team was invited to the school to conduct paired lesson observations with members of Senior and Middle Leadership. This revealed that some variance remained in staff judgement of lessons, which needed to be addressed.

When the introduction of Subject Review was shared with teaching staff, their wariness was apparent. They feared that the process would be a critical, top-down approach – an opportunity for Senior Leaders to play at being Ofsted Inspectors – rather than a tool to develop the quality of Teaching and Learning at the school. It was essential to banish these fears. The school has a long history of co-construction and it was imperative that the Subject Review process harnessed this ethos and continued the dialogue, which had started in 2011.

"We were very anxious about the intensity of the process. It seemed like an in-depth audit that was designed to find everything that was wrong with the department."

Head of Biology

TEACHING AND LEARNING GROUP

In the summer term of 2012, the Deputy Head in charge of Professional Development created a 'Teaching and Learning' working group. Membership of the group was by open invitation to encourage a wide variety of staff to participate: union representatives, Heads of Department, members of Senior Leadership and NQTs gave the group a rich mixture of experiences and viewpoints.

The group's first task was to develop a consistent understanding of effective Teaching and Learning. What would observers expect to see in lessons to show that effective learning was taking place? What evidence would there be that students were making effective progress over time? The group specifically did this without Ofsted criteria to hand. The process needed to come from the staff to give them a sense of ownership. The questions that underpinned every discussion were always: 'What will create the most impact for our students?' 'What will make them the best learners they can be?'

The group met over the summer and autumn terms, including spending an INSET day working with the whole staff to really define and articulate what outstanding Teaching and Learning looked, felt, and sounded like at Newstead Wood. The product of the group's meetings was a new pro forma to be used in lesson observations.

The form contained 'observable indicators' under a list of ten criteria.

Criterion	Top level practice	Examples of good practice	Areas for development	Areas requiring urgent attention
High expectations	An open mind-set is evident (can-do attitude).	Students show confidence and resilience. All students are engaged and motivated. Students and teacher are on time and prepared (correct equipment etc.) Folders and book are up to date (work and marking).	Most students show confidence and engagement. Most students arrive on time and are correctly prepared. The majority of students have up to date books, which have been marked.	Students lack confidence. Many are disengaged. Students are late and many do not have necessary books and equipment. Folders are incomplete and/or unmarked by teacher.
Range of teaching styles	Independent learning is evident	There is an effective balance between teacher directed learning and student activity. There is a mix of approaches and skills (over several lessons).	Balance between teacher-led and student activity is mostly good. There is little variation in approach over several lessons.	Too much time on one approach, which does not hold student interest. Virtually no variety over several lessons.

Extract from the revised lesson pro forma showing 'observable indicators' under two of the ten criteria

To maintain staff ownership, the decision was taken to avoid the direct use of 'Ofsted language'. 'Top-level practice' replaced 'Outstanding', 'Areas For Development' replaced 'Satisfactory', and 'Areas Requiring Urgent Attention' replaced 'Unsatisfactory'. Nevertheless, there is striking similarity between our own and the Ofsted indicators, though not by design. There was also a clear balance between observing teacher actions and student behaviours so that the link between the two would be made clear. The observable indicators aimed to show the impact of teaching over time. For example, 'top-level practice' such as 'An open mind-set is evident' would be difficult to achieve as a result of a sudden change in teaching specifically for an observation.

THE REVIEW PROCESS

A key aim of the review process was not only to enable Middle Leaders to better understand the development points within their department, but to change the school's culture of lesson observation to one which embraced a more 'open door' ethos and enabled best practice to be shared. It is well documented that Middle Leaders are the 'engine room' of schools and that to sustain school improvement they are the people who "must work collaboratively across the school to ensure consistency between departments," (James Toop, *Tackling Educational Disadvantage In England's Secondary Schools, IPPR Report, June 2013.*)

A key decision of the Teaching and Learning group was that each subject review would include a 'Guest Head of Department' and that each observation should be a joint observation between a member of the Leadership Group and a member of the department, under review or the Guest Head of Department. The Head of the department under review and the Deputy Head of the department would co-observe a larger number of lessons where possible. This concept of co-observation was an essential part of developing a shared language of learning and a common understanding of the effect of teaching on learning and a crucial outcome of the working group.

Review team identified by SLT with a team leader and a guest HoD. Timetable of observations provided by the Team Leader who will schedule the 'pre-review' meting to take place in the week before the observations.	Pre-review meeting (with lunch provided) with Team Leader, line manager, HoD and guest HoD. Discuss departmental self-evaluation and any areas for particular focus for the review. Departmental work scrutiny, outcomes of Student Focus Groups and any other monitoring processes form part of the self-evaluation.	Teachers observed for two half-lessons. All observations joint between member of Leadership Group and a member of the department under review, or the guest HoD. All teachers will co-observe at least one other colleague. HoDs and HoD deputies will co-observe a larger number of lessons.
Observers use the observation grid based on observable features developed by staff. Teachers should provide observers with evidence of lesson planning, the appropriate section of SoL, and copy of class progress tracker sheet/mark book page.	Observers discuss and agree feedback.. Feedback to teachers by the SLG observer takes place as soon as possible. Co-observer may sit in on the feedback. Teachers given copies of observations (may choose to use for performance management).	Review team meets and agrees outcomes. SLG leader writes the report using a standard template. Team Leader meets with HoD, line manager and guest HoD to discuss outcomes (lunch time with lunch provided). Team Leader and HoD report back to department.

THE FIRST WAVE OF REVIEWS: PITFALLS AND SUCCESSES

The first round of subject reviews began in the autumn term of 2012 and slowly, as each department experienced the constructive and supportive nature of the review, anxieties dissipated. As departments were given ample warning of when the review would take place, with clear guidelines that had been drawn up by the working group, there was a common sense of purpose established early on. The focus on co-construction also meant that staff felt that they were active, rather than passive participants in the process, having created the tools that were used in the observations themselves. The time invested in creating a shared understanding of effective teaching and learning resulted in closely-aligned lesson judgments between most co-observers, with post-lesson discussions enabling observers to discuss and reconcile any differences of opinion (this was rare).

> **"**The first review provided clear development points which I was able to use as targets for the team development plan, ensuring that the discussion of these targets continued into the New Year. The second review identified clear progress in these areas for development which was highly motivating and encouraging.**"**

Head of English

By the summer term, every department, and therefore every member of teaching staff, had undergone the subject review process, and all but a few part-time staff had co-observed a colleague's lesson. It was clear that both a significant shift in attitudes and a sharpening in Middle Leaders' understanding of development points was taking place.

Colleagues commented that following the review, "direction for improvement was clear" and the process was "invaluable for (my) own understanding of the team and its strengths". Despite their initial concerns, teachers were enthusiastic about observing each other's lessons and the opportunity to "learn from other departments".

> **"**A more positive response to the observation process is seen as it is framed in such a positive way; feedback is helpful and constructive.**"**

Head of History

Whilst staff feedback was positive, the completion of several subject reviews showed that adjustments would need to be made to the mechanics of the process. Firstly, it became clear that the time needed to complete a review had been underestimated. With a significant number of part-time teaching staff and some large departments, it was impossible for some subjects to complete the observation process in the anticipated two-three days.

It was evident that ensuring sufficient time for high-quality feedback following an observation needed to be built into the review timetable. Likewise, even though post-review meetings were planned into the process, it was clear that we needed to ensure more time for these to fully explore the outcomes of the review and to support Middle Leaders in formulating a clear action plan for how to move the department forward. We were also keen to ensure that work scrutiny was a part of the review process; however the time allowed for this was not sufficient.

IMPACT

As a direct result of the subject review process, the 2013-2014 School Development Plan is a better-informed, truly co-constructed platform for school improvement. Middle Leaders are an integral part of the school improvement process and enable the school's vision. The review structure means that they possess a greater understanding of their role in monitoring, and have more confidence and competence in carrying it out.

From an individual perspective, teachers have taken many new teaching strategies away from co-observation. A member of the PE department is now using a wider range of assessment strategies in lessons after co-observing another member of the team. One member of the Science department observed the way a colleague supported students who are underperforming, and is now trying to employ these strategies into his lessons. A History teacher who was observed giving excellent, detailed feedback to his A2 History students said he was "inspired by an assessment framework" he had seen in a colleague's lesson during the subject review.

Most importantly, there has been a cultural shift in attitudes towards observation. Although much harder to quantify, staff have commented on the review as a chance to "reflect more on lessons" and "a chance to show the good things we are doing". Furthermore, this year, a greater number of staff have volunteered to let other colleagues observe them for training and development. The CPD programme for 2013-2014 is built around professional enquiries, which are based on the Teaching and Learning development areas arising from the subject review process. Because of the success of the subject review, staff are much more willing to embrace peer-observation, an important component in any professional enquiry work.

The use of the Guest Head of Department has also proved to be a valuable tool for subject leaders. By seeing the way Teaching and Learning is led in different departments, Guest HoDs are keen to incorporate the most effective tools. The Chemistry department plans to implement the 'skills passport' used in Geography, whilst the Head of History is more "determined to ensure students know where they are going and how to achieve or exceed this" after being a Guest HoD with the Maths department.

Senior Leaders have also seen the power of this part of the process in sharing effective practice and improving the leadership skills of Middle Managers. The development points from the first wave of subject reviews have given Middle Leaders increased focus in their team development planning and those who have undergone a second subject review this year have benefitted from being able to evaluate the team's progress more sharply.

The departments that have undergone their second subject review have demonstrated progress in the areas identified in the first cycle, and in the core areas of the School Development Plan. In each department reviewed in the second cycle, there has been an increase in the number of lessons observed, demonstrating features of 'top level' (Outstanding) practice and a reduction in the number of areas highlighted as 'areas for development.'

Successive subject reviews mean that senior leaders have a clearer understanding of the quality of Teaching and Learning across the school and middle managers have a clearer understanding across their departments. The Subject Reviews build a clear picture of strengths and areas for development in our professional practice, allowing us, together, to identify and address areas of in-school variation more effectively.

> **"**From a leadership perspective, I think the Guest HoD has been a powerful part of the process – initiating conversations between colleagues in different departments about Teaching and Learning; providing different perspectives on classroom practice – particularly, though not exclusively, between practical and non-practical subjects; sharing and developing best practice.**"**

Deputy Head

REFLECTIONS

The impact of the subject review process cannot be underestimated. We have made huge strides forward, not only in addressing Ofsted's observation that "leaders at all levels focus more sharply on improving the quality of students' learning and any development points are followed up" (Ofsted report, 2010), but in changing people's attitudes towards the purpose of observation. The resistance and concern felt by staff in the early stages of the process was only going to be allayed if we embraced co-construction and ensured that the reviews were developmental, not critical.

Now that the majority of staff have found the review to be a positive experience, their capacity for reflection and drive to improve their own teaching, or that within their departments, has dramatically increased. The subject review process has paved the way for other methods of measuring the quality of Teaching and Learning, such as learning walks, and Heads of Department are much more confident to conduct drop-in observations of their own.

NEXT STEPS

We are currently halfway through the second subject review cycle and already looking at how the process can be further improved:

- The lesson observation pro forma needs to be revisited and re-evaluated to see if it is fully fit for purpose.

- The subject review needs to sit alongside other methods, which enable leaders to gain a clear picture of the quality of learning over time and enable professional learning conversations between colleagues. This may include 'learning walks' focusing on specific areas of the SDP and drop-in observations.

- Heads of department should be able to request to be Guest HoD for a specific department.

- A cycle of work scrutiny needs to be embedded more effectively.

- A parallel focus for tutorials is being considered to raise standards in this area.

CHAPTER 17

LEARNING TO BE RESILIENT AND BRILLIANT

ALI KHAN AND MEHMET EMIN, LITTLE ILFORD SCHOOL

FOCUS AREA

This case study seeks to outline the strategies that have been developed to cater for the most able students at Little Ilford School (LIS). It highlights the development and evolution of a system that has one key aim: to give our students the best possible opportunities to reach the highest ranks in the academic world and beyond. Most able learners include the Gifted and Talented students as defined by Government bodies, but also those students recognised internally as having a particular gift or talent.

BACKGROUND CONTEXT

Official statistics around more able learners in the past few years seem to all point in the same direction and tell the same story; that our most able pupils in non-selective secondary schools are not performing as well as they should be. Indeed, a survey commissioned by Ofsted in 2013 highlighted the fact that there is a huge disparity in admissions to the most prestigious universities between a small number of independent and selective schools, and the great majority of state-maintained, non-selective schools and academies. One of the key findings of this report was that 65% of pupils achieving Level 5+ in Maths and English at the end of KS2 failed to attain A/A* at GCSE in 2012.

In 2008, our school's GCSE results for five or more A*-C grades, including English and Maths, were at 42%. The focus for the school was C/D borderline students and there was a particular emphasis on literacy. This was no surprise, as the base rate attainment levels of students starting school at Little Ilford are significantly lower than the national average. Many students come to school with poor reading and writing skills and, living in one of the most densely populated and deprived areas in Newham, our students have many issues that adversely affect their learning. However, it became clear that in trying to deal with C/D borderline students, more often than not the brightest pupils were not stretched or challenged enough and left with grades that didn't reflect their potential.

The GCSE results of 2008 showed that only two subjects were above or in line with national averages for A/A*. In light of this, the last few years have seen a number of changes across the school to try to improve the percentage of students achieving A*/A.

THE STORY

NEW IDENTIFICATION PROCESS DIGS DEEPER
The journey started with revamping the identification process for more able learners. Traditionally, LIS only categorised the top 10% of students as G&T based on KS2 data. Talented students in different subject areas were only identified as and when the teacher recognised their talents. It was clear that this was a very restrictive way of looking at our more able students, and so it was felt that the identification system needed to be reinvented to make it more expansive.

The traditional top 10% were named as G10 on data lists, however there was an additional list added of students who had an APS of 30 or above but fell outside the G&T list. This was usually because they achieved one level 4 at the end of KS2. This additional group was named G30 on data lists. Together, the G10 and G30 students account for around 20-25% of students, depending on the year group. In addition, staff in the Performing Arts and PE were asked to identify students with a talent at the end of the first term.

It was decided that all G10 and G30 students needed to make four levels of progress by the time they left LIS, two whole levels by the end of Year 8, and two further whole levels by the end of Year 11. Moreover, G10 students should be achieving an A grade by the end of Year 10 and an A* by the end of the GCSE course in Year 11.

TEACHING AND LEARNING

LIS has always placed great emphasis on consistency within Teaching and Learning in order to drive change. There was no difference here when it came to accelerating the progress of the most able learners. It was stressed that all departments needed to stretch and challenge pupils in every lesson and that learning must be differentiated for these students right from the beginning of lessons.

There was a lot of time invested in looking at the function and benefits of learning objectives and success criteria. The learning objective dealt with the overarching aim of the lesson and the success criteria broke down the learning into steps that enabled students to achieve the learning objective. It was felt that this was important, as it gave students an insight into their learning and showed them which skills they were using.

It was also important to break away placing emphasis on C/D borderline students, towards all lessons being differentiated downwards and not upwards. This would also ensure that G&T provision was inclusive, rather than exclusive. Many of the lessons now taught at LIS are pitched to a very high level, which has seen all students perform significantly better, not just the more able. The mantra is that there should be no ceiling to learning or, as the Greek historian Plutarch said: "The mind is not a vessel to be filled but a fire to be kindled".

We wanted to ensure that our most able students were getting the best education possible, and therefore departments were urged to think about their teaching and learning before, during and after lessons. The following are some 'dos' of our school in relation to catering for more able students.

BEFORE THE LESSON

Teachers were required to analyse their schemes of learning and to ensure that there were opportunities for higher order skills to be developed in every lesson. Evaluation and application are higher order skills in Science and are incorporated in every scheme of learning from KS3. One example taken from Year 7 would be: 'Evaluate the use of IVF treatment in older women'.

More able learners must have a different starting point, and their learning needs must be addressed. One effective way of doing this is through differentiated questioning. There has been an emphasis on questioning strategies such as 'bounce and pounce', that enable deeper thinking and engagement, and one of the many CPD sessions on offer for staff is on questioning strategies.

Finally, showing students a sophisticated modelled answer on a similar question from a different topic can help them to write independently to a very high standard. A modelled answer has the benefit of giving students structures without inhibiting their learning or copying.

DURING THE LESSON

Questioning should be differentiated so that speculation, inquiry and discussion are aimed at the more able. This will also encourage students to discuss their ideas and add suggestions to the mixing pot. It is important that the teacher facilitates discussions rather than leading them, and picks their moments to interject, allowing collaborative talk to flourish and take greater meaning.

Independent inquiry is integral to the learning of more able students. A strategy labelled 'C3B4ME' is used to do this, where students have to see three classmates for an answer to a problem before they are allowed to approach the teacher for help.

Impact of TLC discussions and inset training day

In addition to your planning, you should also include the following points in your essay:

- In your conclusion, say what you think about the response of some to negative reports of genetic screening in the media.

- Do you think there are any positives to come out of the negative portrayal of genetic screening in the media?

- It was recently said on a radio chat show that 'genetic screening is wrong, even if it is to prevent suffering'. What do you think about this statement?

More challenge does not mean more work. Avoid repetitive extension work and time filling activities. You can encourage deeper thinking by setting challenging questions to work that all students may be doing.

Students must be set the task of drawing individual and unique conclusions that are feasible and backed up with evidence from the main analysis points discussed. More able students may be given new information linked to what they are studying and be required to make use of it appropriately in their work – or they may be asked to research new information themselves. To add further challenge, a word limit may be set, reminding students there are time constraints in an exam.

It is essential that students are given sufficient thinking time when answering questions. This will ensure that key vocabulary and content is embedded appropriately, as well as allowing students to apply knowledge to the world in which we live. In this way, learning is contextualised to students' own lives and experiences so that it is not seen as something that is alien to them.

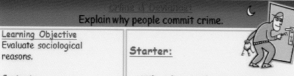

Learning Objective
Evaluate sociological
reasons.
 	
Context:
Crime & Deviance
 	
Success Criteria:
1. Recall information (D/C)
2. Explain Reasons (C-A)
3. Evaluate Reasons (A/A*)
4. Apply Sociological
   perspectives and
   explanations (A/A*)
Keywords:
Crime, Labelling, Relative
   deprivation, and other
   keywords covered last
   lesson, (look at keyword
   sheet).
	Starter:
	
	Why do people commit crime?
	Quiz Quiz Trade
	
	• **What is crime?**
	• **State 3 types of crime.**
	• **Explain the labelling theory.**
	• **Do you think the labelling
	   theory is a good explanation
	   for crime? Justify**
	• **Using a sociological perspective
	   explain why people may commit
	   crime.**

Above is an example of differentiated success criteria and how learning can be differentiated through questioning.

AFTER THE LESSON

In order to consolidate and broaden learning, it is important to set homework on topics covered in lessons but in more complex and unfamiliar contexts. A number of departments now set more project-based homework over a number of weeks that require independence and creativity. By having reflective homework tasks, students are encouraged to revise the topics taught and to ask further questions in their books that they can then bring to lessons. It is important for teachers to think about homework tasks carefully, and to ensure that the work set allows students to evaluate and synthesise, rather than simply regurgitate the work.

WHOLE SCHOOL INITIATIVES

STAFF TRAINING AND CPD SESSIONS

In terms of our Teaching and Learning, we realised that within lessons not all teachers were adequately making provision for their most able students. We also realised that we had a number of teachers who were providing exceptional opportunities for the more able. In light of this, we offered CPD sessions run by our staff to facilitate and support teachers to cater more effectively for their brightest students. Currently, these CPD sessions include Questioning, A/A* and More Able workshops (We felt it was important to differentiate between A/A* and More Able since there are varying abilities within the lower and middle sets.)

These workshops are not stand-alone but are a series of four sessions from which staff can take away concrete strategies for use in lessons. Through pupil performance data, SLT identified departments which had converted C/D borderline students but whose A*/A percentages fell short of the mark. They were then provided with support and training to improve.

Teaching and learning bulletins were shared with all staff to keep the profile of More Able students high and to encourage everyone to do their bit to accelerate the progress of these students. We also periodically held good practice briefings and insets. Furthermore, provision for G&T students is one of the key foci listed on lesson observation forms.

SOFT FEDERATION AND KS2 CO-ORDINATOR

Students needed to be inspired to go to Russell Group Universities. We have set up a Russell Group Programme to raise the aspirations of the G&T students and their parents. We invited a broker, the Brilliant Club to work with our Primary cluster. This independent organisation has a KS4 programme, which trains students to write extended essays (dissertation style) at KS4.

Through careful planning, LIS and the Brilliant Club created a programme for KS2 Y6 students. Year 6 G&T students embarked on a two-week summer school programme on which they received intense mentoring by PhD students. They were trained to write a 1000 word dissertation, which was graded in the same way as essays at degree level. Students were taught how to research and develop skills of independent inquiry – skills that are needed at college and degree-level but being practiced from Year 6. Furthermore, students were sent on a visit to Oxford University for feedback and had the opportunity to experience university life. This programme was then revisited at KS4 for Year 9 and 10 with G10 and G30 students.

DEEP LEARNING WEEKS

Much of the research into More Able learners shows they like to engage in immersive learning where they study a topic in depth. For this reason, it was decided that for two weeks in the year the timetable would be collapsed and students would engage with a deep learning experience. Many of the projects the students are involved with require skills of leadership, teamwork and independence.

One example is the Monopoly trip in Year 7 where students are split into groups of five or six and are asked to independently coordinate and plan a trip around London, visiting as many areas as possible found on the Monopoly board game. They have a limited budget, in which they are required to make allowances for food, travel and any other costs. The teacher takes a back seat and allows the students to coordinate and execute the plan independently, even if they do make mistakes!

IMPACT

The data has shown a significant increase in the number of students achieving A*/A. As was mentioned in the beginning of this case study, the 2008 GCSE results were 42% A*-C including English and Maths, with only a few subjects above the national average for A/A*. The 2013 results showed a 19% increase in A*-C, but notably there were 17 subjects that achieved above the national average for A/A*, including English Language, Literature, Mathematics and the Sciences. In addition to this, subjects such as Sociology and Religious Studies achieved 57.1% and 48% A/A* respectively, compared to a national average of 28.8% and 17.5%% A/A*. As a result, there has been a huge rise (400%) in applications to reputable sixth forms and colleges in the area.

In a recent survey, some of the comments made by our students were as follows:

"I am on target for A/A* in every subject because I take responsibility for my own learning and know that in order to do well in life I have to be the best that I possibly can be."

"We have learnt to be resilient and brilliant."

"In order to help ourselves and the community we let our aspirations be our inspiration."

"Our teachers are the best because they have the knowledge that extends our learning beyond secondary education."

"We want to learn because our teachers make us the focus of our lessons which are challenging, fun and engaging."

"The Russell Group Programme allows us to define and follow our goals and dreams."

"As a graduate, I will look back on my high school with pride and be grateful for the wonderful teachers I had the opportunity to work with."

In addition our Parent Voice feedback has also been very encouraging:

"Little Ilford School has been nothing short of magnificent for my children; everything from academic studies, sport, social skills and extracurricular activities have been of the highest standard."

"Our children love going to school every day and they get the appropriate recognition for doing well."

"Little Ilford School has given our daughter a wonderful experience and she has been able to participate in many different activities organised for the G&T group."

"G&T students are identified at an early stage at Little Ilford School which helps in developing these students and preparing them for the future ahead."

"On the whole, the school has provided great opportunities to students of a mixture of abilities. The G&T group has been assisted and inspired greatly by the school, which has made them the responsible young adults they are now."

NEXT STEPS

As always, the pursuit of perfection never ends and there is always room for improvement. A policy that stagnates and does not reinvent or adapt itself to the changing wave of education will inevitably regress and deteriorate.

The following points address the next challenges that we face:

- Many of our parents have a very narrow perception of what subject areas and degrees will lead to success. Awareness needs to be created of the many pathways and career options available to students and parents views need to be broadened.

- There are certain boys on the G10 and G30 list that can be negatively influenced by their peer group – how do we raise their aspirations?

- There needs to be an increase in the number of students achieving A*/A in five or more subjects to enable them to compete with the best in the country.

- As part of the pastoral programme, our Interview and Guidance Co-ordinator surveys every child in order to establish their future aspirations. This information now needs to be used in order to plan and tailor educational visits for different groups of students.

The biggest challenge has always been to inspire parents to allow students to pursue their dreams and goals. We have therefore piloted a day trip for our students and parents to visit a London-based university and business so that they can experience university life first hand, see its benefits, and overcome the fears of tuition fees. This initiative now needs to be refined and introduced as part of our Russell Group Programme.

CHAPTER 18

PREPARING STUDENTS FOR THE COMMERCIAL AND GLOBALISED WORLD THROUGH A BROAD CURRICULUM

EWA KOLCZYNSKA AND LOREDANA ROBERTS, GUMLEY HOUSE CONVENT SCHOOL FCJ

FOCUS AREA

This case study illustrates how Gumley House School created competency-led learning that supports students' academic education through a broad curriculum.

AIMS

In 2008, the Senior Leadership Team review concluded that students needed to be better prepared with the relevant attitudes, skills and abilities for their post-school life in a rapidly changing world characterised by the digital explosion, the fast-paced emergence of new roles and jobs, global and economic change, and Mandarin becoming the dominant world language. In addition, we wanted to strengthen and make explicit our commitment to girls' education and their career paths by challenging gender inequality and breaking employment barriers.

BACKGROUND CONTEXT

Gumley is a well-established and successful school founded in 1841. As a Catholic school, we have a strong ethos that reflects our Christian values, making our school a vibrant learning community with a commitment to developing our students into fully rounded individuals, looking outwards as they prepare to make a difference in the world.

A number of factors defined our progression to competency-led learning. Firstly, we recognised that our existing curriculum had to more accurately reflect global market changes. We had to identify investment and accreditation that would facilitate these competencies and align student experiences with those of industry and commerce. The school gained Business & Enterprise specialism in 2006, which was valuable in creating an entry platform for business partnerships. The school's success in implementing new Business & Enterprise learning initiatives led to the Specialist Schools and Academies Trust offering us a second specialism in 2008 and we chose Modern Foreign Languages.

At the time, our language curriculum comprised only European languages, but with the new language specialism, we decided to introduce Mandarin from Year 7, thereby addressing one of the main cultural and economic changes in the global market. We were the first school in the Borough of Hounslow to teach Mandarin and remain the only school in the borough to teach it in the curriculum. A-Level Mandarin is now firmly established, and this helps us to leverage external links.

Another factor was the acknowledgement that the school's recruitment strategy had to be revolutionary rather than evolutionary – a leadership position had to be created to drive the vision. We decided that the B & E specialism needed be overseen by an Assistant Headteacher. The language specialism was to be led by the Head of Languages.

THE STORY

It was clear that the creation of a Director of Specialisms had to be a senior responsibility. We looked to appoint someone from the private sector with a proven track record of successful commercial achievements. Above all, the Director of Specialisms had to be in harmony with the school's distinctive ethos and drive the change and innovation we had identified with enthusiasm.

It took three sets of interviews to find an applicant with the potential and vision we were seeking. In addition to possessing the essential personal qualities, our Director of Specialisms offered expertise, which included experience as a Senior Manager and a Board Director for a FTSE 100 media company working with start-ups, acquisitions and mergers. Crucially, her business skills included the leadership and development of internal teams, external commercial partnerships and profits across different operational remits and international territories.

However, appointing a non-teacher to a senior post brought certain challenges, some of which we had anticipated. For example, the existing curriculum arrangements didn't effectively provide students with the understanding of how best to apply what they would learn to the shifting demands of a fast-paced twenty first century world. All teaching and support staff had to be clear that this was a pivotal development. We underlined that the Director of Specialisms would report directly to the Headteacher and that all developments agreed would carry the Head's full support and be represented in the school improvement plan.

The initial key responsibilities were confined to the two specialisms – the role soon expanded to developing work-related competencies, and to involve programme strategies across all curriculum subjects. It was at this point that we encountered a degree of variance in staff response. For senior staff and teachers in the specialist subjects, the purpose of the role was evident and welcome. For others, the professional purpose and role was unknown territory. Staff buy-in was a process, which occurred at different stages. The changes in mind-set and attitude generally came with increasing involvement and a growing realisation that students were acquiring distinctive competences and experiences.

The strategy gradually secured the outcomes and impact we sought, although we needed to allow time for what was clearly a merging between private and public sector methods of procedure and practice. Understandably, teaching staff had to engage with and evaluate the experience before they saw the advantages within their own curricular sphere. Consequently, impact would not be achieved simultaneously across all subjects. The situation called for a strategic initiative which would set an informed and consensual way forward.

The Director of Specialisms decided on a consultative approach that incorporated staff, students and external parties. A 360 degree audit of existing student learning and curricular provision was undertaken, with the findings forming the basis of and setting the priorities for a comprehensive and agreed strategy. The consultation and audit began with the teaching staff in Gumley, and then spread across the broader education establishment, particularly schools with specialisms in a position to share proven practices, successes and obstacles that Gumley could learn from. A key objective of the process was to gain opinion on the various ways external expertise may be successfully integrated. The consultation helped to achieve 'buy-in' with the school's staff through joint proactive planning, as well as forming wider relationships in the education sector.

It was similarly vital to include our students. The focus group approach established a clearer understanding of the positive and negative learning experiences of extra curriculum initiatives and gave an insight into students' perceived future needs, challenges, desires and potential career aspirations.

We wanted to know what the barriers to entering the workplace were, so we approached recruitment influencers from Heads of Talent & Human Resources to Managing and Marketing Directors in local and city-based businesses to gauge their assessment of young people's skill and competency gaps in both the current and predicted future market. All companies responded positively and many offered to extend their involvement, recognising the opportunity of influencing what they would see as commercially prepared students who would one day be their prospective employees. Crucially, the Director of Specialisms established which organisations were able to lead bespoke programmes to shape skills and competencies learning to meet the needs we had identified.

The final focus was on local and international communities. We were fully committed to developing a global citizenship agenda. With forty five home languages spoken by our students, community engagement is integral to the school's ethos. The Director of Specialisms became a member of the steering committees of various community youth groups as well as establishing international links through the British Council to HSBC – a company that had been proactive in initiating international school projects.

The findings from our market intelligence defined our planning and communication strategy. Global citizenship, an ideas culture and life and employability skills spearheaded the initial stages of our student development programme. Other strong indicators emerged; work placements were essential, identified in numerous sources including a Guardian report demonstrating that two thirds of UK graduates in one year had gained employment with companies they had previous experiences with. So a work experience placement programme for sixth form students, which drew on the fresh connections, was implemented. Its success is summed up by a student: "I really wasn't sure what to do for my future before gaining a school work placement at HMRC in Year 12 and the experience opened my eyes to the opportunities out there and gave me confidence which made the experience more enjoyable".

A HSBC survey on UK companies identified languages and financial capabilities as two of the most sought-after skills. Consequently, we decided to merge language and financial learning into preparation for work roles at Key Stage 3. Further research established that in addition to academic achievements, behaviours and transferrable skills were being sought and formed an integral part of many industry interviews. Candidates' ability to 'apply learning' to the different range of tasks and situations facing them was deemed as being as important as what they were studying.

From the student focus groups, it was apparent that building self-belief was essential. We found there was a significant degree of confusion and apprehension, in part created by media coverage of the recession and the fact that future employment would include many jobs in areas and responsibilities, which had not yet been invented. Moving mind-sets for girls and overcoming barriers to entry remains a high focus for the school given two emerging issues – an industry desire in certain sectors, such as engineering and ICT to balance out male-dominated careers – and addressing the ever present 'glass ceiling' effect for women in the work force.

Teacher involvement in the consultation process was also critical. It was one thing to be in agreement with the general purpose, but another to take an active part in the planning and implementation of initiatives. Over time, our planning has become highly structured with discussions held earlier in the academic planning cycle with heads of subjects, year groups and departments. Issues emerging from our external partners and the market are examined, and competency and skills-based needs are identified. Planning cycles, which are prepared well in advance, ensure better outcomes.

Having a Director of Specialisms experienced in project management, and with sole responsibility, guaranteed that relevant advance planning was in place to secure maximum impact. One example was a Year 12 Careers Day event. Instead of assessing the desired subject and career paths of the new Year 12 intake in September, research began earlier. Possible career options and pathways of Year 11 students in their second term allowed us to identify the employers we wished to target so that we would be in a position to provide a strong match for our Year 12 students. This enabled us to attract participation from national and global partners such as Google, GSK, and Accenture, who responded positively to longer lead times. On evaluation, 92% students found the day valuable, 85% felt "more informed in career paths" and 94% reported they were "more confident in preparing for interviews".

One student said: "The two Glaxo Smith Kline interview skills workshops went through all the different interview preparation techniques and processes, which is knowledge usually only gained through experience". Another student added: "The afternoon with CMR Recruitment really helped me in understanding what the business world is really like when it comes to applying for jobs, and the sort of skills that employers both credit and don't credit, in particular regarding CVs – which isn't always made clear. By the end of the day, we knew exactly what we should and shouldn't do to give ourselves the best opportunity to get the job of our dreams. Overall, a brilliant and beneficial day".

Evaluations from our industry partners consistently report a 100% positive experience of working with us and state future commitment to developing their relationship with Gumley.

Establishing and sustaining business relationships and networks which match our student development needs is complicated. We recognise we have to adopt a flexible and informed approach to constant market shifts to ensure our learning programme remains current and innovative. To ensure sustainability, the partner retention strategy remains as important as acquiring new partnerships. Increasingly, company partners turn to us for our advice and it is indeed progress when we are able to influence thinking at that level. The Director Of Specialisms' methodology has been pivotal to the school's success in forming external local and international partnerships. The school prepares a brief for each organisation or individual it approaches, stating our aims, as well as seeking to establish how we can tie in with partner objectives.

Our partnership with an ICT city asset finance consultancy was voted The Times' Top 100 Small-To-Medium Companies To Work For. It also boasts a global expansion objective to encourage more women into the sector, which was ideal for Gumley, providing top-level expertise and resulting in over 14 different work-related initiatives for Key Stages 3, 4 & 5. The school's evaluation of sixth form students attending the company's industry induction days showed a 90% pre to post conversion on students' desire to enter this sector after university. Similarly, attendance at the HR job-planning skills session brought overwhelming feedback from our Year 10 and 11 students, with 100% feeling more confident and better prepared for university and job interviews. A three-year relationship with a city consultancy has involved establishing mentoring sessions between with its HR team and sixth form students to guide them as they move on to university.

Marketing communication is integral to maintaining external partnerships as well as capturing new ones, as we can quickly direct new business targets to our newsletters and website to promote external links. At times, we are asked to participate in a company's Corporate Social Responsibility (CSR) announcements and in addition the school has built press relationships to achieve regular coverage. This is predominantly local, though we have had some national successes that include The Times and The Guardian, covering initiatives such as our Youth Philanthropy Project, as well as the Global Young Leaders Conference for sixth form students.

IMPACT

Gumley has twice achieved the International School Award, in 2009-2012 & 2012-2015. These accreditations acknowledge progress and set fresh goals. The school has gained the Prince's Teaching Institute for Languages, History, Geography and English. Strong partnerships and established reciprocal visits with community groups and schools in Africa, India, Singapore, China and Europe feature prominently in our school calendar – a valuable contribution to students' cultural awareness. In 2013, we initiated our first Global Conference for 260 sixth form students from four schools and invited external speakers representing a spectrum of viewpoints. The conference's purpose was to deepen students' thinking, with a theme, which addressed the ethics, benefits and disadvantages of globalisation.

More knowledge of global issues	Felt able to express my views in the debate	Better understanding of the implications of Globalisation
88%	85%	74%

Individual students in Year 12 who demonstrate exceptional motivation and commitment are offered the opportunity to participate in 'The Global Young Leaders Conference New York & Washington'.

"*Every day we had a guest speaker to talk to us about their role in global affairs and debates held in the United Nations; it was unbelievable to think that we sat in the same seats as current world leaders, discussing similar problems that they have to tackle: development, the environment, health, human rights, peace and security, science and technology and trade and globalisation. It was an experience I will never forget.*"

Annual courses such as 'Go Global', a KS3 language and business skills course for all Year 9 students, focus on understanding the link between languages and work. Results show an 8% increase in GCSE language take-up, students expressing confidence in their language skills and a greater desire to seek language-related careers.

Uptake on Language GCSE	I would like to use my language skills in the workplace	I feel confident speaking in a language that I have never been taught in school
8%	64%	69%

The Warwick Centre of Education and Industry (CEI) Award & Young Enterprise School Award both opened doors to establish strong contacts with companies able and willing to invest quality resources and expertise. 360-degree evaluations, increasingly conducted through online surveys, are carried out after every programme to assess impact and identify future student needs.

YEAR 9 STUDENTS 'LEARN TO EARN' – FINANCIAL CAPABILITY AND CAREER PLANNING

Better understanding of the cost of living	Ability to Identify job roles linked to interests	Understand the qualifications for my career path
97%	96%	94%

The development of competency-led engagement has resulted in our students gaining broader opportunities to develop the skills and attitudes, which form an integral component of this curriculum. Successful programmes such as 'Young Reporter', project involvement with London universities and social enterprise initiatives have created a trickle-down effect with students from lower year groups actively seeking participation in these new learning experiences.

Students feel more confident in preparing for interviews, with one student now in her second year at Loughborough university, stating: "Being selected for the Young Journalist Scheme was a great opportunity as it really helped prepare me for work and university. It required independent thought and motivation to go out and find the news stories. By having a deadline it kept me on my toes and kept me organised. Furthermore, my work experience in the specialisms department gave me a taster for life outside the school walls and what really goes on."

Broadening career options for women and addressing gender inequality continues to be a focus. Our visiting speaker programmes include female pilots, scientists and others whose achievements have made a significant impact. 'International Women's Day', 'Day Of The Girl' and 'Women Of The World' workshops, and mentoring sessions with high profile women are planned to inspire our students.

NEXT STEPS

OUR PRIORITIES ARE NOW:

- To continue to acquire quality partnerships to support our student development plan.

- To secure successful designation as a 'Confucius Classroom' school to use the advantages and the opportunities membership of the Confucius Institute will bring.

- To develop further teacher and support staff involvement so that our curriculum objectives are reflected in all aspects of school life.

- To encourage student feedback channels such as 'learner voice' so that they play a determining role.

CHAPTER 19

OAKS PARK IS ASPIRING HIGHER

LIKHON MUHAMMAD, OAKS PARK HIGH SCHOOL

FOCUS AREA

Aspire Higher is a unique initiative which helps students to become the driver in the 'road trip' of their life. The programme inspires students to get the best out of the opportunities that are available, inside and outside of school, and to prepare them for a happy and successful life.

RATIONALE

In looking to improve the performance of our sixth formers, we realised that there was a huge mismatch between the performance, aspirations, expectations and achievements of our students. As a result of this, many students were choosing the wrong subjects at AS/A2 and aiming for unsuitable destinations beyond our school. Parents' unrealistic expectations did not help the situation either. In addition, we felt that students were too spoon-fed and lacked the ability to be independent. We wanted to create something that helped to solve both these problems.

Oaks Park is an inclusive comprehensive school and therefore has resource constraints to consider. We wanted to level the playing field somewhat, so that our students could compete with the best and be the best, irrespective of what level they were at. This initiative is not just for high achievers. We set out to be fully inclusive in inspiring our students, making sure not to discriminate based on background, ability or opportunity.

BACKGROUND/CONTEXT

In the past, the school provided students with support in their preparation for life beyond Oaks Park. However, this support was formally introduced towards the end of Year 12 and was very piecemeal in its nature. Our new Head of Year 13 wanted to break this trend. She wanted our students to have the same opportunities as those in independent schools and to aim really high. She took a lead on making a difference.

In her words: "Given that our school has a limited budget and is non-selective, we are never going to have the resources I would like to channel into the progression of our students. Therefore, we need to make the best use of what we DO have, which is a very dedicated body of staff, great IT facilities and an extremely progressive, open-minded SMT that lets innovation thrive.

"This kind of environment is perfect for someone like me, who does what they are meant to be doing, but who wants to do much more. I need an intellectual and creative outlet to be truly satisfied and OPHS gives me that outlet. Aspire Higher is a huge undertaking but I am enjoying it as a process and the labours are beginning to bear fruit."

It quickly became apparent that we had a large bank of expertise in the school staff and great opportunities to give to our students both in and out of school. However, these were not being co-ordinated in any meaningful way, which meant that opportunities were missed and it wasn't always obvious to students how to help themselves. Also, there was a malaise pervading some of our students, making them very passive about their learning. This kind of apathy is insidious and, if left unchecked, produces youngsters who are not ready to meet the world when they leave school at 18. After consultation with staff, it became very clear that most staff agreed that something needed to be done.

THE STORY

The Head of Year 13 set about creating an online information, advice and guidance tool for students. She firstly spoke to our online learning platform co-ordinator about what she wanted to establish and just what was technically possible. At this initial stage, the Head of Year planned the basic idea, with the named pathways, the functionality and ideas about content. There was a series of meetings with the sixth form team where the most appropriate categories of pathways were discussed, alongside what grades the pathways should be linked to. Some ideas about content were fleshed out, then the sixth form team spent a whole day in a room adding suggestions to each pathway, and sub-categorised them into year groups. The whole room was submerged in posters, paper, evidence and post-it notes!

It was a mammoth day, but it was totally worth it, as everyone's ideas really made Aspire Higher emerge into reality. The Head of Year 13 then spent her summer holiday building the programme, and it was rolled it out to Years 10 to 13 in September 2013. The form tutors introduced the programme to their tutees. All students had to log on in their own time and choose a pathway. Once logged in to the system, students have complete freedom to explore any pathway they like. However, they are given guidance to match their effort and attainment grades to date.

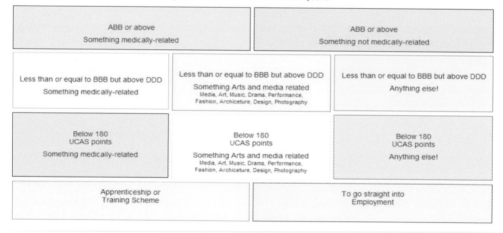

ABB or above: something not medically-related:

THERE ARE 60 BOXES IN THIS PARTICULAR PATHWAY. EACH OF THE BOXES LEADS TO A LINK OR A DOCUMENT.

AT THE BOTTOM OF THE PAGE, THERE ARE CLEAR INSTRUCTIONS FOR STUDENTS.

Things you must do:

- Use Unifrog to find your unis and courses
- London Taster Course Programme – arrange to go on one
- University of Cambridge master classes – look into these and try to get into one
- Register with Access Professions.com, to receive notifications of summer schools, internships, mentoring
- Use your APPLY book – it's a goldmine! Show your form tutor what you found
- Keep browsing through the 6th form notice board for great opportunities -

Things you could do:

- Find out about K+ (Kings Coll)
- See if you're eligible for the fantastic opportunities offered by the Social Mobility Foundation - if you are and you are interested, apply!
- Find out about scholarships, student finance and more - it's all just a click away!
- start revising - look at the "revision advice" button or visit the Get Revising website
- Sign up for a fantastic Curriculum Enrichment oppotunity
- Sutton Trust Summer Schools

ABB OR ABOVE: SOMETHING NOT MEDICALLY-RELATED:

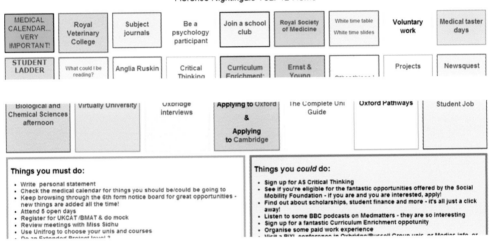

Florence Nightingale Year 12 Home

Things you must do:

- Write personal statement
- Check the medical calendar for things you should be/could be going to
- Keep browsing through the 6th form notice board for great opportunities - new things are added all the time!
- Attend 5 open days
- Register for UKCAT /BMAT & do mock
- Review meetings with Miss Sidhu
- Use Unifrog to choose your unis and courses
- Do an Extended Project level 3

Things you could do:

- Sign up for AS Critical Thinking
- See if you're eligible for the fantastic opportunities offered by the Social Mobility Foundation - if you are and you are interested, apply!
- Find out about scholarships, student finance and more - it's all just a click away!
- Listen to some BBC podcasts on Medmatters - they are so interesting
- Sign up for a fantastic Curriculum Enrichment oppotunity
- Organise some paid work experience
- Visit a BYL conference in Oxbridge/Russell Group unis or Medics info or

TO GO STRAIGHT INTO EMPLOYMENT:

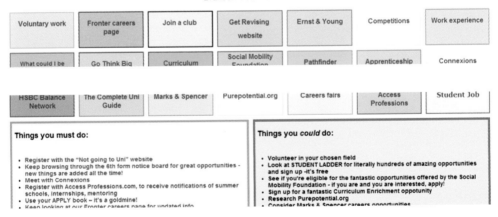

Branson Year 12 Home

Things you must do:

- Register with the "Not going to Uni" website
- Keep browsing through the 6th form notice board for great opportunities - new things are added all the time!
- Meet with Connexions
- Register with Access Professions.com, to receive notifications of summer schools, internships, mentoring
- Use your APPLY book – it's a goldmine!
- Keep looking at our Fronter careers page for updated info

Things you could do:

- Volunteer in your chosen field
- Look at STUDENT LADDER for literally hundreds of amazing opportunities and sign up -it's free
- See if you're eligible for the fantastic opportunities offered by the Social Mobility Foundation - if you are and you are interested, apply!
- Sign up for a fantastic Curriculum Enrichment oppotunity
- Research Purepotential.org
- Consider Marks & Spencer careers opportunities

Aspire Higher gives each child the tools and direction to enable them to start differentiating between themselves and everyone else, so that when they apply for their chosen university place or their preferred career, they stand out from the crowd in meaningful ways.

Often, students don't understand that what they do in Years 7 to 11 heavily impacts on the choices they have when in the sixth form. This applies to their A-Level and BTEC choices, and also to their higher education or employment opportunities. The beauty of Aspire Higher is that it gives them a portal to a huge wealth of resources, but it is still the students themselves who must walk through the portal and do the work, thereby encouraging them to be independent.

The aim is to help each student get to where they really want to go to – their aspirations should be high and their horizons wide. The idea is that now the fantastic opportunities available to our students, both in-house and externally, won't be missed through lack of information or a fractured delivery system. Aspire Higher is centralised and easy to access from school or home. Parents are encouraged to enjoy using it alongside their children and the system is regularly updated with new and exciting things to do, read and see.

THE SYSTEM NOW PROVIDES SUPPORT IN A VARIETY OF WAYS, WHICH INCLUDE:
- Deciding what they want to do after they leave school and how to get there.

- Showing them how to be competitive and to stand out.

- Creating a personal plan.

- Providing resources and guidance.

    – Jobs – careers service.

    – Universities and courses – 50,000.

    – UCAS – applying for HE.

    – Focused work experience and summer school.

    – Relevant and focused visits.

    – Projects – EPQ and others.

    – Online interactive tool to self-select their pathways.

- Providing regular review meetings with mentors every half term (during tutor time).

- Giving guidance to produce essential action points for the year.

The review meetings are conducted in 'coaching' style where students are asked questions on their effective use of the system in building their future. These questions allow students to reflect and plan ahead.

IMPACT

To measure impact, we have interviewed students from Years 10 to 13 and tried to find out what benefit, if any, they are getting. In summary, all students have said that they feel more in control of their own future and that they feel empowered to make well informed decisions.

KS4 students are surer about the subjects they are choosing and have realistic expectations of what they can expect in the future. This was enhanced at the 'Medicore-Fair' we organised, which involved twenty healthcare professionals spending a day with Oaks Park students and being interviewed by the students.

KS5 students are feeling confident about their ability and this is improving their chances of success. Two of our students have been offered a place at Oxford and Cambridge this year.

Many Year 12 students are independently preparing a portfolio to help them during the university application process. Among the variety of enrichment activities, students are independently arranging to attend summer schools, university-led programmes, work experiences as well as reading relevant books and creating contacts outside school.

When asked about the impact of Aspire Higher, a student's response was: *"I went to a free autumn/summer school and it was amazing – I'd never have heard of it if it hadn't been for Aspire Higher"*. Another student said: *"My mind is not closed on one thing now, through explorations I have learnt about things I can do beyond school, which I did not consider before"*. One Year 12 student commented: *"I have been made aware of the Sutton Trust group that has helped me to choose summer schools."*

At a recent Oxbridge Information evening, held at OPHS, the Oxford speaker said: *"This is brilliant – it's exactly what we are trying to tell schools to do for their students!"* Meanwhile, parents have said: *"It's fantastic that you do this for the students here – it shows you really do care about them"*.

NEXT STEPS

All of the students we spoke to said that it would benefit them even better if they had access to something like this from Year 7, so we plan to roll it out to KS3 from September 2014. A few students pointed out that certain pathways are not as well resourced as the rest, so we are planning to work on these. Also, some students have mentioned that they would benefit from a more regular dedicated form time on Aspire Higher so we will collaborate with our Heads of Year during the summer term to make a decision about allocating more tutor time to Aspire Higher. Now that all our students in Years 10-13 have started to use the system, we will implement a more rigorous monitoring system in September 2014. We will also evaluate the increased workload of the sixth form team in running the programme and consider allocating a TLR to another member of staff to increase the capacity of the team.

The ultimate indicator of the success of this programme will be to see how happy and successful our students are in the real world in years to come. Until then, we will continue to Aspire Higher!

CHAPTER 20

LEARNING TO LOVE LANGUAGE – PRIMARY PARTNERS MFL PROJECT

CHARLOTTE SAYED, ST MICHAEL'S CATHOLIC COLLEGE

FOCUS AREA

This case study examines a project designed to build expertise in language teaching within primary schools. MFL specialists from St Michael's work with primary schools, using modelling, team teaching and team planning to build confidence and increase subject specific knowledge and pedagogy, thus enabling the delivery of higher quality teaching and the use of improved subject-specific resources.

AIMS

Introduced in 2008, the project began as part of a government initiative to increase the teaching of MFL within primary schools and its initial aims were:

- To improve the quality and level of provision for MFL within primary schools.

- To build and strengthen cross-phase relationships.

- To ease transition to KS3.

With the government introduction of compulsory language at KS2, the introduction of the EBACC suite of subjects, and the Progress 8 measure – which comes into play from 2016 – the aims have grown to encompass:

- Building student skills and confidence leading to increased uptake of MFL at KS4.

- Improving results at KS3 and 4.

Perhaps most importantly, the aim has been to promote an interest and enthusiasm for learning language and build students' confidence to take risks, their curiosity and greater cultural understanding.

BACKGROUND CONTEXT

St Michael's Catholic College is an 11-18 Catholic comprehensive school situated in Bermondsey. The college has 27 feeder primary schools and the project has allowed us to work closely with up to five of them. St Michael's held a dual specialism in Business and Languages and the MFL department has consistently achieved outstanding results – in 2013, 25% of students achieved A* and A for French, with 43.8% for Spanish and our A*-C results for both subjects were 83.3% and 87.5% respectively.

THE STORY

A termly bespoke programme is currently offered to each of four of the college's feeder schools to support them in meeting their individual priorities for MFL provision. To maintain its profile, the partnership is led by a member of the college Senior Leadership Team.

Each phase of the project begins with a meeting to agree the focus with the primary co-ordinator, and to ensure that the programme of support to be created is tailored to the individual priorities of each school. A programme is created and agreed by the lead practitioner for the project: an MFL teacher from St Michael's. Each school has an allocation of up to eight weeks of half a day's support. Quality assurance takes place at the end of each programme through interview and feedback from staff and the evaluation of these responses informs the planning for the next cycle of the partnership. There is also dedicated time for a regular informal evaluation of the learning for both teacher and students at the end of each of the lessons delivered, to agree aims for the subsequent lessons.

A strength of the programme is that it is entirely flexible. At one of the feeder primaries, a member of staff who has a degree in MFL is now in her second year of working with the college on the project. She plans and delivers the lessons and resources for Years 5 and 6, using St Michael's staff expertise to deliver the lessons to Years 3 and 4. This has built the pupils' confidence at an earlier stage and increases our capacity to deliver high-quality language teaching within the school.

The college lead teacher works differently with an NQT within the same school, team teaching and modelling good practice. With some other partners, the college is the sole deliverer of the language. The focus of the teaching is on speaking and listening: students learn songs and play games using gesture and movement to reinforce the basic vocabulary that they are learning. The primary co-ordinator feels that the language skills that the pupils develop impact on their learning elsewhere, and that their listening skills in particular have improved.

STAFF EVALUATION

ONE OF THE SCHOOLS INVOLVED IN 2012 FED BACK THE FOLLOWING:

What worked well

- Interactive activities incorporated in lessons.

- Paired conversations.

- Opportunities built in to extend written work.

- Students were engaged and planned work met the needs of the mixed ability groups.

- Planning meetings after each lesson to reflect and prepare for next lesson.

- Lesson timing was about right (30 minutes).

- Students enjoyed having lessons delivered by a secondary specialist.

Areas for improvement:

- Pace of delivery could be faster.

- Build in a five-minute slot before the start of each lesson for final preparation/set up.

Student evaluation

The questionnaires elicited a 100% positive response from students. All students were able to explain clearly what they had learnt during the unit of work. The responses indicated that all students had enjoyed their French lessons and the most frequent positive comments made, were:

- They enjoyed active learning – especially games, role plays and pair work.

- They would like to carry on with learning French and also visit France.

- The lessons will help them if they continue with French at secondary school.

Areas for improvement:

- Some students said they would have liked to learn songs.

- Some students said they would have liked to read and write more in French.

- Almost all students said they would like slightly longer lessons and more lessons in the future.

In the next evaluation, from another partner school, the areas for improvement were:

- To differentiate students who already have some knowledge of French.

- Some students would have liked longer lessons.

- Some students would have liked to learn more French songs.

Evaluations are tracked by the member of SLT in charge of the project, to ensure that action has been taken to secure improvement on the basis of the feedback given.

Certainly, in the most recent lesson observation, the request to learn more French songs was being enthusiastically fulfilled.

IMPACT

Five primary schools have worked with us (four had no previous MFL Teaching and Learning). Over the course of the project, this has resulted in:

- 11 primary teachers being trained in planning lessons and teaching French.

- All teachers reporting that their subject knowledge and pedagogy had improved.

- 12 teaching assistants being trained in the teaching of French.

- Schemes of work and lesson plans developed and used in five primaries.

- INSET training sessions on French language acquisition in French MFL held for primary staff.

- Playground Games in French initiative set up and used in primary school.

The response from students is consistently 100% positive. Students from Year 3 said:

"*I like the way she teaches us to say things in a funny way so that we remember things.*"

"*It will help us to learn other languages.*"

"*I find it interesting and I like to know a new language.*"

"*It's a challenging language to learn, there's lots of fun stuff to say and to do.*"

It is clear from these responses that our key aim to build and enthusiasm for language and for learning has been achieved.

In terms of impact at St Michael's, there was a 78% take-up of MFL in Year 10 in the 2011-2012 academic year – the first cohort to benefit from the partnership – and this number has been maintained. This helpfully coincided with the introduction of the EBACC. Staff teaching Year 7 notice a marked difference between students who have experienced the intervention, against those who have not. Students from the primary schools within the partnership participate more confidently in lessons from the outset and show increased aptitude in learning new vocabulary. Due to the quality of teaching that they receive in Year 7, this gap is closed by the first Christmas formal assessment, though analysis of results in Year 7 show that progress to targets for students with high Key Stage 2 results is 1.3 points better than those with a lower starting point.

There is a clear impact in terms of the enthusiasm of students, the confidence that they gain and the positive effect that has on other students within their classes once they arrive in our lessons – which translates into the popularity the subject has within the college. Add to that, the quality of relationship with our key feeder schools and the strong position they are now in, with the introduction of compulsory languages at KS2, then you can appreciate why we consider this project well worth the time and expertise invested.

The key issue for both the college and the partner schools has been ensuring that the project has time allocated to it, not just for the lessons, but for the follow-up conversations; these, rather than email communication, are where the most effective planning for the next lessons take place. Primary colleagues feel the pressure of SATs preparation and they have had to fight quite hard to maintain the time for the MFL project. As a college, we too have had to be flexible to their cycle of preparation. Now that MFL is compulsory at KS2, the issue of sustainability will be key; the college is planning for a role that will involve more consultancy and training than delivery.

NEXT STEPS

St Michael's currently offers master classes in Business and Technology to Year 5 pupils as part of Business and Enterprise Week during the summer term. Positive feedback from primary schools has led us to investigate the possibility of offering languages master classes at the same time, easing transition by giving students the opportunity to develop their confidence in the language skills within a secondary environment. In addition, the college is using the project as CPD, providing staff with training to teach outside of their Key Stage specialism and thereby raising expectations across the department of what students are capable of achieving from the start of Year 7.

CHAPTER 21

ROOTED IN STEWARDSHIP

DHARMINI SHAH AND NEIL GRASSICK,
BISHOP RAMSEY CHURCH OF ENGLAND SCHOOL

FOCUS AREA

This case study shows how the Bishop Ramsey community has used the external school environment in creative ways to improve student experience, but also to motivate and mobilise staff.

BACKGROUND CONTEXT

The school environment is a key component in the context of a school and is important in creating the right ethos. At Bishop Ramsey, we see the environment as a tool to show students about stewardship in the wider world, as well as God's creation.

Our Head of Humanities had a passion for Geography and Environmental education, not just in the classroom, and had begun to explore how these disciplines could extend outside the buildings through small-scale projects in and around the school. However, due to the fact he is a Head of Faculty, the time and attention needed to fully develop this passion was not available. So, a new post was created at the school, entitled Head of Environmental Sustainability. The role involved leading and promoting Environmental Sustainability within the school. The key objectives of the post were to ensure that students gain experience of environmental sustainability through the taught curriculum, pastoral and extracurricular activities. The Head of Humanities was appointed to the position.

THE STORY

THE BIG DIG!

2010 saw the start of an innovative environmental project entitled The Big Dig, which involved approximately 15 members of staff, 20 students, six parents, and governors alike in digging an outside classroom. Students who were taking part in the Duke of Edinburgh programme and International Baccalaureate participate, as it was an initiative that could enhance their University statements and CVs.

Once the outdoor classroom had been dug out, a working group consisting of 10 members of staff from various faculties was established with the key objective to explore ways in which the outdoor classroom could be utilised for Teaching and Learning beyond the Humanities Faculty. PE, Science, Maths, English and Drama also began to use the outdoor classroom for Teaching and Learning, which led to the area being used for one of the central scenes in the school production of A Midsummer Night's Dream.

Before The Big Dig…

And after… introducing our outdoor classroom

DEVELOPING LINKS WITH OUTSIDE AGENCIES

The school began working with Groundwork South – an environmental charity that aims to help children become skilled, healthy and enterprising – with the confidence to make a positive contribution to their local community and environment. The main purpose of this was to help the charity to trial projects with secondary schools (at this point they had mainly worked with primary schools). Since developing links with Groundwork South, Bishop Ramsey has concentrated on projects with environmental sustainability, based on cutting energy and waste and growing local healthy food.

EXTRACURRICULAR AND STUDENT LEADERSHIP

The Head of Environmental Sustainability established an Eco-Champions Club with representatives from Years 7-13. The Club met weekly and began working on several small-scale projects, including building habitat shelters within the outdoor classroom, planting orchard beds around the school, planting wild seeds, designing and building mini poly tunnels, and making a composter from recycled materials. This provided the opportunity for a small group to take a lead on the environmental changes that the Head of Environmental Sustainability had envisaged for the school. One of the key themes developed by this group was 'reduce, reuse and recycle', which was advertised to the rest of the school community through creating and displaying posters around the school and presentations in assemblies.

As well as the voluntary Eco-Champions Club, an Eco-Council consisting of 32 members was established, with representatives from each form in Years 7-11. The group regularly met the Head of Environmental Sustainability and would communicate information to the rest of their form group. The Eco-Council primarily focused on biodiversity and had several sub-groups to ensure that everyone had a specific role within the team.

One of the earlier, larger projects led by the Eco-Champions was the Zero Waste Challenge. The group collected rubbish from classroom waste bins and completed a school eco-audit of rubbish. Students produced and presented videos of their findings through school assemblies, with the intention of creating an awareness of reducing and recycling. This led to recycle bins being installed around the school site. Each classroom and office was given a recycle bin, and recycling was installed around the school site.

CURRICULUM

Through the pastoral curriculum, there has been an emphasis on environmental education, especially at Key Stage 3 where approximately 555 students have engaged with the projects. During the pastoral Learning For Life lesson, a six-week project-based learning initiative was introduced through a series of cross-curricular creative activities encouraging students to reduce, reuse and recycle. For one of the projects, entitled 'Trashion', students had to work resourcefully in groups within their form to produce six items of clothing made from any material, which has been pre-used or recycled, to be shown on the catwalk during a showcase. Members of another form were required to demonstrate their artistic talents by designing and creating four different 3D sculptures based upon the theme of 'The Natural World' using only recycled materials. The projects had a competitive element to them, with each form competing for their House.

Through Learning For Life, students have had several lessons connected with 'Switch Off Fortnight' where students were taught about energy issues impacting upon our country and the importance of using energy efficiently. Leading on from this, one of the homework projects at Key Stage 3 encourages students (and parents) to monitor their waste and energy use over a week. Based upon the consumption of energy, students are required to devise an action plan to reduce consumption and waste in their homes. After some time of using the action plan, the students were then required to monitor the energy consumption at home and measure the effectiveness of their action plans. This project has not only educated students – but also their parents and carers.

CURRICULUM ENRICHMENT DAYS

The opportunity for whole school involvement in the environment comes through Curriculum Days, where Years 7-13 are off-timetable for the day and participate in curriculum-enriching, project-based activities. The Environmental Curriculum Days have led to several projects that approximately 555 students have been involved in, and these increased pupils' knowledge of environmental sustainability. The first project concentrated on creating a vegetable garden for growing the school's own vegetables.

Since then, the vegetable garden has been maintained by the Eco-Champions. An Eco-Champion reflected: "One of the main reasons as to why being a member has been so fulfilling, is the constantly changing school environment. It is always exciting to see the development of the vegetables or plants that have been planted at the start of the academic year, and watch them grow throughout the year."

Other projects have also included the construction of a wooden shed, building fencing around the pond and laying of grass areas. Students have also made sets, costumes and jewellery for the school production on such days through reducing, reusing and recycling other products. The latest Curriculum Day project was the building of poly tunnels.

SWAP SHOPS

A stretch and challenge project was designed to challenge selected Year 13 students to lead a project based on reducing, reusing and recycling. The students were presented with the challenge of organising, publicising and running a 'Swap Shop' for 185 Year 7s. Leaders of the project created a list of good quality items that Year 7 had at home and were no longer using. Year 7 students brought in a shoebox of such items and swapped these items with others that their peers had brought in. This enabled Year 7s to understand that items shouldn't just be thrown away if they are not in use. The idea has also been adopted by Year 11 prefects and a similar Swap Shop for Year 11 has been arranged.

PHOTOGRAPHY COMPETITION

Another way of encouraging student appreciation, awe and wonder of the environment and world we live in was through a photography competition. Students from Years 7-13 were invited to submit a photo of the environment, which they had taken themselves. This led to the 12 best entries being chosen for publication in Bishop Ramsey's own brand calendar for 2014. Copies of the calendar were sold to the school community, raising £70 for Malosa School in Malawi.

WORK BEYOND THE SCHOOL COMMUNITY

In line with one of the school priorities of A Community That Looks Outward And Beyond, some of the students had the opportunity of extending their work of managing the environment beyond the school. A voluntary group of 20 Year 9 students worked with 20 local residents and two Councillors in creating the Highgrove Council Estate Community Garden. This work was part of the Groundwork South project entitled Greener Estates, where the objective was to work in the local community to use green space and build a relationship with the local community.

NATURAL CONNECTIONS PROGRAMME

Some of the students in Key Stage 3 have also benefitted from a kinaesthetic approach in learning about environmental sustainability. The Natural Connections Programme was run in conjunction with Groundwork South East. This was a two-stage programme working with 15 Year 8 students nominated by their form tutors. The students identified were those who usually find certain aspects of school challenging, such as social interactions with peers or attendance – or those who couldn't necessarily concentrate for extended periods of time in a classroom setting.

For stage 1 of this programme, students participated in five sessions, both on and off school site. The sessions encouraged various skills such as team work, problem-solving, ICT and personal reflection. The group had to undertake different challenges and tasks based on the environment. For example, students had to research the environment through a 'Wonder Walk' and learn to prioritise and problem-solve by creating a shelter and a fire.

For stage 2 of this programme, the Bishop Ramsey students organised, planned and worked with Year 3 students from a local primary school. Students devised a Wonder Walk in the outdoor classroom with five stations. Each station had a team challenge or game and an educational aspect to it, to teach Year 3 about the environment.

IMPACT

By focusing on the development of the work on environmental sustainability, Bishop Ramsey School has achieved cumulative benefits in terms of staff development, physical and aesthetic improvement of the school grounds, growth of student skills, as well as education and awareness for students about the environment.

The following quote captures the enthusiasm of the Head of Environmental Sustainability: *"I have a passion for our planet and believe that the awe and wonder is something that everybody can experience – even during the shortest interaction with our environment. From planting a seed and watching it grow into something you can eat, to just feeling the warmth of the sun against your skin on a bright sunny day surrounded by verdant vegetation, simple things can inspire."*

He adds: *"My aim with the work that I do is to expose our students to new experiences outside and to make them think about how precious our planet is. Using creative and fun activities also shows them that they can make a difference to how long our planet can cope with the relentless exploitation it is currently experiencing – through their sound stewardship and decisions they really are key players in the future of their world."*

The various projects that have taken place have also encouraged parental engagement. The Parents' Association at Bishop Ramsey, otherwise known as 'Friends of Bishop Ramsey', has fully supported the projects through donations. This has inspired other parents to get involved and collect the Morrisons Let's Grow vouchers, as well as providing generous donations of materials for Curriculum Days and other projects. Equipment such as bird boxes and insect hotels have also been purchased with the vouchers. The school has also installed recycling bins for batteries, mobile phones and printer ink cartridges that students and parents can use. By recycling such items, we have been able to raise money for Malosa School in Malawi. (A biennial trip for approximately 25 sixth form students, accompanied by three teachers, takes place to Malosa School where students experience Malawian life and learn about its agriculture and natural landscape).

The products that have been grown in the vegetable garden have been sold at the Parents' Association events. This has meant that the vegetable garden has become self-sustainable and more products can be grown each season.

Students have not only learnt about the environment academically, but they have gained in experiential knowledge of the environment, too. This has empowered learners and has led students to a greater appreciation of their surroundings. Many students have also enhanced their skills from group work to communication and leadership. This is in line with the school priority of Every Relationship A Positive Encounter and Every Day At School A Rich School Experience.

The projects that have taken place have also provided an opportunity for an ex-student on a gap year to become an intern before going to university. The intern had the opportunity of leading the Eco-Champions: "The running of the Club is so important for the school as we have cleaned up the school, and created a sustainable environment for future generations at Bishop Ramsey. Some of the main projects that the Club has been involved in are; planting vegetables and selling them, creating a path to the greenhouse, planting the trees for the orchard, cleaning the school's grounds and planting flowers in various points around the school site to make it appear more attractive."

As a result of all the work and experience gained, the student changed university course and was inspired to study a degree based on the environment.

NEXT STEPS

A strong foundation has been laid in terms of managing the environment at Bishop Ramsey School – however, there are still objectives that the Head of Environmental Sustainability would like to achieve for the school environment.

In terms of students, the next steps are to develop the work of the Eco-Council further to focus on litter and recycling in the school, and to continue the work of the Eco-Champions Club to include the development of a more attractive entrance to the school. Another step would be for students to gain a qualification awarded by the Royal Horticultural Society for their green-fingered work around school.

The school has gained the Silver Flag Award for Eco-Schools for all the environmental work that has been carried out. The next step is to work towards achieving the Green Flag Award.

The intention of the Head Of Environmental Sustainability was to change the culture and behaviour of Bishop Ramsey students for the good of the planet and to put stewardship into practice. In the words of Betty Smith from *A Tree Grows in Brooklyn*: *"Look at everything always as though you were seeing it either for the first or last time: thus is your time on earth filled with glory."*

With all these projects, Bishop Ramsey aims to continue to nurture students in a Christian learning community about stewardship in the wider world, and to show stewardship for God's creation.

CHAPTER 22

CAFE PARAMO – YOU CAN TASTE THE JUSTICE

MIKE BETTLES, HEATHFIELD COMMUNITY SCHOOL

FOCUS AREA

This case study outlines a project whereby Heathfield Community School took the entire coffee harvest from a small co-operative in the Podocarpus National Park of Ecuador, and supported students in packaging, marketing and selling this product as Heathfield's Café Paramo, putting all of the profits back into the school that educates the sons and daughters of the co-operative. The initiative allows the students to play seriously and gives them 'the chance to be' – to take on different roles from designer, to sales executive, to eco-warrior.

AIMS/RATIONALE

Café Paramo didn't spring forth out of a clearly structured plan; rather, it developed gradually and organically from a chance meeting and the initial germ of an idea. However, three very clear aims motivated and impelled the project from the very beginning:

1. The project should allow the students to operate within a real-world business context, to come up with realistic solutions to actual problems. This should be true across a wide range of spheres – from traditional school subjects, including English, Art, Design and Maths – to 'vocational' areas such as finance, marketing and sales. Without us having to invent scenarios, the students should have to deal with issues and provide solutions within the context of real-life business needs. They should also come face-to-face with the ambiguous reality behind concepts such as Globalisation, Fairtrade, Freetrade and Ethical Investment.

2. We wished to emphasise the international scope of the project. The project was set up at a time when we had already developed very good European links but we wanted something that would help to broaden the scope of our international work. Heathfield School is 98% white UK heritage and 50% of the students come from our rural catchment.

3. The project must give students the sort of experiences that would imbue them with the confidence that many independent school students take as their birth right. From there, we could confidently expect them to take over the UK and to do a very good job of making it a fairer place.

THE STORY

Heathfield Community School, from the bustling metropolis of Taunton in Somerset, buys, markets and sells the entire coffee harvest of a co-operative in the Podocarpus Mountains of Ecuador. How cool is that?

Actually – we don't anymore, because the co-operative received a better offer from Café Nero, but we certainly did for a long time – from 2007, until 2013. We now have the same arrangement with a co-operative from the Dominican Republic (chosen, amongst other reasons, because of the tragic murder of one of its key workers).

The whole project started with a chance meeting in Watchet between Ian Grant, our then Head of Geography at Heathfield, and Paul Marsh, Managing Director of Miles Coffee Merchants. To cut a long story short, the beatific Paul agreed to source us with the already mentioned coffee harvest, roasted and vacuum-sealed in their factory, and a very generous parent agreed to provide us with the sticky labels.

Our focus, therefore, was simply on designing the labels and associated merchandise (coffee mugs, t-shirts et al) and on marketing and selling the product. This is crucially important to the long-term success of the project: the 'on-site' production of any goods – but especially of perishable goods – involves a responsibility in terms of quality control and food hygiene that is very difficult for a school to maintain over a sustained period of time. Removing that responsibility is certainly one reason for the project's longevity.

Initially, in 2007, the project started on a relatively small scale and involved around ten students from Years 9 and 10. This quickly mushroomed as students and staff were attracted by the project – with both groups seeing in it the potential for some real-life education. It was important to us that, right from the beginning, recruitment for Café Paramo was based entirely on interest and commitment. It has never been a project aimed exclusively at, say, Gifted and Talented students – although it has undoubtedly given many students the opportunity to show just how ferociously talented they are.

Two visits were crucial in terms of giving impetus to the Café Paramo project. Students went to DJ Miles' coffee production facilities, became familiar with the different stages of the roasting and packaging process and met a variety of key individuals from the firm. A reciprocal visit by Paul Marsh and a South American coffee merchant to Heathfield was also important in terms of fostering interest and creating links between the two groups.

Right from the start, the decision was made that every penny of profit should go back to support the schools where the farmworkers' children were educated. Of course, we have always purchased the coffee from them at a price that is higher than the Fairtrade price – 'Fairer Than Fairtrade' is the slogan that the Café Paramo marketing team coined for this. In no sense is this cultural imperialism – they have a product that we want (it is very good coffee) and we are prepared to pay a good price for it. That's business – and a very good business it has been, too. As of last month, we have bought £8,000 of coffee from the two co-operatives and we have also sent back to them some £4,000 in profit.

The 'big bang' for Café Paramo in terms of student organisation and student voice, came in 2011 with the creation of a company structure in which all students involved were asked to take on specific roles. Students opted to become part of the finance, marketing, international or design team. We also set up a managerial board, which, again, students opted into. This structure gave the students both a clear 'job description' and a sense of autonomy that was very empowering. By this stage (and up until the present day) at any one time there would be around sixty to seventy students directly involved in the company, with most of those students coming from Years 9 and 10.

Café Paramo has also become a whole school project that has spread its tentacles out to so many areas of school life. In English, for example, all students in Year 8 undertake a web design project based on the Café Paramo brand. Representatives from the company go into teaching groups and talk to students about the Café Paramo experience. It also forms the basis for projects in Art and this year there has been a whole school multicultural focus on the Caribbean, and on the Dominican Republic in particular.

This project has longevity: the illustrations here are the third generation of designs to be used for the labels.

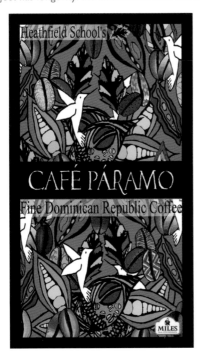 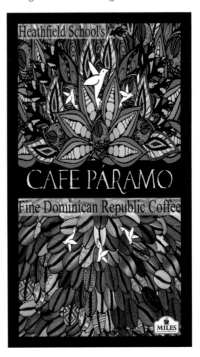

Like most companies, Café Paramo has had its ups and downs, but the commitment and passion of the students and the teachers has pulled us through. One of the main difficulties has been an issue that many successful buisnesses have to address – how do you manage expansion in a way that is not going to destroy the essential nature of the original intentions? This has needed careful managing and the group has, for example, taken the decision not to supply any more local coffee shops because of the supply responsibilities that causes; instead, they have decided to focus on 'one-off' shows such as the local sustainability show, school events, local village fetes and, oh yes, Glastonbury Festival!

Another recurring difficulty is staffing personnel and succession planning. The whole project is reliant on the commitment and dedication of the staff member overseeing it. One lesson a week is given as recompense, but the post holder then has to balance this commitment against all of his/her other duties. Fortunately, the company structure and the enthusiasm of the students have alleviated some of the pressure on the teachers, but it is always a delicate balancing act for the teachers involved. In the end, the continuing existence of Café Paramo relies on both the teacher and the students wanting to do it.

We should not forget the unswerving support of our suppliers – Miles Coffee. Nor should we forget the celebrity cachet that has come with the project. Students (not teachers) have been asked to give presentations at Asia House in London and at Brunel University – where they (students not teachers) have met Michael Eavis, Colin Greenwood, the Managing Director of the Fairtrade Foundation, and Ragee Omaar.

IMPACT

The length of the project (it has now been running for 10 years) means that we have had a number of different results and outcomes:

The project has provided a focus for learning in many areas of the curriculum. In this respect, it has impacted on all of the students in the school. This has included:

- A Year 8 English Café Paramo project centred around writing for advertising copy and on advertising and website design.

- A Year 9 Art scheme of work that focused on traditional Ecuadorian patterns and textiles.

- Year 8 multicultural week in 2014 that concentrates on the Caribbean, and in particular on the Dominican Republic.

The impact on students who have decided to actively engage themselves in the running of the Café Paramo Company (this now amounts to some 300 students) has been nothing short of profound. In terms of the aims of the project, the students have faced the difficulties, problems and the triumphs of running what is, without doubt, a hugely successful company. They have had to adopt a variety of roles and play them out in real-life contexts. They have gained the confidence to give a key presentation at one of the most prestigious business schools in the world, and also the confidence to accost innocent members of the public and persuade them to buy some coffee. And they have definitely had lots of fun.

The Café Paramo project received a real accolade when a team of students was asked to present their project as a part of a conference held at the Said Business School at Oxford University in 2012. This, in turn, led to an invite to present as the keynote address at the following year's conference in London – after which, the accompanying Heathfield Staff were left as wallflowers whilst the students were regaled by the likes of the Managing Director of Fairtrade Europe, and the bassist from Radiohead. They have now been invited to the 2014 Conference at the University of Lund in Sweden.

Our experiences through Café Paramo have had a direct impact on two associated projects: Comenius Bi-Lateral project, and Comenius Multi-Lateral project. Our Bi-Lateral project allowed us to introduce the Spanish language into the school and this, of course, was linked to the Spanish-speaking countries of Ecuador and the Dominican Republic. Students on the Bi-Lateral project who went over to Gijon on the Spanish Exchange were all involved in Café Paramo and the eventual aim is for those students to visit the school in the Dominican Republic. In the Multi-Lateral project, the other schools involved (from the Canary Islands, the Czech Republic, Italy and Holland) have all adopted the idea of combining entrepreneurship with sustainability which is at the heart of Café Paramo.

Another outcome has been outreach work with other schools. A number of other schools, both locally and nationally and both primary and secondary, have expressed an interest in following the Café Paramo model. This has involved both staff and students in visiting schools to advise them on how to set up this kind of project. Disappointingly, however, in only one case has this led to any long-term success at another school.

Café Paramo is well known in the local area because it is marketed and sold in a variety of local outlets (such as local coffee shops) and at a number of special events – such as the Christmas Fair in Taunton Town Centre, or at the Sustainability Show held every year in Taunton. A number of local business people have also become involved through the school's Education Business Partnership to give advice to the students on a wide range of sales, marketing and financial issues.

For many students, Café Paramo has been a central part of their development at Heathfield as they have moved from being assistants in Year 8 to part of the Management team in Years 10 and 11.

Here are the reflections of some students (and a parent) who have been involved for a number of years, and who have contributed significantly to the growth and development of Café Paramo:

"*I feel that Café Paramo is a very good club to be involved in, because you are able to develop skills that will be very useful in the future. It also offers you many opportunities, such as selling at events, learning a new language and even on going on trips abroad. But most of all, it has helped me to gain confidence by talking to new people.*"

– Esme

"*Students have gained confidence, learnt business skills and had great fun. A wonderful project that helps communities internationally…*"

– Mrs Codrington (Esme's Mum)

"*I have always been happy to know that everything that I did was to help the school in Ecuador and now the Dominican Republic. I have been privileged to speak in public at many prestigious places and I was a special guest speaker at Brunel University. I have enjoyed selling the coffee at various events and meeting Deborah Meaden and Michael Eavis!*"

– Sean

"*I've been involved in Café Paramo since Year 8 and continued to work for the project all the way up to my last year of school. It's taken me all over the place – not just in Somerset, but nationally as well. A group of us were lucky enough to travel to Oxford to give a presentation at a conference. Although I am at college now and no longer involved, I have fond memories of being part of Café Paramo and I will take all the skills I have gained into later life.*"

– Ellen

"*Café Paramo has been a part of my life for four years now. Before I decided to join, my sister Ellen was a Managing Director. I saw all the opportunities she was given – speeches, radio interviews and school trips – and I knew I was keen to take part. Our whole family are aware of Café Paramo and the work that they do – they also very much enjoy the coffee! Mum has taken a lead role in driving us to all the events and admits that she wishes there had been something like that when she was at school. I am now in Year 10 and still very much a part of the project and I hope that will continue – a lot has changed, such as our move of cooperatives from Ecuador to the Dominican Republic – but the work we do continues to stay the same and I am thankful to be a part of it.*"

– Katy

"*Café Paramo has given me an insight into the business world and it has given me valuable skills through real-life experience. I have marketed our product to corporate business owners and this has allowed me to network and set up pathways for the future. Café Paramo has allowed me to start my career early. I now know how to sell, be part of/run a business and I have gained some real-life knowledge of the coffee industry. This summer, I intend to do a work experience placement with a coffee importing/exporting company in London.*"

– Robbie

The project has also had a significant effect on teachers:

"*Café Paramo is about adding value to a student's educational experience. It is a brilliant project, which inspires and engages not only myself, but all the student members of the team. I strongly believe in a sustainable and fair future for the world, and through Café Paramo, we are able to create an education which allows everyone the opportunity to understand the issues, promote intercultural understanding and be part of the solutions.*"

– Heather Essadiq

"*Café Paramo's impact has exceeded my expectations. The project, driven by staff, and more recently by students has enriched the curriculum immeasurably. In many ways, it encapsulates the ethos of the school. It has become organic and celebrates that part of school life, which is hard to quantify. Café Paramo will continue to grow and, with other schools buying into the project, have a bigger impact on students in the South West. Just as importantly, the impact on the students and communities in the Dominican Republic will be enhanced —and this will mirror impacts in the UK. This project has always had fairness between partners at its heart. With students at its core it can only get better and better!*"

– Ian Grant, initiator of the whole project

NEXT STEPS

In order to progress Café Paramo even further, we need to invest more time linking with our friends in the Dominican Republic. By forming friendships with the communities we are working with, we can help to develop our mutual inspiration. Our proposed trip to the Dominican Republic in 2015, with students from Year 11 who have been involved in the project for the last five years, is a key part of this process.

The project has a good model and many schools have been enthusiastic to do something similar. However, in only one case has it led to a long-term, sustained project. It is one of our aims to reach out to other schools to see if we can change this situation.

The last word goes to Paul Marsh, Managing Director at Miles Coffee. When asked what the project meant to him, he penned the following:

"From my point of view, I love working with a local school that wants to do something different, which in the long term, will help communities who do not have so many of the benefits we take for granted."

"It is hard to quantify or explain it, but I find there is just something brilliant about young people doing something that has such a big impact on people they do not know. I suppose, without wanting to sound cheesy, it is just great being part of something that isn't all about the money and does involve so many wider benefits."

"Regarding perception, if anything it reinforces my belief that the State system can deliver fantastic achievements. In this case, teachers are allowed to think outside the box and are then encouraged to try and see what will happen. I appreciate this cannot have been easy with all the constraints that are imposed on their time, as some of it would have been outside work hours. The quality of work that the students produce is superb and I am always so impressed with how courteous and enthusiastic they are when I deal with them."

CHAPTER 23

WHAT CAN WE DO TO BE BETTER? A CASE STUDY IN THE POWER OF SPORT TO BE TRANSFORMATIVE

RAY WHYMS AND JACQUIE SMITH, LAMPTON SCHOOL

FOCUS AREA

This case study will look at the power of sports leadership to motivate students to develop positive behaviours and attitudes towards school and education. This is within the context of a relatively new but highly successful Basketball Academy which develops elite athletes who learn to exercise responsible leadership. It sees sport as a means of breaking social disadvantage and enabling students to develop academic and sporting excellence, which will allow them to achieve to their potential in the future. The importance of 'true grit' or character development is also a key outcome.

It is an example of the impact of strategic talent spotting and development achieved by investing in the entrepreneurial vision of an emerging teacher.

AIMS/RATIONALE

The Basketball Academy was established about four years ago with the support of the PE Department. This necessitated an investment, significantly reducing the teaching time of the Academy Director. It aimed to:

- Build successful basketball teams, through the development of athletes, to play at professional, regional and national level in a school with a limited basketball tradition.

- Use elite sport to develop habits associated with successful people e.g. punctuality, reliability, resilience, and self-discipline. We hoped that basketball, in particular, would enable groups of students who might not access the more traditional sports to seize alternative pathways to success.

- Capitalise on the power of membership of an elite academy to break patterns of under-achievement among some students.

- Use sport to unite students across the school and to develop a sense of belonging and pride beyond social groups in a school with unusually high patterns of diversity.

The study seeks to evaluate how successful this strategy has been, and in particular whether we have achieved sustained changes of behaviour among the members of the Basketball Academy.

BACKGROUND CONTEXT

Sport is very popular among boys and girls at Lampton, where there is a comprehensive competitive sports programme across a range of sports alongside a culture of 'no excuses' participation by all students in lessons. The PE Department has been externally evaluated as 'Outstanding'. This has been achieved, in part, through the development of a curriculum that engages and challenges students of great 'talent' and is accessible to students of all social, faith and cultural backgrounds.

The school is located in central Hounslow. Lampton School's deprivation index of 0.29 is well above the national average (0.22) and puts us in the top 25% of most deprived schools nationally. Many students live in social housing or in multi-occupancy dwellings which are over-crowded and without gardens. Local parks are problematic places to 'hang out' – unacceptable to many families, and unsafe at times. The school's grounds therefore offer students the opportunity to exercise and to socialise with friends in a safe environment. It is noticeable that many areas of the site are used by students until well into the early evening. Students defended long and unstaggered lunch hours as an opportunity to enjoy unstructured time to develop social bonds when lunchtime was reviewed by the SLT and the School Council.

The school has a limited, if celebrated, tradition of elite sportsmen and women. Past students include Owais Shah (England/Middlesex cricketer), Carlton Cole (West Ham/England footballer) and Stephen Caulker (Cardiff Captain/England U21 footballer). These three are local heroes, in addition to Mo Farah – a local 'boy' who has proved particularly inspirational to the Somali community.

The power of sports to model 'grit' in difficult circumstances was made clear when J.J. Jegede (Sky Sports Living For Sport athlete, mentor and GB long jumper) visited the school in 2012. Students asked for private conversations with him to discuss how to resist 'wrong choices' involving gang behaviours.

Basketball is a popular sport with boys and now increasingly with girls. While social housing developments lack football pitches, they always have room for Basketball hoops. Local sports teams do recruit healthy numbers, but really talented athletes find the training and exposure they need in regional centres outside of school. Caulker was a member of the Tottenham Youth Academy. The arrival of Alan Keane (Basketball Academy Director) at Lampton, coincided with the emergence of basketball as the sport of choice amongst many of our urban youth.

THE STORY: THE EMERGENCE OF A BASKETBALL ACADEMY

Keane's background could not be more different from that of his students. Raised in small town, rural Ireland, he espouses a tradition of commitment to community, to service, and to the value of sacrifice. He also has a strong belief in 'grit'.

Like many students, he saw basketball as a means to a life with purpose and excitement, a life a little less ordinary: *"I found my passion for basketball when I was 12 years old, watching the local national league senior team play. After seeing the excitement of the first game, I was hooked. I would go to the games every Saturday night. There would be close to 1500 people at the game and I would soak up the atmosphere, dreaming one day I would play for that team. Little did I know at the time that I would play semi-professionally for that team for eight years."*

Qualification as a PE teacher in the UK was the means by which Keane could also further his basketball career – first as a professional player, and then as a national coach. He joined Lampton in 2006 as a PE teacher with a dream. Within four years, he was seeing a crossover between his blossoming coaching career and his school role. From London Regional Head Coach, he was promoted first to England U15, and then U16 national coach. Recognised Regional Development Programme 'Coach Of The Year' twice and National 'Dave Fisher' award for coach of the year, Keane was determined to invent a tradition of basketball at Lampton.

In the early years, basketball had a low profile; practice sessions took place in out of school hours as the squad developed. However, within two years, Keane presented a case for a Basketball Academy. Talented athletes were identified for coaching sessions in the day. Alongside technical coaching and deliberative practice, went mentoring sessions. Students began to understand that athletic success requires resilience, commitment and grit. Committed to the notion of discipline as a factor in success, but working with students often on the edge of anti-social behaviours or on the edge of non-participation in school, Keane was striving for the level of self-discipline normally found in musicians and orchestra players.

He saw little difference between the world of the classroom and that of the basketball court in transforming lives: *"The basketball court is our classroom. Our philosophy is simple – what can we do to be better? At Lampton Basketball Academy, we don't set rules – we set standards – and these standards begin in the home, the classroom, and finally on the basketball court. We simply want to use the tools of basketball and what it is to be part of a team to develop and grow upstanding young people. If you are positive, work hard and want to improve, you can do it."*

The success of the Academy reflects the results of research pioneered by Anders Ericsson and quoted by Carol Dweck into the impact of praise that focuses on hard work and resilience rather 'intelligence'. It supports Matthew Syed's findings in Bounce. Syed sought to explain sporting success and to dispel the myth of 'born or natural talent' through highlighting the impact of access to a top coach and 24/7 facilities, as well as the power of practice.

The Basketball Academy opens at 7am and closes long after school. On a daily basis, 70 students spend lunchtimes training and many sessions are run by students themselves. This enables them to build towards their 10,000 hours (cited by academics as the required practice time to become world class). The school site staff, now understanding of the power of basketball, support and enable students' access to sports facilities throughout the holidays. An academy graduate and current university Sports Studies undergraduate, Viom Wadhaa, has been hired as a part-time coach to increase capacity.

Ever entrepreneurial, the school has developed links with BSkyB Sports to access the facilities of their sporting academy in west London to develop professional training facilities. We are in negotiations with Greenhouse Pioneers (a national charity) to establish a formal academy for the wider local community throughout the holidays to further enable committed and elite athletes to access the training they need.

The Academy seeks to replicate the dedication shown by professional athletes. The Academy has built in the squad a sense of family, with all the ties that this brings. The Basketball Academy students look different in school – their 'Academy' ties are preciously won and a badge of honour. Members can be suspended from the Academy if their attendance, behaviour or work ethic in the main school drops. This has worked as a real game changer for some student, and is particularly effective with students who find organisation difficult and who might historically have caused real challenges in KS4. To lose the right to wear the tie is, for many, the most severe of deterrents.

The experience of a current member, suspended for poor learning behaviour in lessons and poor attitudes towards school, is an example of Dweck's findings in practice: *"When Mr Keane suspended me I had to crawl my way back. He never sought me out. I had to seek him again and again to prove to him that I had changed. I had to get the teachers to tell him that I was doing better. He never once came to find me."*

IMPACT

In seeking to evaluate the impact of the Academy, we have interrogated our student performance data. The range of data is still limited as we are only just experiencing the progress of significant numbers of Academy members to KS4 and KS5. We have triangulated our school Management Information data with student and staff interviews to try to establish the impact of the Academy.

At Lampton, centralised and electronic detention records enable us to map those who transgress school rules. Of 45 Academy students with complete data, 76% saw a reduction in detentions from 2012-2013, at a time when, with a comparison group, numbers increased. In individual cases, there was a 66% reduction. It is worth noting that all the students involved in the Basketball Academy in Year 10 have an attendance figure above 90%, with 83% of them having an attendance rate over 95%. Many of these had dipped below the 90% mark prior to joining the Academy.

The same success can be seen in terms of progress. Lampton sets ambitious targets for students: in terms of levels, from Year 7 to the end of KS3 students are expected to achieve four to five sub-levels of progress in English and Science and six to seven for Maths. In Year 9, 95% of Academy students in English, 75% in Maths and 93% in Science exceeded their targets.

Of the 14 students designated as Pupil Premium at Key Stage 3, 79% are on track to achieve their target levels in English, Maths and Science. However, this picture is not so positive at Key Stage 4 where only 20% of the Pupil Premium students are on target to achieve their GCSE targets at the current time (the Academy was embryonic when these students were in KS3). However, with extensive revision and individualised interventions programme in place for these students, this picture is expected to improve substantially.

REFLECTIONS AND EVALUATION

The discipline instilled on the court and the loyalty to the 'family' is being replicated in the absence of exclusions for Academy members, some of whom were on the edge of criminality. For many students, the power of the coach to inspire is matched by their fear of letting him down.

When one of the Academy students left last year, his father said: *"Mr Keane, thank you for everything you have done for my son. You have been a father figure, a friend and somebody he can trust. He will miss you, the boys, and the environment you have set here at Lampton Basketball Academy."*

London teachers will understand that for many of our students, a powerful 'father figure' is transformative in its own right. Teachers in the school have recognised the transformation in the learning behaviours of students once in the Academy. Testimonies about students begin with changes in the wearing of the uniform and swiftly encompass the transfer of behaviours such as resilience, relentless practice, and risk-taking to their work across the curriculum. Dweck's 'growth mind-set', once learned in basketball through constant practice and a refusal to admit defeat till the final whistle, can be more easily applied to the mathematics classroom.

The following testimonial is typical: *"N is beginning to mature and recognise that it is he who is in control of his destiny – taking responsibility for his actions and becoming more confident within the lesson. The Basketball Academy has helped with their drive, focus and desire in lessons."*

We have been particularly pleased with a more recent initiative in which the Academy has championed: reading. Academy members now act as reading mentors to younger students, modelling that even 'cool' students read. Further developments are showing early promise, with members of the Academy mentoring students with support for homework.

Match days demonstrate the power of the Academy to develop a culture in which the wider school shows loyalty to the family of the school through basketball. Matches, at home and away, have hundreds of spectators. They are intensely theatrical: the spectators bring music and dol drums. Psychological strategies are used by both players and the audience. In all of this, no matter what their own experience of being intimidated or provoked is, the Academy members have to remain 'Lampton gentlemen'. For the first time in the memory of those in the school, coaches have been hired to take spectators to matches around the nation. Students who at one time might have been infamous or revered for their defiance of school rules are now lauded as representatives of the school. Partisanship has united staff and students.

The Academy has been a study in the efficacy of commitment, resilience and team work, from playing (and losing) at a local level, the school teams now compete on the national stage and routinely reaching the finals of U14 and U18 competitions. We are beginning to see students being selected for advanced professional academies, such as the GB Academy in Bristol, and being sponsored for basketball camps in the US. For students at Lampton who often come from ethnic communities with little tradition of living away from home, such experiences can only be endured with plenty of 'grit'. The students remain intensely aware of their role as trail blazers for those who come after them and trips home always include training sessions in the Academy.

We are committed to the power of sport to transform lives and are determined that the Academy should enable students to begin to earn money in recognition of their skills. Thus, the introduction of Level 1 National Governing Body coaching and refereeing qualifications, which enable students to referee and gain match fees. In a recent development, members of the Academy are allocated to local primary schools. They take responsibility for coaching primary students in basketball for a half term at a time.

We are also prepared to give time to helping other colleagues who are seeking to replicate the success we have had. Many academy directors request visits to gain an insight into how to set up a successful programme. One recent visitor from the South West of England made the following comment: *"I wanted to thank you once again for giving up your time. You, your programme and your pupils were all extremely impressive and inspiring and only make me want to improve our own program further."*

NEXT STEPS

The Academy has produced excellent outcomes for the students and the school in a relatively short space of time. We aim to capitalise on the outreach work in the local community by providing further quality opportunities to the primary education sector in Hounslow.

Alongside this, is the proposal to be a centre for delivering the Advanced Apprenticeship in Sporting Excellence. AASE is designed to meet the needs of elite athletes aged 16-18 who wish to continue their sporting career and gain qualifications at the same time.

Building opportunities for girls is at the forefront of the development of the Academy. The girls' Basketball Academy has now grown to 35 official members, with up to 30 more attending open practice sessions. We have an under-13 team competing at National League level and girls assist in officiating roles at our junior games. Girls also go into the primary sector to provide coaching sessions.

Much of the success of the Academy has been due to the right person, at the right time, in an area, which has enabled students to taste success. Sport has helped to break social disadvantage while providing students with the structure and discipline to achieve their potential. It is concrete evidence of what can be achieved by a committed and talented member of staff given the human and physical resources to kick start change. It is evidence of the impact of a talent-spotting mind-set, underpinned by creating the capacity to enable innovation.

CHAPTER 24

SUCCEEDING WITH SUCCESSION

SIMON APPLEMAN AND DEB MELLOR, JFS SCHOOL

FOCUS AREA

The issue of developing leaders from within is one that occupied many pages of past years' *Going For Great* publications. Indeed, at a time when future recruitment in the profession is said to be at a crisis point, such initiatives take on increased importance. Previous case studies in this area are worth reading as each school that has contributed to the debate has focussed on a different approach. JFS has its own unique programme and we hope that the contents and philosophy of this, supported by systems for feedback and impact, will be of interest.

Whilst others have taken the approach of Acting Up (Oaks Park School – G4G, 2013) or *A Ticket To The Next Bus Stop* (Claremont High School – G4G, 2012), a few years ago we introduced the JFS Enrichment Programme with a focus on Leadership and Management and Teaching and Learning. This case study focuses on the Leadership and Management strand – the overall aim of which has been to equip teachers with the skills to lead and manage their sections and teams in an effective and motivating way. It aims to allow managers to develop personally and professionally and, potentially, to become the Middle and Senior Leaders of the future, addressing issues of future succession.

BACKGROUND CONTEXT

JFS is a Jewish comprehensive school with a roll of over 2000 students, 160 teachers and over 50 support staff. We have sustained consistently high results over the last ten years and were graded Outstanding in our last two Ofsted inspections. Staffing is, generally, very stable. However, recruitment – especially at Middle Leadership level, has proven to be problematic – too often we do not receive the quantity or the quality of applications that we would hope for when advertising some key positions.

The first part of our story, therefore, examines the Leadership and Management programme we have put in place, whilst the second part seeks to evaluate the success of the programme, the impact on recruitment and to draw out lessons learnt.

THE STORY

Our Leadership and Management Enrichment Programme has been running since 2008-2009. Each year, we tweak the courses available, responding to feedback and building on skills previously covered. Crucially, the programme is facilitated by external consultants who specialise in training and coaching for leadership and team development. Their experience of leadership across a vast range of sectors, not just education, is a key aspect. Their ability to create an open, non-judgmental environment for discussion is inspirational itself and a model for leadership. Knowing what questions to ask (and not to ask) and when to ask them is a real skill, allowing the course to remain truly developmental and for colleagues to speak openly and freely. These are complemented by a range of engaging activities, thoughtful and supportive discussion. Collectively, these have helped raise self and team awareness and instilled a positive approach to challenging issues.

A further key principle has been to allow all staff to participate in the programme – which has evolved into a series of four two-hour after-school workshops over three months, concluding with a keynote speaker – regardless of their current role, responsibility or experience. Although there is a logical sequence through the courses, this is not always followed and colleagues are encouraged to opt for the course they feel is most suitable for them. The inclusion of NQTs, support staff and, more recently, colleagues from other schools, has proven to be a highly positive aspect. While no guarantee is given about future promotion, there is an explicit expectation that staff will use new-found skills in their day-to-day work which, in turn, will reflect itself in increased self-awareness, finer leadership skills and – directly or indirectly – better outcomes for students.

Over the years a suite of eight programmes has been developed:

Aspiring Middle Leaders 1: Preparing for leadership

- To understand some principles of leadership – what are the personal qualities needed to be a future manager/leader? Applying these qualities in a school context, and decision making.

- To understand the difference between leadership and management – what are the different leadership styles? Setting goals and achieving results, and the transition to management.

- To understand the principles of change management and to engage positively with them. Understanding the change management curve – how to manage yourself and others through change, and dealing with change.

- To understand what Senior Leaders expect – how will I know if I am capable? How will I know if I am successful?

Aspiring Middle Leaders 2: Preparing yourself for a future leadership role (includes insights discovery)

- So you want to be a manager – where am I now and where do I need to be? Making the move from peer to manager, what a good manager does and are you fit and ready?

- Knowing me, knowing you – excellent managers are excellent communicators, understand yourself, understand others – use a model of behaviour to improve communication and relationship, and learn to deal with difficult people.

- Developing as a manager – the key skills needed early on, decision taking, delegation and motivation.

- Putting it all together – preparing to put yourself forward – what do I have to offer? Packaging yourself in the best way, plus essential interview skills.

Middle Leaders 1: Exploration of issues for those in first years of L&M role

- Approaches for leadership – to understand the underlying beliefs for effective leadership, support and challenge – finding the balance, positive regard and genuineness, expectancy and reinforcement, assessing your underlying beliefs.

- What successful leaders do (part 1) – to identify the four key stages of leading high performance, building your vision and mobilising your staff, feedback, explicitness, developing resilience and motivation.

- What successful leaders do (part 2) – to identify the four key stages of leading high performance, developing staff, situational consistency and enabling, building capacity, delegation.

- Leading change – preparing people for change, getting the process right, understanding people's response to change – making it real, and making it stick.

Middle Leaders 2: Exploration of issues for those more than three years' of L&M experience
(includes insights full circle)

- Preparing for behaviour change – what got you here won't get you there, so what needs to change? Examine the bad habits of senior leaders, address some of your own irritants that you would like to change and commit to behaviour change.

- Planning for 360-degree feedback – understanding self and others to help you pick your feedback respondents, an insights discovery refresher, feedback – giving it constructively, receiving it elegantly and coaching for performance.

- Full-circle feedback debrief and action planning – coaching each other to get full value from your discovery full-circle profile, reactions and responses to your profile – where are you now and where do you want to be? Actions you need to take to get there.

- Lucky dip – to address your outstanding priorities – you decide what and how, a master class in key subject(s), action learning with real-life case studies, action planning for the future.

Middle Leaders 3: Towards outstanding leadership

This programme was less structured than other Leadership and Management Programmes. Each workshop was centred around themes suggested by participants, including: How to Have Difficult Conversations, Time Management, Motivating Others and Holding Others To Account.

- What is a team? Groups and teams, communicating your vision to the team, establishing team purpose and team goals.

- Who is on the team? Different team types, radiators and drains, building trust, accountability, commitment and focus, team strengths, weaknesses and ones to watch, roles and responsibilities around challenge and support.

- What should teams be measuring themselves against? Testing the team against an effectiveness model – where are the gaps or opportunities? Understanding the four pillars of team effectiveness and getting to the next stage – what will it take?

- Honing the high-performance team, being the team leader, valuing and using expertise – supporting and delegating, moving flexibly between teams – what makes you marketable? Image and PR outside of the team.

Coaching and mentoring: An introduction to coaching and mentoring with practical time for coaching each other

- From Transactional to Transformational Leadership – understanding how leadership manifests itself and mastering the essentials of transformational leadership – results, vision, relationships and leading from within.

- Leading from within and developing others – coaching and mentoring defined, their differences, uses and associated skills, a structure for both and practising the process and skills.

- Practising the process and skills continued – what hinders coaching? Peer Coaching, coaching to bring about change.

- Coaching students – review and action planning, applying the skills in your own environment, next steps.

First and foremost, the 360 coaching programme is an extended conversation. It is an opportunity for participants to discuss in confidence their professional development, to celebrate strengths and to identify areas for development. In doing so, the 360 helps to reveal potential 'blind spots' and areas that the participant might be less aware of. It takes the form of collated responses to agreed questions and lasts for four sessions. Responsibility to continue work on the issues is that of the participant, supported by their SLT line manager.

There are five notable features of the courses, which we believe have been integral to its success:

1. The first session of the Aspiring Middle Leaders 1, Exploring Leadership Versus Management, has always been delivered by the Headteacher. This makes an important statement and has been much valued by participants.

2. The INSIGHTS model mentioned above deserves further comment. It is a behavioural model designed to help others to be more effective in their dealings with people. Based solidly upon the work of psychologist Carl Jung, the INSIGHTS model uses four colours to represent different types of work behaviour: Fiery Red, Sunshine Yellow, Earth Green and Cool Blue. Each person has a unique blend of these colours, which help to explain their own style, their strengths and weaknesses, endearing little foibles and irritating bad habits. Through a detailed and practical personal profile, leaders, teams and individuals can learn more about themselves and can gain a competitive edge by learning to be that little bit better at all things people-related.

3. The final session – a keynote lecture – has been delivered from those in education and those who work in the wider world of leadership, including CEOs of major companies. After all, leadership is leadership and the specific sector seems not to make a difference to the lessons to be learnt. Previous guest speakers include Walter Goldsmith (a retired Corporate Vice President and Chief Executive at Black & Decker), Arnold Wagner (former Chair of Governors and Director of Human Resources, Smiths Group PLC), Rachel MacFarlane (Headteacher at Isaac Newton Academy) and Andy Buck (Director of Secondary Education, Academies at United Learning).

4. The 360 coaching programme, in its first year, was introduced to reach those colleagues who, for whatever reason, had not participated in previous programmes. Colleagues were invited to participate and many, though not all, found it a highly valuable experience.

5. Purely logistical, but the most important thing – don't forget the food! We have catered each session with enough tea and coffee, biscuits, cake and fruit ready for the start of each session and a break, taken at the will of the facilitator. After the keynote lecture, we conclude with a catered supper.

When to schedule such a programme is a challenge. When is a good time? Never! Colleagues have faced pressures with marking or reports and occasionally this has impacted on attendance. The dark days of winter can be problematic and sessions have had to be rearranged because of snow. Maintaining an awareness of the balance and dynamics of each group has been important. How and when to seek feedback from participants is important and we have varied the strategy each year. This year, in addition to a full end-of-course evaluation, we have also sent out a short online questionnaire after each session – this is designed to help us in the planning, but also to help colleagues reflect on their learning.

Feedback has been highly positive:

"I have already started implementing ideas and methods into the way that I conduct myself in school. I would hope to be able to continue to move up in my career and pass on information to help others. The course will allow me to have greater insight into understanding the people I am dealing with – leaders, peers or members of my team – how to get along with them and motivate them to give their best."

– Subject Leader

"I just wanted to say thank you for leading the four sessions that I was a part of during the last few months. Teachers can be an unforgiving audience when they are the ones being educated, but I was thoroughly engaged and left each one feeling like I had learnt something new and innovative. In particular, yesterday's session was exceptionally useful as it tackled the hands-on issues that managers face on a day-to-day basis. I'm hoping that further sessions will occur in the future that will build upon the ones you have just run."

– Classroom teacher since appointed to Deputy Subject Leader role

"The programme has inspired me to think and take a different approach to the way in which I would handle and deal with situations in the future. It has also given me an insight into how my approach may impact on others."

– Year Manager

"I hope to be able to put the coaching skills that I learnt into practice during lessons, 1:1s, etc. It has made a huge difference to the way in which I will work! It has already changed the way I approach matters with individuals and groups of all types, in order that they can become more self-reliant."

– Senior Administrator

Participation rates have been fairly consistent and followed expected patterns:

	2008-09	2009-10	2010-11	2011-12	2012-13	2013-14
Asp. Middle Leaders 1	26	24	17			13
Asp. Middle Leaders 2		10	9			
Middle Leaders 1		11	6			
Middle Leaders 2			6		12	
Middle Leaders 3					13	
Middle Leaders 4						15
Coaching and Mentoring				18		
Bespoke 360 Coaching					5	5
TOTAL	**26**	**45**	**38**	**18**	**30**	**33**

Some colleagues have participated in a number of programmes. In total, almost 100 different staff have attended over 200 sessions – a significant programme of leadership development impacting on a great number of staff. However, the numbers are not the only part of the story.

EVALUATION

How does one evaluate such a programme? We have found the Kirkpatrick model – first created by Donald Kirkpatrick in 1959 and since revised – to be particularly effective, with its four stages of:

- **Reaction** – to what extent do participants respond favourably to the training?

- **Skills and knowledge (learning)** – to what degree do participants acquire the intended knowledge, skills, attributes, confidence and commitment based on their participation?

- **Application (behaviour)** – to what degree do participants apply what they learnt during the training when they are back on the job?

- **Impact (results)** – to what degree do targeted outcomes occur as a result of the training and subsequent reinforcement?

After each session, and at the end of each programme, we ask colleagues to complete an online evaluation form. This has proven very helpful in informing us of any tweaks along the way, but it has also been designed to help participants to reflect on their learning.

REACTIONS

The immediate reactions to the sessions have been very positive. Colleagues often comment on and value the dialogue with different staff, the time for guided reflection, the time to stop and think, and realistic yet practical and easy-to-apply strategies for day-to-day work. Critical comments, though few, tend to focus on too much material and not enough time to reflect and review. Occasionally, feedback can be contradictory – for example, some have suggested a more concentrated programme – whilst others would like more time between sessions.

SKILLS AND KNOWLEDGE (LEARNING)

There is no doubt that colleagues benefit from and value greater self-awareness, leadership skills, an ability to understand and relate to others, questioning techniques, affirmation of their own practice and active listening skills, to name but a few. Occasionally, colleagues lack awareness or confidence in applying some of the skills as a Middle Leader, especially where they may not have direct line management responsibilities.

APPLICATION (BEHAVIOUR)

The first two stages of evaluation are important and necessary parts of the process. However, it is when we change behaviours that we can truly consider the Leadership and Management Programme successful. Feedback from colleagues indicates that we do this. Colleagues tell us that they have gone on to improve relationships with those they line-manage, they have developed after-school programmes for students, used questioning techniques in mid-year reviews, used coaching techniques with students and in academic monitoring meetings, reflected more on their own and others' actions/reactions and used a more flexible style of communication. All of this has stemmed from the session attended.

IMPACT (RESULTS)

The Leadership and Management programme is one of the highest-rated CPD programmes we run. Colleagues who have participated in the programme benefit from boosted morale and greater confidence in communication and decision making. In terms of recruitment, out of the 100+ different participants, over half have gone on to receive promotion to a Subject Leader, Deputy Subject Leader, Director of Studies, Year Manager or other post of responsibility, reflecting the increased capacity for and aspiration to Middle Leadership. Additionally, the JFS programme was commended in a recent Ofsted report, which stated: *"Links with JFS School have helped middle leaders improve their practice."*

NEXT STEPS

The Enrichment programme is well established in the JFS calendar. In May/June of each year we start planning the programme and identifying dates for the following academic year. For next year, we anticipate a return of the 'Coaching' programme and further use of the INSIGHT discovery module. Additionally, we will have a discussion as to which individuals or groups of staff will benefit from the 360 bespoke coaching.

CONCLUSION

The JFS Leadership and Management Programme has inspired many of our staff to consider, develop and realise their leadership abilities through a combination of group workshops and individual coaching, utilising aspects of the Insights Discovery and Full Circle Programmes, and their own rich experience. It has been accessed by over 100 teaching and support staff across all levels of experience, offering just the right amount of support and challenge. In addition to raising individual and team awareness, the courses have provided an open environment in which colleagues can reflect on what they do, plus how and why they do it.

The results are clear to see. A significant number of participants in the programmes have gone on to promotion. Additionally, supportive feedback has helped us to evaluate our own programme and to alter provision, leading to the development of new programmes.

CHAPTER 25

MENTORING MATTERS – HERE'S HOW

STEPHANIE GEORGE AND PATRICIA ST LOUIS, PLASHET SCHOOL

FOCUS AREA

This case study describes how the Plashet School Learning Mentor team, based in the school's Learning Support unit, developed its practice to have a greater impact upon student development, achievement and progress, academically, socially and personally.

BACKGROUND CONTEXT

The Learning Support Team at Plashet School consists of three Learning Mentors, a Learning Support Teacher and a Head of Department. The aim of the department is to work with students to overcome barriers to learning. These barriers range in nature and severity from 'return from illness' to 'parental bereavement', 'relationship breakdown', 'social isolation', and 'friendship difficulties'. The team is engaged in working with students to secure a pathway towards achievement.

In 2007, a new Head of Department was appointed. At the time, the team had two Learning Mentors and a temporary Learning Support teacher. The team quickly grew to three Learning Mentors and one permanent teacher. The development of the team and work of the Learning Mentors were linked to aspects of the school development plan. The departmental development plan detailed this specifically – below is a snapshot of part of the plan.

Area for development (linked to one-year SDP Strategic Priorities)	Desired Outcomes	Actions	Evidence of successful completion
1. Achievement	1.3 Learning Personalisation	1.3.1 Interventions to enhance progress/attainment thereby narrowing the gaps in rates of progress a) AQA Progress with Learning Mentor Course b) AQA Peer Mediation Course c) Craft Club	Quantitative and qualitative evaluation of the impact of interventions a) AQA Progress with Learning Mentor Course b) AQA Peer Mediation Course

Linking the department's Development Plan directly into the School Development Plan gave a direction for the department's work with students that had both qualitative and quantitative tangible outcomes.

THE STORY

In 2009, with a team of three, the team developed a highly structured and formal system of working with staff and students. The process looked like this:

Learning Mentor Intervention	Learning Mentor Intervention as part of whole school pastoral support	Whole School Pastoral Involvement
All referrals are completed on a form, following an agreement on criteria for referral after full consultation with year leaders. The referral is counter-signed by the Year Leader, who obtains parental consent.		All Learning Mentors are attached to a year team and attend all Year team and pastoral meetings.
All students, after initial rapport building appointment, are baseline assessed using an assessment tool designed by the Plashet team.		Learning Mentors attend Year team assemblies.
A shared and student focussed mentoring action plan is devised with the student, and all action plans are SMART with subject progress, teacher input, curriculum, personal, social information and student input		Learning Mentors attend parents' evenings and year group events.
Mentoring monitoring meetings take place and a review of targets and action plans may follow.		Learning Mentors are involved in pastoral plans, SEN meetings, attendance meetings and EWO meetings.
Reassessment follows, with a scrutiny of progress academically, socially and personally, to examine for upward movement and progress.		Learning Mentors support the Year Leader and SLT member with student matters.
Termly review of the Learning Mentor's caseload by the Head of Department takes place with a report back to the referring Year Team Leader to complete the cycle. The Head of Department and Learning Mentor make a decision about when the mentoring should end.		Evaluating the impact of their work and reporting to the pastoral team on a termly basis following case work monitoring by the Head of Department.
At the end of the mentoring intervention, (which may take six, 12, or more weeks) the student evaluates the mentoring intervention.		Data tracking incidents and events and providing information to pastoral team leaders.

The team members contribute to the school newsletters and internal bulletins and they participate in and lead a variety of events – for example, Anti-Bullying Week, where the mentors run a 'chat board'. This is usually a topical issue that students discuss and comment on throughout the week. Reference book albums that mark each Anti-Bullying Week since 2009 have been created and held for viewing in the department. There is also a student-led, and mentor staffed, drop-in during the week, together with peer mediators offering short restorative justice sessions.

The team has been involved in a number of events over the past five years, including making two programmes with Teachers TV – Learning Mentors In Schools and Behaviour Resource Review, hosting visits from staff from other schools to share good practice and a round table discussion between the Chair of Governors and the Peer Mediators.

Students are identified by the pastoral teams for intervention. The criteria for referral was agreed with Year Co-ordinators and shared with all Year teams. The Year Co-ordinator is responsible for making referrals. The criteria is transparent and includes: unresolved friendship issues, social isolation, bereavement, family or domestic concerns, attendance, assertiveness and confidence issues, self-esteem and emotional literacy concerns. The Learning Mentors publish their appointments list each week in the staff bulletin so that staff are clear about when the students are to attend appointments. Additionally, the Learning Mentors keep a daily log of all appointments and drop-ins for data and statistically monitoring.

Each term, the Head of Department conducts a review with each Learning Mentor, examining the progress of each student, and a decision is made to close, continue or monitor a particular student case. At this meeting, the action plan is reviewed and amended. A student may have Learning Mentor intervention for between six and 30 weeks, but cases are always reviewed every term. At the end of each term, the case is evaluated by the student and the Learning Mentor.

A range of resources is used in the Learning Support Unit for assistance with a number of issues and interventions. Firstly, the team uses self-assessments to gauge the baseline for the students. The assessment provides a measure of the student's attitude to learning. The assessment covers the following areas: self-esteem, academic achievement, attendance, behaviour and empathy. The assessment is completed at the start and end of each mentoring case to measure the impact of mentoring.

The Learning Mentors use a formalised process with key documentation to ensure consistency of approach: a referral form, a baseline assessment, an introduction to mentoring protocol and confidentiality statement, a curriculum assessment, a target setting sheet and an action plan. These resources are differentiated for KS3 and KS4. Curriculum data and attendance data are also scrutinised. At the end of the mentoring cycle, students complete an evaluation form and all mentoring intervention is monitored by the Head of Department who conducts termly reviews of every Mentor's caseload.

The initial mentoring assessments cover aspects of students' approaches to learning, which include confidence, attendance at school, punctuality, peer relationships, relationships with teachers and preparedness for learning, organisation skills and participation in extracurricular activities. The assessment aims to build a full picture of the student to enable the Learning Mentor to focus on the issues that impede learning, participation and achievement.

The action plan is then negotiated with the student to work through the identified issues. For example, a mentoring session to support a student experiencing peer group issues might include using the *Mentoring Questioning Dice, The Sunshine Thinking Activity,* the *Show Me The Difference Activity, or The Top Five Cards.* These resources would help the student to get underneath the skin of the issue to work out how and why the peer group issue is affecting their participation in learning, and to effectively manage and/or overcome the issue. The team uses a range of interactive resources to support their work, such as PASS, (Pupil Attitude to Self and School) and SNAP-B (Special Educational Needs Programme: Behaviour). However, the most effective assessment tool has been the one that the team has developed and designed for the school's students and context themselves.

The Head of Department and one of the Learning Mentors attended an AQA Award Development course and learnt how to write AQA qualifications. They then developed a national qualification for demonstrating the progress students made. *The AQA Progress And Learning With A Learning Mentor 77261* was the first qualification they penned. Three more followed: *Anger Management, Peer Mediation and Relating Skills.* The AQA 77261 provides an opportunity for students to demonstrate progress in a formalised way, which is accredited. It is the first national award for assessing progress made by students when working with a Learning Mentor.

The outcomes of the award include:

- The student and mentor feedback.

- Individual target setting and action planning.

- Opportunities to discuss progress and ways forward.

- Identifying strengths, weaknesses and barriers to learning.

IMPACT

Feedback from the students who have been supported by a Learning Mentor is extremely encouraging:

"The first time I had a Learning Mentor was in Year 8. I didn't know what to expect. As the appointments continued, I began to let my guard down (not fully) and was able to trust her and tell her things. Now when she asks me questions, I don't worry about being judged or looked at in a certain way. I know she is there to help. I don't normally have a bond with a member of staff or in fact anyone with authority however I felt comfortable talking to her."

"In the past, I had a problem with attendance and punctuality. I find timing quite difficult and am late for most things i.e. school in the morning. I had a wake-up call when I had a talk with my Learning Mentor regarding this issue and she told me I really need to improve for the future or else colleges and universities won't be impressed and I would be rejected. Therefore, I have become more punctual and even set my clock forward 10 minutes to ensure I'm not late. This has helped as my form tutor has recognised my improvement and praised my achievement. It felt good to have my behaviour and punctuality reviewed as improving as opposed to deteriorating."

"Two people I'd apologise to before I leave THIS school? My two mentors, they've seen me in my angriest, my downfall and my up rise. I'm grateful that I have had them. My family are proud of me and are no longer disappointed. Going off to college will be hard, but I'll take everything I've learnt from my second home, the LSU, and always use it."

"My mentor helped me change and look at school with a new attitude. I feel that I could talk to her about anything and anyone. She pushed me and encouraged me to become a better student and told me I could achieve my potential if I tried hard, which made me gain confidence about what I could do. I just finished some of my exams and have a couple more exams left to do and I revised really hard for them and I think I did well. My mentor gave me some ideas on how to revise through revision timetables and other revision skills. I used these ideas to revise with which is one of the main reasons why I think I did well in my exams. I was really focused on it so I think I have made some progress."

The team's book Activities To Help Young People Deal With Bullying was published in spring 2014. In July 2013, the team won the Times Educational Award for Support Team Of The Year 2013.

NEXT STEPS

The team will move forward by developing assessment tools for mentoring, using the Apple iPad device, and also plans to develop further accreditation.

CHAPTER 26

A TASTE OF VOCATIONAL LEARNING: THE TUESDAY PROGRAMME

PAULINE WILLIAMS AND LISA COAKLEY, CLAPTON GIRLS' ACADEMY

FOCUS AREA

This study focuses on the establishment of an alternative vocational programme at Clapton Girls' Academy and evaluates the impact of this initiative on students' re-engagement, motivation, attendance, behaviour and aspirations.

AIMS

We wanted to address the needs of a small group of students at KS3 who we thought would benefit from some alternative provision, whilst at the same time reducing the number of students at KS4 who needed an alternative provision placement off site. We felt that if we addressed the needs of these students earlier on, then we would have fewer students needing an alternative programme at KS4.

Given that there was no suitable provision available in the borough at the time, we fully embraced the opportunity to create our own bespoke programme. We secured some funding for one year and had the opportunity to work closely with one of the borough's alternative provision providers (New Regent's College). Together, we came up with the idea of a vocational programme, using external providers who would deliver sessions both on and off site.

The aims of our vocational programme were fivefold:

Aims	Measured
1. To improve student motivation, self-confidence and engagement with education.	Through attendance and grades.
2. To improve student behaviour and staff and student relations.	Through frequency of behaviour incidents and staff observations.
3. To improve emotional well-being to help students to overcome barriers to attainment.	Through staff observations, student responses and parental feedback.
4. To gain good academic attainment with successful completion of accredited units.	By whether the students fulfil the assessment criteria.
5. To identify which students may benefit from full time alternative provision in Years 10 and 11, thereby ensuring clearly defined pathways post the programme.	By whether the students fulfil the assessment criteria.

BACKGROUND CONTEXT

The consideration of a bespoke programme really began at least a year before its implementation. Students in KS3 who were at risk of fixed term exclusions or permanent exclusions, the disaffected or disengaged, those at risk of becoming NEETs, or students who would benefit from a more flexible, vocational programme – were already being tracked and monitored, and the consideration of providing something alternative was already on the discussion table.

Although the actual programme had not been developed in full detail, we were clear that we wanted (and needed) to provide something for the girls who were showing that the curriculum on offer at the time did not meet their needs. Although the traditional KS4 off-site alternative provision pathway was available, we were focused on providing a course for students at KS3 to see if this could mean that they might not need KS4 alternative provision.

THE STORY

Spring term 2011 was when the programme initially began to take shape. Following conversations with a representative from Hackney Learning Trust and Regent's College, and the sharing of our expectations of the programme, we decided that four positive and engaged students – two Year 9 girls and two Year 10s – were ideal candidates for the initial course. The idea of a practical, vocational taster programme made sense when we considered the needs of these students. They had found the full-time academic curriculum challenging and showed that they would benefit from a more flexible or practical input to their curriculum diet. They also lacked confidence and self-esteem.

Providing them with the opportunity to experience vocational taster sessions on a weekly basis would, and did, make these four students feel very special. They worked effectively within this small group and established good group dynamics considering that they had not interacted previously. Had these girls been referred to the more 'traditional' off-site provision, they would not have experienced the range of vocational tasters that they did. Learning new tasks and being put into unfamiliar situations in a very small group increased the students' participation and required them to be very confident from the beginning of each new session.

The outside providers (who were selected by Hackney Learning Trust in conjunction with New Regent's College's alternative provision team) provided the students with a four-week cooking course held at Shoreditch Spa and a four-week introduction to film making and music video making. They also had an introduction to fashion, hair and beauty, retail, and to the range of work carried out at Hackney City Farm. The students took part in the programme for a half-day a week over two terms. They were given a clear set of guidelines they needed to follow in order to take part in the programme. At the end of the programme, both of the older students were accepted onto appropriate courses at the local college, something they had previously been reluctant to consider due to poor self-perception and low aspirations.

During 2011-2012, we moved towards a longer day. By September 2012, the offer became a one-day weekly project run with INSPIRE (which provides a range of vocational facilitators in the borough). Students followed their usual timetable for four days in school and had one day involved in an alternative vocational curriculum. There was the possibility for accreditation and progression routes post KS3/KS4 if needed. We also earmarked the funding to support one full-time Learning Assistant whose role was to facilitate the whole programme and to monitor the students involved, as well as act as a mentor to the students who were participating in the programme.

The programme had a change of name and a confirmed day. The Tuesday Programme was born. It was shaped to address the needs of the most appropriate Year group, which for us, was Year 9. We chose the longest day of our week because it allowed us to fit in more activities. This bespoke course now allowed for students to have input into the units, choosing one or two vocational aspects that they wished to explore (depending on availability). Students were selected on the basis of need and had to have parental agreement. Students selected were discussed at Leadership level and baseline data was used to inform decisions. Parents were contacted by the Learning Assistant to share good news and to discuss any concerns. There was a 'contract' that both students and parents signed, and expectations were explained clearly within this. The Learning Assistant met with all parents/carers of the students participating (at the parents' consultation evening) and there was the opportunity to discuss wider issues, consolidating the joined-up nature of the programme and the students' holistic experience. Home and Academy links were also further strengthened.

We feel that we were providing a relevant and engaging vocational curriculum that ensured that the Year 9 students involved would remain in education, have improved attendance, fewer behaviour issues and would gain the experience and knowledge of vocational courses; thus providing a pathway to alternative provision at KS4, should they need it. There has been a reduction in the number of students we plan alternative provision for.

The nature of the course, being comprised of a small group with a high adult-to-student ratio and being centred around creative and practical work, has meant that the girls' individual, emotional and social needs are well met, and that their emotional and social development is encouraged through individualised support. It has been good value for money at about £40 per head per session, based on a group of six students in 2012-2013. This has proved to be an effective use of Pupil Premium funding.

A sample Tuesday Programme timetable

Tuesday	Course	Venue
25th September	Catering	Shoreditch Spa
2nd October	Catering	Shoreditch Spa
9th October	Catering	Shoreditch Spa
16th October	Catering	Shoreditch Spa
23rd October	Catering	Shoreditch Spa
HALF TERM		
6th November	Film Making	Clapton Girls Academy (CGA)
20th November	Film Making	CGA
27th November	Film Making	CGA
4th December	Fashion and Textiles	CGA
11th December	Fashion and Textiles	CGA
18th December	Fashion and Textiles	CGA
CHRISTMAS HOLIDAYS		
8th January	Sport and Leisure	CGA
15th January	Sport and Leisure	CGA
22nd January	Sport and Leisure	Footsteps Sports Academy
29th January	Hair Styling	CGA
5th February	Hair Styling	CGA
12th February	Hair Styling	The Hair Project

HALF TERM		
26th February	Hair Styling	The Hair Project
5th March	Nail Art	CGA
12th March	Nail Art	CGA
19th March	Art and Design	CGA
26th March	Alternative Timetable Day	CGA
EASTER HOLIDAY		
16th April	Art and Design	CGA
23rd April	Construction and Mechanics	Camden Job Train
30th April	Construction and Mechanics	Camden Job Train
7th May	Outdoor Cooking & Farm Skills	Hackney City Farm
14th May	Outdoor Cooking & Farm Skills	Hackney City Farm
21st May	Outdoor Cooking & Farm Skills	Hackney City Farm

IMPACT

As previously stipulated, one of the aims of the programme was to either maintain or improve the girls' grades. In the most recent cohort, all students either maintained their grade levels or moved up a grade level in English. The same trend could be seen for Mathematics. These were important findings, since they indicated that *The Tuesday Programme,* despite requiring students to miss a whole day of curricular study, did not appear to have an adverse impact upon academic achievements. The girls' portfolios, consisting of written work, designs, artefacts and research, have been assessed and students have been awarded with the NOCN Key Skills Level 3 qualification.

There has been a marked reduction in the number of students requiring alternative placements at KS4. (We were planning for eight students in 2012, now we plan for four students in 2014). *The Tuesday Programme* is replacing some alternative provision expenditure now, since we do not need to fund as many alternative provision places at KS4.

Looking at students' attendance in the autumn term compared to the spring and summer terms, two students that were of particular concern in relation to poor attendance showed a dramatic improvement, another student's attendance improved consistently throughout the year. The rest of the students' attendance remained above 96% which was the academy's required minimum attendance level. Throughout the year, the average attendance of the Tuesday group was marginally higher than the rest of Year 9. This was very promising considering poor attendance was a concern for some of the girls who were selected for the programme.

From discussions with a number of the girls' teachers and support staff, it is clear that the girls' behaviour had gradually improved throughout the year. Staff commented that the girls were calmer and more mature in class and seemed happier. Evidence of improvement in behaviour was particularly well illustrated by increased positive staff comments regarding off-site visits with the girls.

All of the students' parents have expressed support and gratitude for the programme and stated that their child enjoyed it. One mother was particularly positive about the programme, stating: *"I think it is amazing (The Tuesday Programme). M's really improved. She goes to school more, she tries harder and she goes to PE now. I am really proud of her."*

Students have said:

"*The Tuesday Programme is my favourite day of the week, we are really lucky.*"

"*I think I behave better now. I used to get angry but now I'm better at walking away.*"

(In response to the sports and leisure taster): "I want to start playing football again. It's made me realise how good I am at it and I want to join a girls' team."

"*I like learning something new each week and meeting different people.*"

"*I was proud of my football and boxing certificate and I learned new skills.*"

"*We do fun things and we are lucky we get to do it. Some of (the) things we have done can help us in life.*"

The facilitators are also very positive:

"*These girls show amazing potential, some of the styles I have seen today are as good as some of our college students'. The girls' effort and behaviour have been great; they are welcome at the salon anytime.*"
– Hair Styling Facilitator, (Andrew Curtis) from The Hair Project

"*It's been so great having girls here for a change; we hardly ever have girls' schools come. It's been really interesting for me and I hope to try and get more girls involved in mechanics.*"
– Mechanics Workshop Facilitator.

The Learning Assistant involved commented: *"The variety of the tasters set and the diversity within the facilitators meant the girls had a number of new, exciting and educational experiences that have broadened their horizons and given them a great insight into what is available to them."*

Aims	Measured	Achieved
1. To improve student motivation, self-confidence and engagement with education.	Through attendance and grades.	96% or higher attendance. Maintained grades for English and Maths or improved by at least one grade.
2. To improve student behaviour and staff and student relations.	Through behaviour call-out frequency (and staff observations)	Marked reduction in call-outs for these students compared to when they first started the programme.
3. To improve emotional well-being to help students to overcome barriers to attainment.	Through staff observations, student responses and parental feedback.	Sample of quotes from students, parents and staff indicate wellbeing and addressing underlying issues that could lead to disengagement.
4. To gain good academic attainment with successful completion of accredited units.	By whether the students fulfil the assessment criteria.	All students in both cohorts have completed the units to achieve accreditation.
5. To identify which students may benefit from full time alternative provision in Years 10 and 11, thereby ensuring clearly defined pathways post-programme.	By a reduction in the number of students who need full time alternative provision.	One out of the nine students (2012-2013) needed alternative placement at KS4. One out of the 10 students in 2013-2014 will need an alternative placement at KS4.

REFLECTIONS AND EVALUATION

Now, in 2014, the programme is fully embedded as part of the Year 9 curriculum. The students follow a clear overall outline for the course, including the accredited NOCN elements. Each year, the units will be fine-tuned and adapted according to the cohort. Each year, disengaged students are re-engaged. Students have their achievements publicly recognised during the Year 9 End of Year Achievement Assembly. Our link person from Regent's College and the Learning Assistant, who facilitates the programme, present the girls with their awards.

NEXT STEPS

The challenge of recruiting the right facilitator continues! Perhaps we will combine this role with a Home/Academy Liaison Officer role. We need to continually review and revise the programme so there is a link that runs throughout the whole programme (a set of tasks or a project) to ensure cohesion.

We plan to monitor the new KS4 Teens and Toddlers Programme that is running from January 2014 and will allow for progression for some of the students from *The Tuesday Programme*.

This programme gives teens the skills to consider issues that can lead to disengagement, whilst on a work experience scheme where they mentor a child in a nursery. We are mindful of what place there can be for *The Tuesday Programme* in the great 'unknown/known' proposed changes to the curriculum, 2015 and beyond.

THE 9 PILLARS OF GREATNESS

PILLAR 1: A SHARED VISION, VALUES, CULTURE AND ETHOS, BASED ON THE HIGHEST EXPECTATIONS OF ALL MEMBERS OF THE SCHOOL COMMUNITY

- The vision of the school is clear, understood and shared by all and underpinned by the school's values, philosophy and ethos.

- There is a compelling and inclusive moral purpose driving the school forward, based on equity, social justice and unshakeable principles.

- All those connected with the school are able to articulate their collective values and beliefs and their attention is focused on working to a common ideal and shared goals.

- The vision and aspirations of the school are optimistic and based on a 'growth mind-set' philosophy. There is no ceiling on the expectations of the performance of any member of the school community.

- The vision looks confidently forward — redirecting approaches, anticipating developments and inspiring changes through being bold, positive and ambitious.

- The school's culture and ethos result from the application of its vision and values and manifest themselves in customs, rituals, symbols, stories and language. They are successfully expressed through the ways that members of the school community relate to each other and work together, through the organisation of the school's structures, systems and physical environment and through the quality of learning for both pupils and adults.

- The culture and ethos are embedded in the basic assumptions and beliefs that are shared by all members of the school community and are the 'glue' that holds everyone together.

- There is a commitment to excellence, to remaining open to new ideas and to thinking in new ways.

- Leaders at all levels act in a way that is consistent with the vision and values of the school.

- The collective vision permeates the whole institution and is felt by everyone who visits.

PILLAR 2: INSPIRATIONAL LEADERSHIP AT ALL LEVELS THROUGHOUT THE SCHOOL

- The school's leadership is transformational — visionary, inspiring and values-based. Leaders are able to envision and share a compelling view of the school in the future, they communicate this effectively to the entire school community. Leaders are cheerleaders, enthusiasts, forecasters and dramatists.

- There is excellent operational leadership. Leaders are planners, organisers, resourcers, tacticians and deliverers. They pay attention to detail and get results — they are resilient and determined.

- The school's leadership is transactional — based on building and sustaining high-quality relationships between leaders and led. Leaders are nurturers, trainers, mentors and coaches.

- The school practises invitational and distributed leadership (between staff and students), based on the belief that all have the potential for growth and development, in the knowledge that everyone has a different profile of leadership qualities and with an understanding that the best leaders in one situation may not be the most effective in another. Shared leadership demonstrates mutual respect and trust.

- Leaders deliberately build the capacity for growth and adaptation to change through careful recruitment and retention, developing the workforce and fostering learning in the workplace. They see innovation as part of their day-to-day activity.

- Leaders strive to create and embed aspiration and ambition and develop creativity, wider learning and supported risk-taking.

- Leaders develop an optimistic, lively, energising environment to maximise the additional effort of members of the school community.

- Extended and system-wide leadership is widely practised through school-to-school collaboration, the building of networks and quality relationships with outside agencies, and the provision of an infrastructure for new approaches to innovation and change.

- Leadership characteristics widely observed in the school include a sense of moral purpose, clarity, creativity, transparency, trust, conviction, consistency, courage, resilience, energy, enthusiasm, hope and humility.

PILLAR 3: EXCEPTIONAL TEACHING, LEARNING, ASSESSMENT AND FEEDBACK TO SUPPORT THE HIGHEST LEVELS OF ATTAINMENT AND ACHIEVEMENT

- The promotion of high-quality learning is at the heart of the school's endeavours – learning without limits and success for all are guiding principles.

- There is a clear view of pedagogy that promotes expert teaching and enquiry-based learning.

- Teachers provide appropriate challenges and employ excellent classroom management and organisational skills.

- Staff members have considered collectively what constitutes effective learning and put in place effective processes and practices and varied teaching techniques to maximise achievement and attainment.

- Teachers' excellent subject knowledge consistently challenges and inspires pupils.

- Learning is personalised to individual needs, interests and current attainment levels, so as to maximise students' engagement and enable excellent rates of progress.

- Assessment for learning is very well developed and consistently utilised, with regular opportunities for learning dialogues, self and peer assessment and diagnostic and developmental feedback based on accurate and robust pupil performance data.

- A variety of learning technologies and resources, which encourage independent thinking and learning, are used highly effectively and imaginatively across the curriculum.

- Students are taught to learn independently so that homework becomes an effective opportunity for learning through practice, preparation, elaboration and exploration, paving the way for future learning and seamlessly linking learning in one lesson to the next.

- The constant promotion of self-esteem through high expectations and ambition leads to the pupils assuming responsibility for their learning and behaviour.

- Children and young people are encouraged to aim high. They are provided with information, advice and guidance on future opportunities to enable them to make informed and aspirational choices and to prepare them for the next stage of their learning.

- Enrichment is every pupil's entitlement: opportunities to learn beyond the classroom inspire and motivate pupils and lead to outstanding achievement.

PILLAR 4: A RELENTLESS FOCUS ON ENGAGING AND INVOLVING STUDENTS

- Students are involved in leading, managing and planning their educational experience at all levels.

- The student voice is strong throughout the school, through the Student Council and student leadership teams but also through day-to-day opportunities in every classroom, such as active expression technology, student surveys, feedback and evaluations which capture every voice on school matters.

- The school is a 'Learning Commons' where everyone is considered a learner and everyone has a responsibility to support and encourage each other in their learning.

- Students are citizens of the school in a real sense, playing a key part in the appointment of staff, editing and contributing to school publications and communications, observing and evaluating learning, being represented on school working parties and the governing body and its committees, and acting as ambassadors in representing the school.

- Student focus groups are tasked with researching, investigating and reporting back on school issues such as marking, homework, sanctions and rewards.

- Students are regularly used as peer tutors and co-teachers. They co-plan schemes of learning and co-construct learning activities with staff.

- Peer counsellors, mediators and mentors are used to aid behaviour management and maintain and re-build student relationships.

- Students design, plan and carry out extended projects and produce publicly exhibited outputs such as publications, shows and presentations.

- The school celebrates and supports the achievements of students in their lives as members of the wider community.

PILLAR 5: PERSONALISED AND HIGHLY EFFECTIVE CONTINUOUS PROFESSIONAL DEVELOPMENT WITHIN A LEARNING COMMUNITY

- The school continually emphasises the importance of the study of learning and teaching as the core business of the school.

- There is effective staff development which involves discussion, coaching, mentoring and observing. It develops staff as teachers and leaders.

- All members of staff feel valued, invested in and developed.

- The school is a knowledge-creating institution which audits professional knowledge and manages, validates and disseminates new knowledge.

- High performance is sustained through effective knowledge transfer between schools and other leading organisations.

- The school is a learning community. Staff and governors, as well as students, regularly and openly model their learning and articulate their own learning challenges and goals.

- Learning groups/communities are fostered and developed, which present, review and adapt existing practice and provide quality CPD led by professionals for professionals.

- Innovation and improvement promote critical thinking, build capacity and sustain the vision.

- The school is enquiry-minded, geared to innovation and research, and has a commitment to publishing case studies and organising learning seminars and conferences.

- The school fully mobilises its intellectual, social and organisational capital to produce excellent educational outcomes.

PILLAR 6: A STIMULATING AND INCLUSIVE ENVIRONMENT AND CLIMATE FOR LEARNING

- The school has consistent and high expectations of the behaviour of children, young people and adults and the relationships between them, based on mutual respect, honour, trust and kindness.

- A stimulating visual backdrop to learning is created by the public presentation of pupils' work, learning walls, whole school displays and exhibitions, the use of photographs, pictures, quotations and plasma screens. Displays reinforce the love of subjects and learning, celebrate achievement and progress and raise aspirations.

- Considerable attention is paid to the whole school environment and the quality of the daily experience of those who work and learn in the school: the entrance foyer as a welcoming area, the playground, lunch facilities, toilets, corridors and social spaces as bright, safe and quality places that enhance the climate.

- The school is outward-facing, welcoming to parents and the community, inviting and encouraging them into school to use resources and facilities.

- There is a high quality infrastructure in place to support learning – the library, resource bases, the use of teaching assistants and learning mentors.

- The school is flexibly designed for personalised learning, with spaces allowing for a variety of learning and teaching approaches, supporting knowledge sharing and learning amongst teachers and support staff and emphasising participation and collaboration.

- Individual classrooms and learning areas are planned to encourage pupils' autonomous learning, their ownership of and responsibility for spaces and risk-taking within a safe environment.

- The use of digital technologies – both within and outside the classrooms and schools – enhance learning.

- Pupils are taught about healthy lifestyles, how to avoid risky behaviours, build successful relationships, manage emotions and act responsibly as mature citizens.

PILLAR 7: A RICH AND CREATIVE CURRICULUM, WITHIN AND BEYOND THE CLASSROOM, FULLY MEETING THE NEEDS OF INDIVIDUALS AND GROUPS OF STUDENTS

- The curriculum is concerned with the acquisition of knowledge and understanding, the development of learning skills and the fostering of positive character traits. It supports the development of lively, enquiring minds and the ability to question and argue rationally.

- The curriculum helps pupils to understand the world in which they live, and the interdependence of individuals, groups and nations, enabling them to enter the wider world as active and responsible participants in society.

- Pupils have the opportunity to learn and practice skills that will prepare them for careers in a fast-changing world.

- The school's curriculum provides memorable experiences and rich opportunities for high-quality learning and wider personal development.

- Learning and teaching are personalised throughout the curriculum through pathways and tailored programmes for a wide range of pupils with differing needs, so that all are able to participate, progress and achieve.

- Students are provided with cultural opportunities beyond their prior experience and their horizons are widened by a comprehensive programme of trips, activities, speakers, field work and extracurricular sessions.

- Engagement in enrichment activities is an expectation of all staff and students.

- The curriculum provides a context for moral learning and experience and overtly focuses on, recognises and celebrates character development.

- Excellent cross-curricular links and the promotion of literacy, numeracy, communication and ICT skills in every subject area, contribute to an outstanding whole curriculum.

- Pupils' enjoyment of learning is evident from their interest, concentration, enthusiasm, engagement and progress across a range of subjects and experiences.

- The school is at the forefront of successful and innovative curriculum design.

PILLAR 8: HIGH QUALITY PARTNERSHIPS WITH PARENTS, THE COMMUNITY, OTHER SCHOOLS AND NETWORKS, LOCALLY, NATIONALLY AND INTERNATIONALLY

- The school recognises its responsibility for supporting the education of young people throughout the local area and developing leadership in the system. It establishes links with local schools, especially those in challenging circumstances. It makes a system-wide contribution through a sustained and substantial contribution to the local, national and/or international community.

- The school looks globally to learn from best educational practice and seeks to forge and develop links with schools across the world for mutual improvement.

- The school seeks to build positive interactions with all parents and successfully engages with those who are hard to reach, working in partnership to support their children's learning and maximise their progress.

- The staff appreciate that they cannot fully understand their students if they do not have knowledge of their out-of-school lives, influences and experiences. The staff members have systems for developing their knowledge of the students' lives out of school and they reflect on and utilise the knowledge they glean.

- The staff members understand and celebrate the opportunities, but also appreciate and face up to the challenges, presented by their particular community context.

- The school understands that community links are not just about reaching out to help the community, but to learn from and make better use of existing resources.

- The school and its community create shared beliefs about what they can achieve together.

- The school is clear about what it means by community cohesion and is united in its conviction about its duty to promote it.

- All students, supported and encouraged by the school, are contributing to and enriching the local community.

- The school's facilities and resources are utilised fully by the local community. A wealth of community groups are linked with the school and involved in enriching the curriculum. Through these strong links, the school's ethos permeates the local community.

PILLAR 9: ROBUST AND RIGOROUS SELF-EVALUATION, DATA ANALYSIS AND COLLECTIVE REVIEW

- The school has a self-evaluating culture where collective review, books looks, learning walks and lesson observations are used as an opportunity to increase the common wealth of intellectual curiosity, leading to an extension and sharing of knowledge and ensuring consistently high standards.

- The school as an organisation learns its way forward, building in time for collective enquiry, reviewing evidence and continually striving for betterment.

- There is a regular and forensic analysis of performance data, leading to discussions about strategies for improvement, the implementation of effective action plans and the securing of accountability.

- The school practises appreciative enquiry by distinguishing the best of 'what is', fostering a dialogue for new knowledge around 'what should be' and creating a vision for 'what will be'.

- There is a continuous process of reflection that becomes implicit in the way in which all within the school community talk about their work and learning and which keeps the school aware of its inner life.

- Self-evaluation at all levels is grounded in sophisticated, accurate and open analysis and is used unflinchingly to compare performance against the most stretching of benchmarks.

- The school regularly seeks feedback from and takes full account of the views of students, parents and the community in evaluating its progress. It learns from its mistakes and accepts the challenge of continual improvement.

- The school makes good use of external critical friends, including peer schools, at key points in its journey to provide an open and rigorous reality check.

BIBLIOGRAPHY

Barber, M and Mourshed, M.
How The World's Best Performing Systems Come Out On Top (2007), McKinsey & Co.

Barber, M, and Chijoke, C and Mourshed, M.
How The World's Most Important Improved School Systems Keep Getting Better (2010), McKinsey & Co.

Berwick, G.
Engaging In Excellence (2010), 2 Vols: 'The Approach' and 'Moral Capital'.

Brighouse, T.M and Woods, D.C.
Inspirations – A Collection Of Commentaries To Promote School Improvement (2006), Network Continuum.

Brighouse, T.M and Woods, D.C.
What Makes A Good School Now? (2008), Network Continuum.

Brighouse, T.M and Woods, D.C.
The A-Z Of School Improvement – Principles And Practices (2013), Bloomsbury.

Bubb, S and Earley, P.
Leading And Managing Continuous Professional Development (2007), Sage Publications.

Bubb, S and Earley, P.
Helping Staff Development In Schools (2010), Sage Publications.

Buck, A.
What Makes A Great School? (2013), 2nd Edition, The London Leadership Strategy & National College.

Claxton, G. Building Learning Power (2002).
Claxton, G and Lucas, B. New Kinds Of Smart (2010), Open University Press.

Coates, M. (Ed)
Shaping A New Education Landscape (2010), Continuum.

Collins, J.
Good To Great (2001), Random House.

Covey, S.
The Speed Of Trust (2006), Simon & Schuster.

DfE
The Importance Of Teaching – The Schools White Paper (2010).

Dweck, C.
Mindset, The New Psychology Of Success (2006), Random House.

Earley, P and Porritt, V. (Ed)
Effective Practices In Continuous Professional Development: Lessons From Schools (2009).

Fullan, M.
The Moral Imperative Of School Leadership (2004), Sage Publications.

Fullan, M.
Leadership Development – The Larger Context (2008), Jossey-Bass.

Fullan, M.
The Six Secrets Of Change (2009), Corwin Press.

Fullan, M.
The Principal – Three Keys To Maximising Impact (2014), Jossey-Bass.

Gladwell, M.
The Tipping Point (2000), Little Brown & Company.

Gladwell, M.
Outliers: The Story Of Success (2008), Allen Lane.

Goleman, D.
Focus: The Hidden Driver of Excellence (2013), Bloomsbury.

Gray, S.P and Streshley, W.A.
From Good Schools To Great Schools (2008), Corwin Press.

Hargreaves, A and Fullan, M.
Professional Capital (2012).

Hargreaves, D.H.
A New Shape for Schooling? (2006), SSAT.

Hargreaves, D.H.
The Four Deeps In Action (2008), SSAT.

Harris, A.
Distributed School Leadership (2008), Routledge.

Hattie, J.
Visible Learning: A Synthesis Of Over 800 Meta-Analyses Relating To Achievement (2008).

Hattie, J.
Visible Learning For Teachers (2011).

Hopkins, D.
Every School A Great School (2007), OUP.

Levin, B.
How To Change 5000 Schools (2008),
Harvard Education Press.

Lucas, B.
Revolution – How to Thrive in Crazy Times (2009), Crown House Publishing.

Macfarlane, R and Woods, D.C. (Eds)
Going For Great (2010),
The London Leadership Strategy & National College.

Macfarlane, R and Woods, D.C. (Eds)
Glimpses Of Greatness (2011),
The London Leadership Strategy & National College.

Macfarlane, R and Woods, D.C. (Eds)
Growing Greatness (2012),
The London Leadership Strategy & National College.

Macfarlane, R and Woods, D.C. (Eds)
Generating Greatness (2013),
The London Leadership Strategy & National College.

Marshall, P. (Ed)
The Tail – How England's Schools Fail One Child In Five And What Can Be Done (2013), Profile Books.

Matthews, P.
Twelve Outstanding Secondary Schools – Excelling Against The Odds (2010), Ofsted.

Matthews, P and Mclaughin, C.
Up For It? How Good Schools Become Great With A Little Help From Their Friends (2010),
The London Leadership Strategy & National College.

National College
Review Of The Landscape: Leadership & Leadership Development (2008).

Ofsted
Unseen Children: Access And Achievement 20 Years On (2013).

Ofsted
More Able Children (2013).

Pendleton, D and Furnham, A.
Leadership: All You Need To Know (2012).

Smith, A.
High Performers, The Secret Of Successful Schools (2011), Crown House Publishing.

Syed, M.
Bounce – The Myth Of Talent And The Power Of Practice (2010), Fourth Estate.

Taylor, C and Ryan, C.
Excellence In Education: The Making Of Great Schools (2005), David Fulton.